the farm his scotch bailiff —

home but his daughter is
she's a doosed nice gal,
gal indeed.

Muck's your man for giving
one an appetite, says the Squire

The Squire has a
day at the home farm

THE AFTER-BREAKFAST CIGAR

Selected Memoirs of a King Country Settler

THE AFTER-BREAKFAST
CIGAR

Selected Memoirs of a King Country Settler

by

SPENCER WESTMACOTT

edited by

H. F. WESTMACOTT

A. H. & A. W. REED

WELLINGTON   SYDNEY   LONDON

0747790

43793

First published 1977

A.H. & A.W. REED LTD
65-67 Taranaki Street, Wellington
53 Myoora Road, Terrey Hills, Sydney 2084
11 Southampton Row, London, WC1B 5HA
also
16-18 Beresford Street, Auckland
Cnr Mowbray & Thackeray Streets,
Waltham, Christchurch 2

ISBN 0 589 01011 5

Typeset by Printset Processes (1973) Ltd. Christchurch
Printed by Kyodo-Shing Loong Printing Industries Pte. Ltd, Singapore.

For S. W.'s son

So to the land our hearts we give,
Till the sure magic strike;
And memory, use and love make live
Us and our fields alike.
                    Rudyard Kipling

CONTENTS

ACKNOWLEDGMENTS

The line-drawings are by Romola Wigley, a grand-daughter of Spencer Westmacott. The jacket shows an original watercolour by Spencer Westmacott himself.

Acknowledgment is made to Hodder and Stoughton Ltd. for the quotations from Rudyard Kipling.

INTRODUCTION

MY FATHER-IN-LAW did sometimes smoke a cigar after breakfast, but that was after the Second World War. In the life which he describes in these pages, in the first decade of the century, there was no place for cigars.

Spencer Westmacott, whom I have called S. W., was born at Christchurch in 1885, and educated at Christchurch Boys' High School and later at Waitaki Boys' High School. His father, Herbert Westmacott, had been manager of the Clifford and Weld properties of Flaxbourne and Stoneyhurst, and later farmed at Waikakahi. It was here that S. W. first worked on the land, and it was here that he and his father first heard reports of bush country in the North Island that could be taken up cheaply and was full of potential. They leased their first block of this land in 1910, and S. W. came north to develop it.

This book consists of extracts from the memoirs left by S. W., and tells the story of the property in the Rangitoto Range from its lease in 1910 to the outbreak of the First World War.

The experiences described are not unique. They are typical of those of the pioneer settlers who developed the King Country. It must have been hard to believe that the great areas of virgin bush could ever be turned into pasture. But the settlers did believe it, and they were right.

H. F. W.

The quotations which preface each Part are all from "The Five Nations" by Rudyard Kipling.

PART ONE

S. W. GOES NORTH

*Thence I ran my first rough survey — chose my trees
and blazed and ringed 'em —*

PART ONE

S. W. GOES NORTH

MY FATHER LEFT England in 1862 and came to New Zealand. He returned to England for visits in 1872 and 1882, and from the second of these visits he brought back a folio of sketches of country life by Finch Mason, in which certain pages were devoted to the life of a squire. The first sketch begins with the line: "The after-breakfast cigar lit, the squire trots off to the farm."

A stout, well-fed squire he is, with a healthy liver, that he can light up his cigar after breakfast. Fancy being able to afford it, too. His horse is brought round; he does not have to catch and saddle him. He mounts in comfort. It does not rain, or blow unpleasantly enough to be noticed. The gates are well hung, he never needs to get off and lift them. His bailiff is good. His labourers are industrious. Oh yes. His corn is all stacked neatly in a clean rickyard. The shorthorn bull is never where he ought not to be. Nothing ever gets bogged in a drain. And when at last after a pleasant day our squire stands before a blazing fire, one feels that his household knows no domestic worries and that debts and mortgages are unknown to such a man.

A very good life, I hope you will agree, and very much the life that when I left school, reconciled to the idea that the Army was not for me, I was willing to take up, and, I hoped, eventually, adorn. How to achieve it was the problem to which I must devote my energies when I returned from Waitaki to begin the serious business of making my way in the world.

When my father met me with the dog-cart at Glenavy railway station, I can hardly have looked a very promising figure. I was already six foot tall, but without breadth or depth, sadly pale-faced, thin and loose-jointed. Certainly I could ride a bit, but otherwise I was shamefully inexperienced. I could not even milk a cow.

At first I did only the boys' jobs such as tending the spinning jenny off which ran the wire which they threaded through the iron standards and posts, which were bored. In the swamps, though, we used stakes, and I held a hammer against them while the staples were driven in. Easy things to do, and so I found them; but then I took to digging the post-holes and ramming them. It gave one a feeling of satisfaction to see the new fence being completed strain by strain.

My dog, Mac, taught me to handle sheep. After all, his ancestors had been doing it for countless generations. His sorry appearance caused much contemptuous comment, but when people saw him work it was a different story.

By now I had learned to kill and butcher a sheep. At first I had such a horror of taking life that my father would kill it, and I would carry on from there; but I managed to overcome my nausea after a while, and did the whole job. Now I had a dog, I volunteered to get the sheep in and yard them myself.

The "killers" ran in a long eighteen-acre paddock above the sheepyards on a ridge on the west of the place. There were about twenty of them, half-breds, and very active old ladies. Mac had just learned to follow me. I went to the top of the field and tried to drive the sheep down before me. Mac disappointed me, as he did not seem to understand me, but the sheep ran in the way I wanted over the crest and down towards the yards out of sight. When I got to the brow of the hill they were still running below, but when I followed on down they headed away and disappeared round to the right and over the hill. Mac now seemed a complete failure, for he did not come, though I called. But the sheep presently appeared again, coming, to my surprise, directly towards me. Then I saw a dog's tail waving behind them, and there was Mac, bringing them on to me. Whichever way they tried to run, he got there before them, and presently they were entering the open gate into the yard. Never a sound did he make during the whole proceedings, nor when working sheep did he ever emit a bark in the years that he and I spent together. He remained my constant companion until I left for the north.

During the years at Waikakahi S. W. acquired other skills. He spent five years on his father's farm, and gained a great deal of confidence, and some breadth and weight to balance his height. He worked with his father's employees and neighbours, and developed his own opinions in farming matters.

By 1908 a good many people were beginning to talk about North Island bush country, among them a friend of the Westmacotts named Andrew Hegarty, who was now a run-holder in Poverty Bay. He invited S. W. to come and see the country, of which he gave glowing accounts.

Hegarty met me in Gisborne, and said he had just sold a place of 2000 acres in the Hangaroa and had to give delivery of it, but he lent me a horse and directed me how to ride out to his place in the Mangatu forty-six miles away.

I found the cleared bush country with its gaunt trees and stumps and logs lying everywhere hard to get used to, but I had done so by the time Hegarty returned, and then I began to hear the details of bush farming and to be convinced that it offered prospects to the beginner with small capital that were not available in Canterbury.

Hegarty had sold the Hangaroa place to my old friend, Eric Garcia, and by his invitation we went to stay with him for a few days.

Eric had bought the 2000 acres, part-improved, for £7000. He was already carrying 2000 sheep and hoped to double that in two or three years. He asked me to remain and work with him. He was lonely and wanted a man. I liked the idea; but did not feel I could leave my father suddenly like that.

Hegarty swore by bush country, and well he might. He had leased 4000 acres from the natives for twenty-one years at a shilling an acre, with the option of renewal for a further twenty-one years and compensation for improvement of £2. 10s an acre. In grass this country easily carried two sheep to the acre. It cost about £1. 5s an acre to clear it by contract, 10s to grass it and about 15s an acre to fence; £2. 10s in all, but what was so astonishing to me was the crop of turnip, rape and mustard sown down with the grass upon the burn. On this Hegarty would graze the first winter an average of nine hoggets per acre, thereby paying for fencing and grassing and making a clear profit the first year. He had 400 acres of new burn the first winter I visited him, and his older grass looked in good order. As far as I was able I went into all the details of bush farming.

My host was a good teacher. He told me how to judge bush by the growth upon it, showing that where the big tawa grew was sweet, good country for sheep. That was the best; but all bush was convertible into grass country. To my. enquiry as to whether one could depend on the grass holding he pointed to the next valley which had been cleared for twenty years and where certainly there was a good sole of grass. All the stock on his place looked well. I saw his sheep crutched; they were Lincolns and nothing could be in better condition. I wrote fully of these things to my father, during an absence lasting about five weeks.

I went again to Poverty Bay the following year, but everything had risen in the last twelve months. I was still ready to go into bush country at a valuation of £1 to 25s an acre, but a telegram from my father asking me to return for some cattle work cut short this visit.

*   *   *

Another friend, Hargreaves, went to the North Island at this time, and presently revisiting the South, told me that he had leased a block of land from the Maoris at a place called Honikiwi near Otorohanga, on the main trunk line recently completed and opened. He described land equal to Canterbury country such as Willowbridge, very cheap and with plenty more available. The main trunk lands had a bad reputation because it was said the areas near the line were held by land-sharks and speculators.

Nevertheless, Hargreaves' account was so glowing that I resolved to go and see for myself. He said that if one kept one's business to oneself one could find plenty of unoccupied land and could avoid the land-sharks by leasing or buying direct from the native owners.

The journey north was interesting, in a crowded train from Wellington. The passengers craned out to see the viaducts and spiral, though it was too dark. I slept at Taumarunui, Meredith House, and went on by early train next morning. The country along the line looked rough and wild; there was little livestock to be seen. I was disappointed. Hargreaves met me at Te Kuiti. There were a number of pleasant, frank-looking men on the platform, but when I enquired who anyone was he warned me against him.

"Beware, Spen. He would take you down to your socks. If you are introduced to him, don't whatever you do say that you are after land."

It seemed the land agents met all the trains, and would sell you anything.

The township was crowded with natives. We went on by train to Otorohanga, a primitive place with a Maori pa, two boarding houses and a sawmill. A wide river, the Waipa, ran through it. The main street was a sea of mud. The only wheels in it were those of a wag-gon drawn by two yoke of oxen. From there we started early one morning to ride out to Hargreaves'. The road was mud a foot deep. Across the Waitomo we saw a gig stuck in it. The owner had removed the horse and gone on. We followed, and began to climb round the hills through which ran the only thoroughfare; "fern above the saddle bow", as Kipling wrote, pressing in upon us on each side — thrilling to read about in a poem, not so attractive here. The mud got deeper; the horses wallowed in up to the girths, their bellies leaving a trail in it between the tracks of their feet which they lifted from one pothole to another. We were five hours doing six miles.

I stayed some days and was interested in what I saw. I rather disappointed Hargreaves by saying after our first ride round, "But it is not Willowbridge land." All the same I thought it had possibilities if properly farmed, and said so.

Hargreaves took me along and introduced me to Finlay, his lawyer, of the legal firm of Watts & Broadfoot, who looked me over kindly and said that as a young prospective settler I should find land business in the King Country was a problematical venture at any time. Broadfoot, on the other hand, who was freshfaced and boyishly young in manner, told me not to worry about what people might say, the King Country was progressive, with a great future. It only needed capital and energetic settlers to keep on going ahead. If I let them know what I wanted he had no doubt they could get it for me. I caught the express south feeling I was getting along.

*   *   *

My father did not share my enthusiasm; still, he was reluctant to relinquish the idea, so now he went to see for himself, and on arrival at Te Kuiti went to Broadfoot's office. Broadfoot was most active in the work of leasing and the legal transfer of land from the natives in the King Country. He showed my father the map. There was at least one block in the Rangitoto of over 4500 acres of bush that might be got. It sounded likely, and our opinion being formed on what we had seen in Poverty Bay, we favoured bush. There were other blocks in the same area, but this one had the advantage of having only the one owner, King Mahuta. The others, being held tribally, had a number of owners who would have to agree, and the process of arranging this was expensive and tedious, often dragging on for months.

Who could find out if Mahuta would lease or sell? One Falwasser, a licensed interpreter, was said to be a favourite with him and would be the best man to negotiate. When he arrived he proved to be a handsome young quarter-caste who said he felt confident he could arrange matters with the King.

The King was at Ngaruawahia. He received Falwasser warmly and heard his proposition on my father's behalf. After considering it in the usual leisurely native manner, he said, "Your pakeha friend is ready to buy this place for one pound an acre. Is that so?"

Falwasser told him that was so and that my father had given him £100 on account towards paying for it, which was the case.

"Well," said Mahuta, "listen now. I have never seen this land you speak of nor set foot upon it, but those people down there, my relatives of Maniapoto gave it to me. I should not like them to think I have sold their present. It is however useless to me as it is now. I would like some revenue from it. I will therefore lease it to your pakeha friend, and I am glad to be able to do that for you, Ted. The natives who gave it to me will doubtless approve of my action. Let them get used to a pakeha being there. In this way their feelings will in no way be wounded. Then after a year or so if your friend still wants to buy the place and will pay for it, I have no doubt we can arrange the matter to the satisfaction of both of us."

On that they shook hands. Falwasser reported to my father, who approved so far, but said, "I have not been on the place. I have a son who will live here and work the country. He will come up here and go and look at it. Do not finalise matters until he has reported that the land is what we believed it to be. I would rather lose the £100 paid into your hands if on further examination the land is not suitable."

7

The instructions he gave me were along these lines, and I left for the north a day or two after his return, a further £100 being placed at my disposal.

*　　　*　　　*

On my arrival in Te Kuiti I sent straight to Broadfoot's office. He took me for a walk in the bright sunshine after a frosty night. He told me someone else was already after the place, and feared that if we delayed we might lose it. For that reason he had had the lease prepared, and signed by Mahuta; the rent to be one shilling an acre. I felt he had exceeded his instructions, but if the land was what we believed, it seemed in our interests. I said it seemed all right but before we signed anything I must go over the place myself. He agreed, and introduced me to Sandy Macardle, a large speculator with land east of Te Kuiti, who could tell me how to get over to the block known as Rangitoto 28A. It seemed it would take me a day to get out there, at least a day to explore the section, and another to return. The man to go to was one MacLuckie, who was already settled there. He was coming in to attend the Land Board, and I met him on arrival that night.

Ian Lachlan MacLuckie proved to be a pleasant, slow-smiling, fresh-faced Scot from Falkirk, who had been out in Rangitoto nearly a year, and already had a hundred acres of bush cleared and sown there. He seemed glad to see me, and at the prospect of having me as a neighbour. I was pleased to find a Scot before me; it gave me added confidence. He said he could lend me a horse, and that I could stay with him and he would lend me a native whom he employed as a guide. It turned out to be a week before we started, however. His business with the Land Board did not come up any quicker for him being in town, though he went to the Court House where they sat every morning.

The Maoris had a saying, "Taihoa the Land Court". "Taihoa" means "Wait a bit". This applied to all native business. Before a native sale or lease could be considered in order it had to be approved by the native Land Court composed of a so-called judge and two assessors, one European and one native, with a secretary. The Board had to be satisfied that any land transaction was in the interests of the natives. The pakeha purchaser or lessee usually fumed at the pettifogging and delays; but it was in their interest too, inasmuch as it prevented many disputes as to ownership, and prevented the owner from selling to two or three people at once and getting any money that way, as one need not pay till the Board approved. This made the natives eager for the Board to put the business through.

At Land Board time the Maoris used to crowd into the township bringing their families on horseback or in four-wheeled buggies. Those who were expected to be paid money were accompanied by their relatives and friends to help them spend it. They slept at the homes of their local tribesmen or in the huge carved wharepuni on the little hill above the railway station, where they lay, men, women, boys, girls and little children in the blankets all hugger-mugger on the floor, as happy as sandboys.

Each morning they would stroll leisurely along the street to the Land Board. On fine days they sat about on the grass in the sun with their backs to the railway and watched the traffic pass. If it were wet they seated themselves along the footpaths, their backs to the shop windows or in the entrance on the steps. Most shopkeepers did not object to this as they were good customers and spent freely; those who resented it fumed, until one bethought him and sprinkled the path in front of his shop with a watering can, a proceeding the old native women considered in very bad taste.

The men crowded the billiard rooms, and many became very expert at the game. Others, and these the more important of the landowners, were eternally discussing land sales, describing situation and access, and drawing maps and plans of blocks in the dirt of the footpaths with their walking sticks. The passers by had to walk round them. Sometimes they succeeded in buying strong drink, though it was illegal to supply them and there were no public houses.

The women wore European clothing, certainly, but blouses and skirts of the loosest kind, and of brilliant colouring, with yellow, red, or vari-coloured scarves round their heads. Each had a shawl, and the gaudiest coloured tartans of obscure clans were very popular. Most went bare footed and the married women were tattooed deeply on the lips and chin. They carried their beautiful brown-eyed babies on their backs, the shawl keeping them comfortably in place. There were plenty of these and there needed to be, for they gave the children any European food they fancied, which, when they were in funds, might be crayfish, tinned salmon, or fruit; anything that looked nice, in fact. The fish shop did a roaring trade, not only in the fish I knew, but in mussels and mutton-birds. Their money spent, they would troop off to their houses in the backblocks where potatoes were their chief article of diet and they lived more healthy natural lives.

The local white inhabitants were affected by the easy-going spirit of the natives, and strolled about transacting much of their business out of doors. They met each of the express trains that came in the daytime, the one from the south in the morning and that from the north at three in the afternoon, when they would have a bun and a cup of tea or coffee at the railway refreshment room. These trains seldom ran to time, but that did not matter.

One of these local inhabitants, a man named Macdonald, who represented a Waikato firm, was both interesting and useful. He knew the King Country and found me a little horse of just the kind I needed. I had stipulated that I must have one I could catch anywhere. He said the milkman had one to sell and took me to see him. The milkman — I imagined the sort of person who delivered the milk in Christchurch — turned out to be one of a family of brothers named Self from Norfolk who milked the cows about three miles out and brought the milk in cans on pack horses over the very muddy road into town for delivery from a whare on a township section. I was unused to a milkman who wore good English breeches and gaiters of a cut better than my own, as Dick Self did, and when he asked only £5 for a very useful bay pony, I was rather astonished at its cheapness and bought it without further parley, though Macardle told me later it was top price. He was a good purchase for me. I called him Jeff.

* * *

At last, after what seemed an age, MacLuckie's business was arranged and one bright morning I had my pony saddled at the livery stables and with overcoat, blanket and a few underclothes strapped in a swag before me, I rode out with him to see the Rangitoto Bush 28A, and make the final decision whether or not to exercise our option over it.

We crossed a stream about a mile south of the town and followed a track up into the hills. As we progressed the fern and scrub closed in on each side of us. This was not a formed road, though the wheel marks showed us that waggons went this way, but a native track that picked its way so as to follow the driest route and keep out of the swampy places. Mostly it contrived to avoid the hollows and kept along spurs and on the higher ground. Where it did have to descend to cross the marshy ground, manuka branches had been cut and thrown down as a rough sort of fascine. Here and there were patches of bush; but grass fields ceased at the edge of the little town which, as we looked back at it from the top of the first ridge, looked quite pretty, even the corrugated iron of which all the roofs and many of the buildings were composed, with the hard edges softened by distance and the colour a light blue.

We rode on, and as we rose to the top of a further ridge, Mac-Luckie rose in his stirrups and raising an arm called, "Hail Rangi-toto!"

I joined him. We reined in and looked before us. The middle distance seemed to merge into a solid forest of heavy bush which rose to a long tree-clad hill on the horizon which, though high and large, appeared easy of approach, not too steep, and the forest nowhere broken by cliffs. Yes, it looked all right, yet young and keen though I was, a slight chill took me, a foreboding that the task in front of me would not be easy.

On we went again and crossing a stream we saw a mile or two away some grass and the native whares of a pa called Aharoa and signs of bush falling beyond which Mac said was a place recently taken up by a man called Sutherland from Southland. Presently the track led us along the edge of some bush in the afternoon sun, and then began to descend steeply some hundreds of feet to a wide shingle-bottomed river, the Waipa. Tall manuka, high above our heads, covered the flat to the water's edge on each side.

We splashed through the water up to the horses' girths, lifting our feet in the stirrups, until we climbed out the other side and rode along the flat some distance and the ascent began. For the last few miles Mac told me he and a Maori had made the track which now began to climb and was mattocked out of the almost precipitous hillside in zigzag lengths of thirty to forty yards. We soon got off and led our horses to ease them of our weight, and seemed to me to climb interminably. I was very glad when we emerged on a clearing which opened before us on what appeared to be a flat tableland.

The bush had been cleared the year before, a hundred acres of it. The larger trees, blackened by fire, stood gaunt and high; and new grass was showing well, giving great promise for the future. The camp, a little way to our right, was a welcome sight. We went to it and unsaddling the horses turned them down the track again, putting up a rail behind them. We entered the camp which was a tent about twelve foot by ten with a three-foot wall and a galley about the same length and height attached to and in front of it. A low door of sacking gave entrance at the side, and at the far end from the tent was an open fireplace of upright logs with a bar across it in the chimney and attached thereto a number of wire hooks. A camp oven stood on one side of the fireplace and several billets on the other. Two squared blocks of black punga, or mamaku, stood close by as seats. The embers of a fire were still smouldering in the centre in a pile of white woodash. Along one side of the galley was a table of three wide slabs of timber rough-dressed with an axe or adze, beside which was a round rail of green sapling with the bark still on, at a suitable height to sit on; the knives and forks, enamelled mugs and plates, together with a tin pan and a tin or two of jam and condensed milk lay on the table. On the other side of the galley were several kerosene boxes on poles about three feet high in which the food and spare utensils were stored, and a bag of flour stood on an empty sack on the floor of clean swept dirt. A number of short

11

branches of manuka tied to a longer stick as a broom, stood by the fireplace.

A grey tom-cat came stretching himself from the back tent where he had been sleeping, and welcomed us with a pleased miaou. Mac introduced him as "the best little cat in the Rangitoto"; I believe he was at that time the only one. I was bidden to enter and put my things on the spare bed across the end of the whare. There were two others along the sides made of a framework of green saplings for legs and sides, with split sacks stretched between, and soft bedding of fern.

"Make yourself at home," said my host. "I'll get the fire going. The men'll be in soon."

He commenced gathering sticks and I, wishing to be helpful, assisted him. I was not yet good at lighting fires.

Presently we heard voices coming along a track from the clearing and a tall, pleasant-looking half-caste appeared with a shorter white youth whose name was Kercher. To these I was introduced and we shook hands. The newcomers wore a minimum of clothing: grey flannel singlets, dungaree trousers and heavy sprigged boots. The white boy wore a hat from which the band and lining had long since disappeared and which, from having been a smart enough grey affair with a dent along the crown, had lost all shape except that of its wearer's head, and rose to a rounded peak at the top. This, I was to note later, was the usual form that hats assumed in backblocks places everywhere, and so I have seen them depicted in the mountain districts of America.

Everyone settled at once to the task of preparing tea. While Mac tended the fire, now blazing merrily, Ngahihi Hughes, the half-caste, went for water in a square bucket made from a kerosene tin from which the top had been cut, fitted with a wire handle. He took soap and water, and after filling the tin with water for the camp washed in a nearby creek. On return he commenced with an axe splitting tawa into three-foot lengths for firewood. Kercher got straight to work peeling potatoes and onions which were soon boiling in billies on the fire, in the centre of which the meat was sizzling in a camp oven, flanked on the other side by a billy of water for tea.

Not being so busy, I felt hungry till I bethought myself to go and wash, as dark was falling, and returning found tea was being put on the log table. It was a good meal of the things I have named, topped off with bread and jam. The others drank tea with condensed milk and were suprised that I preferred a mug of water. I was soon to acquire the tea habit but had not done so at the time. A round log is not the most comfortable seat; but I was pleasantly tired and that did not worry me. We ate a lot of onions. Mac said he ate them every day, cooked and raw, and bought them by the sack.

"An onion a day keeps the doctor away," said he. "They go well raw with jam and cheese on a bit of bread and butter."

He proved right in that too. It was just the food for a hard-working man.

The dishes washed, we sat in front of the fire after tea while Hughes baked bread in the camp oven. I noted the process with great interest and eagerness to learn. The sponge, as it is called, had been made in the morning before the men went out to work, by mixing a panful of flour flavoured with a little sugar and salt, with a cupful of liquid yeast from a bottle and enough warm water to make a thick paste. This had been covered with an empty sack and stood in the chimney where it could derive warmth from the embers. It had slowly risen through the day and Hughes had kneaded it for about twenty minutes before tea, making it up into four lumps which he had placed in the warm camp oven to rise during and after the meal, with the lid of the oven set half over the top so as to warm it up but not heat it too quickly.

Now it was ready to bake; the four lumps of dough had risen and joined together. Hughes put the lid on and shovelled some glowing hot tawa embers on top. He stood the oven on the hearth and shovelled a ring of the red embers round it and sat down on his haunches to watch it.

The conversation that evening was about the land, the bush and the queer things in it. Mac, Kercher and I were all more or less new to it. Hughes had been born and brought up on the edge of it and loved it. He knew it in all its aspects. He was a mighty hunter of wild cattle and pig. His Welsh blood came from a grandfather who had been a pakeha Maori. He himself, then, was three parts Maori in breeding, but wholly so in upbringing and outlook on life, and when full fed, as now, in the warmth of the fireside, he was a great talker. MacLuckie had told me of Tara-pikau, the malign spirit of the Rangitoto forest; but only a little. Hughes could tell of him, and also of the Patu-paiarehe, the little folk of the dense leafy depths who are only found in quiet and undisturbed places. Very sensitive, they are, and known only to people close to nature, who have faith, avoiding vulgar society in the cities and on the plains.

Tara-pikau himself was a haunting terror of the trackless bush who lay in wait to lure women into the darkness. To these he would call. If they went to the voice they were never seen again. Several women were named who had disappeared that way, down to recent times, so now no Maori woman or girl ever entered this vast forest which stretched for many miles right out to the open Taupo plains.

"If you are in the bush and you hear a call," said Hughes, "do not go to it, but sit down and call back. If it is Tara-pikau — ah! — he will draw you further and further in after him until you are lost and cannot ever return. It is easy to know the Tara-pikau country if you follow up the streams and see a red eel. When you see that, turn back. That is the boundary of where he lives. Go no further or an evil will happen to you."

Mac smiled reflectively at the fire.

"I think we are all ready for bed," he said. "That bread should be about done, Hughes."

Hughes got a knife, removed the lid of the camp oven and struck it with the knife against the inside. It gave a clear, ringing sound.

"She's done all right," he said, and to make quite sure drove the knife in between the four loaves. Withdrawing it, he saw it come away clean, and said, "She's good," and turned it out into a clean, empty flour bag on the table.

"Haere kia te moe," said he. "Let's go to bed," which, after trooping outside to look at the starlight of a clear frosty night, we all did, and were soon fast asleep.

I awoke to hear Hughes stirring at daybreak. He preferred to sleep on the floor in front of the fire in the galley. He was to guide me further on my journey into the bush. He was only an occasional employee of Mac's, at ten shillings a day, and this time was there to construct a pataka to store the food where the rats could not reach it. The timber for this was to be split on the far side of a gully, and needed to be brought over before erection. Mac asked if I minded his finishing the job whilst the weather was fine, and we postponed our start for two days. To get the logs across the gully would have been heavy work if it meant carrying them, so to avoid this Hughes rigged a wire on to which we stapled them, and slid them over.

Whilst preparing for this on the second day, three Europeans came out of the bush, each with a swag on his back and carrying axes and slashers. These proved to be Cheal, the surveyor, his assistant, Macdonald, and a stranger, who, when their party had finished its work and gone off to town, had gone for a pleasure trip into the bush for nearly a week. It seemed a sort of busman's holiday to me; but each to his taste.

While Macdonald was resting lazily in the sun, he remarked, "What a country, and what solitude. We are only about twelve miles east of the railway yet we are completely cut off from the world and it's days since we had any news of it."

"Yes," I said, "the King might die and we should not hear of it till we went to town."

It was a curious remark to make on that afternoon of May 6th 1910. We none of us knew the King was ill.

*   *   *

That night down came the rain as it can in the bush, steady and strong, setting in slowly and lasting for days. Each morning as we looked for a break in the clouds, Mac would say, "Ye cannot go into the bush today," and I was glad to remain in the camp, till Monday morning came round. Then, after a wet Sunday night we went out to find it still drizzling and no sign of a break.

"It looks like going on," said I.

"Aye," said Mac, "I'm thinking ye'll never make a start this winter."

I turned to the tent door and said, "Hughes, can you boil a billy in the rain?"

To which he replied, "I can make a fire and cook the kai on it in any weather."

"Well then, we'll start as soon as we've rolled our swags."

After breakfast we were ready, Hughes showed me how to tie flax to the two bottom corners of a sack into which we put our blankets, and the billies and stores, and then to fasten the ends round the top and slip our arms through for the journey. Each of us carried one of these loads, but Hughes, being the seasoned man, insisted on carrying twice what I did. We were each dressed in dungaree trousers and flannels with sleeves ending at the elbow. He wore no hat. I did, but regretted it later. He carried a slasher; I an axe. As we were starting, Mac told Kercher to go with us and try to kill a pig, as the camp was out of meat.

The rain abated. It was fine as we started, by which I mean it was not pouring, though all round was wet, the atmosphere was thick above us and the grass was steaming, while wisps of mist were rising from the bush where the tops of the great trees were visible.

"Good luck to ye," said Mac, as we trailed off across the clearing, Hughes in front to pick the way, then myself, and Kercher, carrying a rifle, following in single file, in the forest formation of the savage the world over.

In that order we entered the bush half a mile further on. There was a track to the abandoned site of a survey camp about a mile on. I say a track, inasmuch as the supplejacks had been cut; but coming off open, hilly country in the south, where the gaze roams for miles, I should not have seen it by myself at all, and had yet to learn to look for signs within three feet of me, such as blazes on the tree-trunks, cut supplejacks and twigs bent over. It was half dark in the bush, and to me depressing. I was relieved to see a sky above me, even though only a grey one, when we reached a deserted camp-site and rested. It had taken us nearly two hours to reach it, in what Hughes said was good going, so slow was I in these unfamiliar surroundings.

Shouldering our packs we went on again. Presently all signs of cuts on the creepers and trees disappeared. As far as I was concerned we were in trackless forest; but really we were following the tracks of wild cattle and pigs which mainly kept to the tops of the low ridges. So I was told, and took Hughes' word for it, for in the semi-darkness and thick tangle of undergrowth I knew not ridge or gully. The gloom had a most depressing effect on me which I tried to conceal. I was content to follow Hughes as he slashed his way foward foot by foot. Content, I say, but that is hardly the word. The pack seemed as heavy as lead and kept catching in the supplejacks and lawyers, even though I stooped. If I kept my eyes up to watch for these, my feet stumbled over roots and I fell forward.

Lunchtime brought some relief, to be able to lay aside the load and lie down while the billy boiled; but I was little refreshed when again we pushed on. An unlooked-for break came when my nose started to bleed. There was nothing to be done but to sit down and let it flow till there was quite a splash on the ground. It horrified Hughes, who ever after in recounting the journey, which he often did, would pause in his story and say, "and then he bleed" — which I did several times in the next two days.

Thereafter we began slowly to rise, as I could tell by the extra effort in walking. Had I been fresher and not struggling to get my pack along through the undergrowth, I would have been more interested in the quality of the land, which I felt must be good by the amount of heavy growth everywhere, the tall ratas, and especially the big tawas which I had been taught to look for. Surely the land which grew supplejacks in such profusion would grow anything, while the strong smell of damp decayed vegetation seemed to me to indicate great richness in the soil.

Hughes was looking for other things with a hunter's eye. He would have paused often to shoot pigeons which sat and gazed at us from nearby branches without attempting to fly away; but I said there was no use doing that to carry them on with us, and being my employee for the moment, he paid heed. He had with him a wonderful half-bred bulldog called Ginger and when Ginger got on to a pig that crossed our track, he dropped his pack and sped after it as I could not have believed possible in that tangle of vines. One minute he was listening to the noise of flight in the gully to our right, and the next minute he was gone. In my exhausted state I lay down on the ground feeling I could never get up again.

Presently he returned, sheath knife in hand, dragging a half-grown pig that he had slain, followed by the grinning bloody-jawed Ginger, and Kercher. For the first time I realised that the light was not as strong as it had been. I also realised the afternoon was drawing late and Kercher was still with us. I asked when he meant to return to MacLuckie. He said Mac would not expect him now and I accepted his presence with us. Hughes suggested we make camp, to my inward relief. We selected a tall rata and dropped our swags under it. He started Kercher making a fire, told me to sit with my feet to it under the rata, and prepared half the pig by taking the skin off — not an easy thing to do — but it was a fat one.

Kercher went for water from the gully. Hughes stuck two forked sticks in the ground, one at each end of the fire, and a long green one on top of them. He then stuck another through the ribs of the pig, and driving the point into the ground on the far side of the fire, told me, "Maybe you turn him sometimes when he sizzle, he roast beautiful"; so I became a turnspit.

Kercher hooked four small billies on the cross-stick over the blaze to boil, whilst Hughes chopped down a small green tawa and split it up into three-foot lengths, some of which he laid along the fire, and piled the rest handy for the night. As it was now growing dark he struck a candle in a branch, but as the blaze from the fire increased it lit up the scene and we needed no other light.

Between them the two rummaged through our packs, unfolding blankets, on which we sat, and producing the food. Hughes had packed this and seemed to have forgotten nothing: bread, butter, sugar, salt, condensed milk, jam, onions, potatoes and even dried apples. The billies soon boiled. Potatoes and onions went into one, apples into another and rice into a third. He seemed to have forgotten nothing, as I said. After all, why should he? He was an experienced hunter and he had MacLuckie's larder to draw upon; but when he came to make the tea, that was the one thing overlooked. I did not miss it much as I had an idea then that tea-drinking was pernicious, and stuck to water.

What a meal followed when the roasting was done! The chops were split off three at a time. Our plates contained potatoes, onions, and some of the dried apples, boiled soft, as sauce. Roast pork and apple sauce. Never have I enjoyed it more than I did by the glancing red glare of that fire in the heart of the Rangitoto bush. We discarded knives for the meat, and gnawed it from the bones; the best sauce was hunger and honest weariness, with the physique of youth to recover strength as we ate. We rinsed our plates with boiling water when we were satisfied, and started the second course, boiled rice and stewed apples. Then we lay on the blankets, our feet to the fire, and discussed our position as we smoked our pipes lazily.

Before leaving Te Kuiti I had carefully got all the information about the country that Cheal's survey office could provide. Rangitoto was not then surveyed. But the country was divided up on the map by straight lines which showed the areas allotted amongst the Maniapoto tribe by the native land court. No heed had been paid to contour or to natural boundaries such as ridges and streams.

17

I had a tracing of the map with me. This showed a trig station on top of Rangitoto mountain, and the western boundary of 28A ran through it. The whole of the vast area was largely unexplored; but in 1879 a Government party of surveyors had, with the concurrence and assistance of most of the native chiefs, passed through the country, setting up trigs on the principal heights. Since then no European had passed through it, it was said, with one exception which I will mention later.

The erection of the trig station was called a "flying survey", and the stations were many miles apart. When erecting them the survey parties had cleared the sites of bush enough to get a sight all round with a theodolite, and by picking up bearings on two or more trigs already erected behind them, the surveyors were able to plot their own position with exactness. They also noted in their field books any prominent feature within view, and sketched what they thought to be the general lie of the country. From these notes the existing maps had been compiled. We were finding here that these maps were wrong. They showed a watershed to the south-east of Rangitoto, with small streams running to a larger one, making a basin lying towards the south from a ridge between Rangitoto and a trig three and a half miles to the east, on a still higher point called Ranginui.

Instead of the streams trending to the south as shown on the map, we found that one, on our left as we progressed, flowed west and north-west to the Waipa, between us and Rangitoto mountain, making almost a gorge there. This stream was called the Owa-wenga. The basin simply did not exist, if Hughes' deduction was right; but that need not affect our plans. We knew that by going south and east of Rangitoto mountain we would be traversing the block 28A, and in that way getting a rough idea of its nature. We considered that by now we were about on the line of the western boundary and a mile to the west of Rangitoto. My father's distant view from open country had satisfied him that the northern end was all dense forest. We wished to find out if the remainder was of the same nature. We decided that we ought to be able to do this in a day. So we planned to leave the swags here, and carrying only food for lunch, to take slasher and rifle and cast round to the east through the bush, returning to sleep where we were.

Despite the lowering appearance of the sky at starting, the weather had, on the whole, been kind to us. There had been showers that wetted us, and the bush was dripping anyway, but it had not been cold and now as we lay, we were prevented from being chilled by the heat of the fire which had long since burned through the first green tawa, leaving a long heap of red glowing embers, on which Hughes from time to time laid more and more of the white split shards so as to let the fire get through them and first dry them, after which they added to the blaze. He was certainly as good as his word. It was a good fire and would last till morning even if unattended. With our feet to it we stretched out, and close together under the same blankets, we soon went to sleep.

If the weather had been comparatively mild, this state of affairs did not continue through the night. How long I had been slumbering I know not when I was awakened by a torrential downpour beating on my face and soaking the blankets. We grabbed for the top edge, and pulling it up got our heads under it and lay for a while in wet misery. Nothing lasts for ever, though, and when it ceased Hughes got out and piled more wood on the fire which nothing could quench. It blazed and sizzled as the raindrops fell on it, and gave us cheer. Wet as we were, we soon slept again, although this happened several times in the night.

For the first time in my life I woke to the note of the tui in the treetops nearby.

"Aha," said Hughes, from the blankets beside me, "daybreak he soon come now. No need to go to sleep again."

"And how do you know that?" I asked.

"Mr Tui, he tell me," replied Hughes, "he always call out before the light come. He tells you, 'Wake up now; soon it is daytime. Make the fire go. Get the kai for breakfast.' " And suiting the action to the words, Hughes himself turned out and piled the firewood on to the heap of glowing embers. I noted the ease with which he left his resting place. One minute asleep, the next on his feet, getting ready for the day, while I was still drowsy and loath to leave the blankets. However I soon got going too, and with towel and soap went down to the stream as soon as the light, true to Tui's promise, began to make the trunks of the trees visible.

Porridge warmed the inner man, and we had more roast pork. We drank hot water and condensed milk, and folding the blankets which we had dried a bit at the fire whilst breakfast cooked, we stowed them under the rata in case it rained, and started, Hughes leading the way. Kercher came on with us, saying that Mac would not expect him back now, and there was no sense in going as he had as yet no meat to take back with him. I was not entirely convinced; but he was not my man. We were in a free country and I could not order him. Later, when I had gained more confidence, I would have sent him back.

Though I had some apprehension at the start as to how I could travel after my weariness of the night before, it soon disappeared and I began to enjoy myself, feeling, as we made more progress, a certain pride too that I suffered little discomfort and was keeping up with my companions. The tall forest overhead still kept us in subdued light, but I was getting used to it and it did not depress me, whilst as we went on the country grew more level, and the undergrowth not so thick. I asked Hughes if this was only my imagination. He said no, it really was so, that the scrub was largely eaten by wild cattle whose footprints we now saw everywhere. The trees seemed if anything larger; the tawas were huge, a sure sign, I had been told in Poverty Bay, of good country.

Having walked east about a mile and a half as Hughes judged the distance, we believed ourselves to be about the centre of 28A, in beautiful easy country. We then turned south and by midday had reached a fair-sized shingle-bottomed stream which we believed must be the Tunawaia. Here we boiled the billy and had lunch. Such glimpses, as openings in the foliage permitted us, of the adjacent country, showed it to be all bush for miles in every direction, whilst to the south it rose again to a ridge, the forward slope lying towards the sun — not that there was any sun that day — which should make ideal sheep country. The map showed that this should be a block of 1137 acres belonging to King Mahuta's brother, Wherowhero.

When rested a little, we turned and circled towards our sleeping site. The day cleared somewhat, and going down a ridge we came to an uprooted tree. Climbing on it we had, through the opening made by its branches, a good outlook to the north. Hughes pointed out the landmarks. Away to the north-west, perhaps thirty miles off, was Pirongia, the sacred mountain, forest covered; and east of it was Kakepuku, much lower, and Kawa hill.

"That easy country you see is all farms around Kihikihi, and there is Orakau where the battle was fought. My father was in it."

"Was he?" said I, with fresh interest. "Did he know Rewi?" I knew the story of Rewi's heroic defiance of our troops when called upon to surrender.

"He was with Rewi all the time and was at his side in the battle."

"And how did he get away," I asked, "when surrounded by the troops?"

"Oh, he was very good on the leg, you know. He run very fast."

I smiled at this quaint way of putting it, and that was all I heard of the story then, but much more later, for Hughes' father, Poupatatae, was a famous fighting man.

This view of open country, distant and vague as it was, cheered me considerably; to think that once opened up Rangitoto was not too far from some kind of civilisation after all. My ideas of the romance of pioneering had been somewhat damped during this journey, and in any case I must always give the business side first place in my calculations, and the presence of farmers and settlements within twenty miles or so would be likely to give us markets for our stock and a property value, should we prove to have miscalculated and have insufficient capital to see the thing through. Though not very businesslike, I had vision, and though I knew any idea I had had of soldiering was now dismissed from my mind, my outlook — steeped as I was in martial lore and history — was distinctly military in its application to daily problems. I knew that the greatest generals, especially "The Duke", had not shirked the decision to retreat when they had overreached themselves, thereby husbanding their resources to fight another day and win. Retreat for us here would be to sell out.

"Lead on, Hughes," said I, and we once more took the trail beneath the trees. He sighted a kaka high above us and shot at it with the rifle. The bird came slipping through the branches making noises that sounded angry rather than concerned.

"He doesn't like it, being shot," said Hughes, finishing it off. "Kuku now, he don't worry. If you miss him first shot, he waits and gives you another chance, but old kaka he has the riri — the bad temper like an old man — and swears werry bad unless you kill him straight away. We have poultry in our stew tonight."

And so, when we reached our last night's bivouac, we did. Pork, potatoes, onions and kaka all went into the billy together, but personally I found the bird flesh tough.

The weather was kind enough to let us sit by the fire and talk before we slept, though it rained again at intervals after we had turned into our blankets. Hughes told of his father who had fought at Waitara in Taranaki, and everywhere else since, until Orakau; of his uncle who joined the Navy and served on our side, and of Rewi and his followers. I always loved the stories that fighting men had to tell of the days that were gone, and I am afraid wished we might enjoy a little excitement of the same kind, regretting that nowadays people seemed able to settle their affairs amicably enough, and that the growing tendency to compromise was an indication that war was a thing of the past. Hughes could tell the details of centuries-old battles, as if they had happened yesterday. He needed little encouragement from me to go on far into the night.

Neither the rain in the night nor the journey home next day, once more carrying our packs, seemed to trouble me as much as on the outward trip. Perhaps one becomes used to anything. Certainly I seemed to walk less clumsily and did not stumble so often.

At the old survey camp, whilst we rested, Mac appeared. As soon as he saw Kercher he cried out, "Oh, there's that swine that did not come home."

He had spent half the first night shouting to the bush to show the way back to camp, and the rest of the time worrying, believing the man was lost. Kercher did not deserve such consideration.

21

That evening, after a full meal, for we had carried back the remains of the wild pork, we discussed the future. I had seen enough to make me decide to go on with the venture. I thought of *Julius Caesar*: "There is a tide in the affairs of men which taken at the flood leads on to fortune." I had learned that, somewhat unwillingly, from Doctor Don at school. I believed that we were at the "flood". The quality of the land, judged by the growth upon it, impressed me that it would grow wonderful grass to feed stock on, and compared to anything I had seen elsewhere it was dirt-cheap at our rental of a shilling an acre. When I thought of the prices people paid for land in Canterbury for grazing purposes, I believed I would be a fool if I did not acquire what I had seen, before the price rose, as I had seen it do in Poverty Bay, and assist any of my friends who were ready to rough it, to do the same.

On return to Te Kuiti I saw a full-page picture, edged in black from the *Weekly News*, prominently displayed in a shop window. It was a portrait of King Edward VII and the printing underneath said it was "Our late dearly beloved King". I removed my hat as I stood astounded and saddened. My remark in the bush to Macdonald came back to me. Had it been prompted by his spirit passing? Who can tell?

A period of waiting then ensued, though, having decided to plunge in, I was naturally eager to get on with the work of opening up the country. I found that our deal with Mahuta had to come before the Land Board for its approval, and they would not be sitting for several weeks in Te Kuiti. Broadfoot advised me that it would be sheer folly to spend a penny more till we were assured of our titles, so I must possess my soul in patience.

At last the Land Board confirmed my title. The latest official valuation of the land was 17/6 an acre, so our price, based on £1, was fair enough. Mahuta had lots of other land. He had not set foot on the place. It seemed in his interest to lease it.

At this time several of S. W.'s friends were beginning to come up from the South Island, to look at bush country and consider its possibilities. Among the first of these was Stanley Brittan, who, together with Rowley Hill and John Rolleston, shared with S. W. the early days of opening up the Rangitoto Range.

The place was unsurveyed. We could not get a sealed title or the plans approved until this was done. The block was divided into three blocks of 1000 acres, and the remainder, of 1552, into a fourth. To prevent aggregation more than 3000 acres could not be taken in one name. I took the first three blocks, the fourth being assigned to my mother. It was a family concern and did not mean that I would expect more than my share of the profits.

It was unusual to do any improvements before survey, but it was considered safe enough, and as we did not want to lose a year, we prepared to get some bush laid off and make a start. It was already June, which left us about five months to fall the bush in time to let it lie long enough to dry for burning. I decided to get 400 acres measured off at the north-western end, and for this purpose engaged Mr Cashel, an authorised assistant surveyor, to come out with me and lay off this by compass, starting from the corner peg which had been located in the survey of the adjacent section.

The first problem was how to get to this corner peg, which was shown a little over a mile north of Rangitoto trig. I had seen enough on my journey with Hughes to know that it would take three or four days to get there if I went to MacLuckie's and on through the bush, for though on the map it was only twelve miles in a straight line from Te Kuiti to the trig station, we would have the same thick bush to negotiate, and the Owawenga gorge to cross. Needs must we use that route if there was no other, but I was told there was an easier way in by following a watercourse out from Otorohanga. On the map it was sixteen miles to the trig, but we hoped the going would be better.

Brittan had come up to join me, and he and I were for starting at once, but not so Mr Cashel, whom I now went to see. He proved to be a handsome, grey-haired man, with a pointed beard and a moustache.

"Start tomorrow?" said he. "Next week will do, won't it? Can't start in the middle of the week."

It never occurred to me to ask why not. He seemed to be a man who knew, and looked so venerable one would sooner have argued the matter with St Paul. Indeed I felt I was rather honoured that he consented to come on the Monday. He lived in a wooden hut in a back section behind the billiard rooms. I did go on Saturday evening to make sure he had not changed his mind. In response to my knocks, two of them at intervals whilst I stood first on one foot then on the other and listened to his progress across the floor within, he thrust his head out of the half-opened door, and enquired my business. I said I had just come to make certain of the time of starting.

"Monday. Monday. I said Monday, didn't I? We'll start on Monday."

"Yes, of course Monday, so it was," said I diffidently. He stared at me, truculently, I thought; his face seemed redder than when we had met in the street, and did I smell whiskey? I sincerely hoped not, and bidding him goodnight, I beat a hasty retreat.

The next thing was to get stores and equipment for the journey. We found we could get these from the local branch of Greene and Colebrook at Otorohanga. We made a list of everything we were likely to require and on the Sunday afternoon Dick Self came and sat with us in the boarding house sitting room and we went through it again with him to make sure we had forgotten nothing and then struck from it all items not indispensible until we had a fair pack horse load.

On the Monday it rained hard enough to make Mr Cashel confirm any doubts I might have had about starting in wet weather. We didn't. On Tuesday morning it did not rain but he said it looked as if it might, and anyway he had turned his horse out again when it rained on Monday, and it would be too late to start when he did catch him, and anyhow he had cast a shoe, must get that fixed up. I perforce had to agree. On Tuesday evening it was fine. He said it looked like holding. What about starting next day? I thought the idea a good one and went to bed hopeful.

Brittan was to go by the morning train to Otorohanga, and Mr Cashel and I riding our horses were to proceed by road and join him there, I hoped before noon. The first part went well enough, Brittan taking our swags, was ready for the train after breakfast; but Mr Cashel said there was no great hurry. He had to catch his horse and then get some things, he said. Outwardly polite, I fumed inwardly, and at last suggested that, as I had to get equipment in Otorohanga, I start. He agreed saying, "Yes. You go on. You can't miss the road."

I went with unvoiced misgivings as to whether he would bother to follow me. He seemed so casual. The road was unmetalled and the preceding day having been dry, it was good to ride upon. I was glad to find how well my pony went, and reached Otorohanga before midday where I stood him a feed of corn and Brittan and I had lunch. He had brought my order for stores and tent, and these were ready. I had meant to hire a pack horse here, and a hack for Brittan; but Davie Ormsby, the half-caste keeper of the livery stable, said he had no pack saddles and suggested we drive out to Otewa and hire from the natives there. He would provide a buggy and driver to take us that far. It seemed a sound enough idea, so we only awaited Mr Cashel's arrival to start; but as yet no sign of him. It was a lovely afternoon and Brittan, smoking his pipe, as yet free from care, seemed to enjoy sauntering up the main street in the sun. It was again my turn to fume; but there seemed no course open to us whereby we could hurry matters.

The town seemed to doze. It was a primitive little place. The main street and footpaths were just plain earth, dry enough for the moment; but deeply rutted by the wheels of bullock waggons.

There was a small wooden railway station and post office facing the railway. On the north side of the little street leading from the station post office was a large store that called itself a Farmers' Co-op. A little house of about four rooms stood next to it, standing a few yards back from the footpath, and on the corner a store belonging to a Syrian called Isaacs. Opposite Isaacs, on the corner, was a two-storeyed boarding house where we had lunched, and going toward the railway again was a tiny butcher's shop.

Across the main street and on the south side was Greene and Colebrook's store with corrugated iron roof and sides, all other buildings being built of wood, whilst some distance on the north side well back from the road was a Maori meeting house. There were no other buildings of note up the main street to the north so we turned southward round the corner from the boarding house and came to the livery stable. Here we lingered awhile and then strolling in the same direction, noted the Commercial Hotel on the opposite side, large and box-like, despite a balcony. At the next corner looking east across the railway we both saw and heard Ellis & Burnand's timber mill at work. In front of it stood a medium sized kahikatea or white pine tree where the advanced party of Hongi's invasion had been slaughtered less than ninety years before. The tree was on that account "tapu". But that is another story and we did not know it then. A number of unpainted white pine shacks, in which dwelt many of the mill hands, completed the picture, which seemed to me, and Brittan too, a singularly unattractive one. The Waipa river meandered round three sides of the township area.

As the afternoon wore on we began to think Mr Cashel was going to fail us, and I wondered what to do. Without him we were really helpless to begin the work at all. Should he not come, I supposed we must stay here and experience more vexatious delay. I was ready to vent my wrath on anyone who spoke to me, and my manner then gave the few who did the idea I was haughty and impatient.

At last we espied Mr Cashel slowly riding over the bridge. Why should he hurry? He was being paid a pound a day. It was nearly four o'clock by now. We were all ready to start and as daylight would go soon after five I was impatient to be off; but he had had no lunch. Couldn't start without something to eat. Where could he get it? I told him we had lunched at the boarding house hours before. He said he would try there. I told him we would go on and make camp at Otewa.

The half-caste driver of the hired buggy was frothing to go so as to be back before dark, so Brittan climbed up beside him. Crack

25

went the whip, off went the horses and I followed at a smart canter. We drove up the main street, turned to the right across the railway, followed a wheel track along the shady side of a hill just above a river, passed some Maori whares and crossed some unfenced native cultivations, without drawing rein until the horses splashed down into a ford which took us over, the water being up above the axles of the buggy.

On we went again up the other side of the river bed to cross once more and follow the track again where it ran through tall manuka above our heads and the right of way was just wide enough to let a waggon through. The pace was terrific for my poor pony, who as he galloped, caught his hoof in a root and went head over heels, sending me well beyond him, my knife flying from its sheath nearly into the buggy. This amused the driver, who pulled up. I was not hurt, nor was the pony; but I told him that, whilst eager to get on, he need not go so fast; but it made little difference. Several more fords, and the same track, brought us after only three-quarters of an hour to an open flat with little grass and many rabbit holes, and across this we pursued our way to some Maori whares, which the driver, pulling up with a flourish, told me was Otewa pa.

The chief's name was, I had been told, Te Ngoi Maika, who, I had also been informed, would find pack horses, hacks, or anything we needed. I enquired for him from two bare-legged giggling girls. They waved in silence towards a large timbered whare with a high open door. I rode up to this and seeing some natives sitting round some food on a mat on the earth floor, again asked for Ngoi. A brown man of medium height with delicate features and black moustache stood up and pointed to himself in silence.

"You are Te Ngoi Maika?" I asked. He nodded his head.

"Then," said I, "I want to hire a pack horse and a saddle horse tomorrow."

"Ten shillings the pack horse," said he, "ten shillings the other horse?"

"Right," said I. "At eight o'clock?" He nodded his head. "Then I want Waiotapu from Mangaorongo to come with us. Can you send him a message to let him know?" I had heard about Waiotapu at Cheal's office, and gathered that he knew the area.

He put his head on one side and looked doubtful.

"Maybe Waiotapu does not come. We will see about that," he answered.

"Oh, but he must come," said I. "Tell him we depend on him to show us the line. He was on Mr Cheal's survey party."

"We will try," came the non-committal reply. Once again I felt alarm that he might not, as I did not know how to commence operations without him. Te Ngoi did not seem conversational. His silence did not put me at my ease. I was to realise later that he was equally embarrassed. To end it, I asked if we might camp in the scrub beyond the pa. He nodded his head. I waved the buggy driver on and set off across the grass to where it was bounded by tall manuka, and cantered after it. There the driver dumped Stanley, the camp gear, and the rations, and, swiftly turning the horses, set off for Otorohanga even faster than he had come.

As we watched him go my sense of forlornness deepened; but it was no use to show it. Here we were, dumped beside the track, in a strange country amongst natives, with only about half an hour's daylight in which to make ourselves comfortable for the night and get an evening meal. Neither of us were good at camping then; but we got to it. I tied the pony to a bush and Stanley commenced making a fire. Fortunately there was plenty of dry manuka. I gathered armfuls and set them handy. We soon had a billy hanging over it full of water. We decided not to pitch a tent; but unrolled the fly which we fastened over a rail about five feet high so as to shelter us from the south should a wind get up, and put our blankets under it. The side towards the fire was open.

At this stage Mr Cashel rode up and asked what we were doing. I told him we were going to sleep here. He said we ought to have slept at the pa. I told him we had been there, but I did not know them, and they had not invited us. He replied that did not matter. However as dark was falling and the fire beginning to make a cheerful blaze, he agreed we might as well stop where we were, as it was going to be a fine night, and he let his horse go on the grass. I tethered mine on a long rope. The grass was short, and he did not appear to be going to have much to eat; but he fell to grazing, as did the other horse, straight away.

Somehow we all felt better after our meal which consisted of tinned beef, bread and butter, and jam, with several pannikins of hot tea with condensed milk and sugar. Life was not so bad. The stars came out above us in a clear sky. The fire spread a red glow in which we basked contentedly and all smoked our pipes. Mr Cashel became conversational. He said this would do for tonight; but another time we should sleep in the pa, if close at hand, as a matter of course. The natives expected it. The stranger was always welcome and no payment was sought. If one desired to make return one could leave them a tin or two of jam or golden syrup. Visitors brought news and they liked to talk a while before they went to bed.

"They will be talking about us tonight," he said, "and the whole district will know tomorrow. Everyone will want to know what you are like, how many men are with you, and what is your business. There will be great speculations as to where you have come from and where you are going. You in your turn would find them an interesting people, I think. I have known them for thirty years, and seen the life amongst them changing; but in many ways they remain the same, very different to ourselves in their outlook. Certainly they wear our clothes; but they are still very primitive at heart, gentle and good natured. The coming of the railway is spoiling those who live near it. They get money and squander it and it does them no good; but in these places like Otewa away from it they are not so demoralised as yet."

That Mr Cashel should talk like this surprised me. I had heard about him, that he was what men called "a hard old case" who drank heavily at times, and had been a real rolling stone. I had not yet learned that men could drink and still make their way in the world. The fact was, he only had a bust occasionally and was no soaker. He was of good Irish family, and had gone to sea as a merchant service apprentice in sail. There he had learned navigation which had enabled him to take up the work of survey. He was an authorised assistant. That meant he could work for a licensed surveyor, command a party in the field and do all the work a surveyor could himself do; but his plans, to be approved, must go through a surveyor's office and be adopted by the licensed man who would be responsible were there any errors. For work in the rough, such as laying off my bush before falling, he was entitled to act as he liked and receive any pay he chose, by private arrangement. He had worked up quite a good business for himself at this, and was now very comfortably off with money invested in town sections in Te Kuiti.

His life had been varied. He had early left the sea and joined a cavalry regiment, the Carabineers, in which he served two years. Coming to New Zealand he had soon found his way into survey, and being so handy, as were all sailors whatever their rank or rating, had been early entrusted with responsibility and men worked well for him as he was pleasant natured. He had actually been on the flying survey in 1879 in this very district and at Taupo had acquired a Maori wife, who for a while had accompanied him in the bush carrying her share of stores and equipment. Later he told me what a good sort she was, and how difficult it had been to abandon her in her native village. Not because she tried to follow him; she was too proud for that, when at length she realised he wanted her no longer; but because he did not, at first, find it easy to live without her. This night I did not know these details; but treated him as head of our party and called him Mr Cashel.

His talk was soothing, and his easygoing mood infectious. When later we rolled ourselves in our blankets I was content enough that all would go well on the morrow.

A touch of frost gave us a clear bright sunrise. Mr Cashel and

Brittan both were up before me, rather to my shame. I was learning to sleep well anywhere and was getting used to doing without sheets in camp, though down south at home, I hated the rough feel of blankets round my neck. Another meal exactly as the night before made us fit for anything that might lie before us. We went over to the pa, and this time found the natives smiling and communicative owing to the fact that Mr Cashel talked Maori like one of them. I now let him do the negotiation, having told him the night before about my own efforts in that direction, and after much converse he reported as follows:

"The pack horse, with a man, will be ready when wanted. It is being caught now, also the hack for Brittan; but Waiotapu is at Mangaorongo, four miles away. The boys are riding over presently with a message. It seems likely he may not come. Yes, I have told them how important it is. If he does not join us, we must try to get someone else. We can do with another man anyway, and send the packman back when we reach our destination. There seems little else to be done until Waiotapu turns up. So we may as well go back to our camp and wait."

Again I fumed at the prospect of further delay. We lit our pipes and smoked by the fire, as the boys galloped past us towards Mangaorongo. It annoyed me to calculate that Waiotapu could not be with us for at least an hour and a half even if he came straight away. Presently another native turned up. He had been on survey two years before in the Rangitoto when they had run a parallel and cross line to my corner peg. Should Waiotapu not come, this might be useful to us. He offered his services. He said his name was Waho Emery.

"What wages do you want?" said I.

"Ten bob," said he.

Mr Cashel chipped in, "I think nine bob, eh? That is enough."

"Kapai, that is good," said Waho contentedly as he sat on his horse.

Mr Cashel turned to me saying, "It is the usual wage. Apparently here they have decided to ask ten shillings for everything, pack horse, hack and all; but there is no need to pay it."

We waited long. Presently the pack horse arrived led by a full-blooded native with face and bristly moustache like those seen on the masks of old Japanese armour. His name was Peta Tahatika. He had a look of perpetual good humour, and when I told him it was nine-thirty he smiled disarmingly and replied, "Mr Te Ngoi he say eight the time you say all right; but I no come before. I know Waiotapu not be here yet. Maybe he not come at all."

Explosively I turned to Mr Cashel. "You hear that. What is all this mystery about this confounded Waiotapu? Has he seen him this morning? Are we never going to get anything definite about him? Here we are, ready to start, and are losing valuable time, all on account of a man we have never seen, and who it appears we may not see at all. I suppose he does exist?"

Mr Cashel was soothing. He gabbled away to the pack man and presently said, "It does seem improbable he is coming. It seems he has only just married."

In my impatience I could not see that this should affect matters; but there was nothing for it now, having sent for him, but to await his arrival, or at least the return of the boys from the Mangaorongo. We caught and saddled our horses, rolled up our coats and blankets and strapped them on the pack saddle which I now observed to be a worn-out tattered thing, the only sound parts being the frame and hooks. The breast plate and crupper were mended and tied with green flax.

Again we waited until the sun rising high and growing hunger reminded us that noon was approaching. We decided to have lunch, at which the two natives, hitherto maddeningly inert, showed an interest in the proceedings. On went the billy again and, the tea made, all fell to and felt better.

As we were finishing, the native boys galloped up from Manga-orongo as if they had been going at that pace there and back, whilst really they had been dawdling with their friends, to say: "Waiotapu he no come. He say he don't like. He say kapai you go yourselves. He no care."

This after four hours' waiting for him, for the last two of which I had been feeling the same way.

"All right, we'll start," said I.

The way the two natives now got to the business of the day was reassuring. They said little; but together they worked without at any time getting in each other's way or hesitating. In a surprisingly short time the gear was rolled up into three sacks; two of even weight, judged by eye and hand, were hooked on each side of the pack saddle, and a large one containing chiefly the tent and fly was placed on top. A long flax rope was passed under the bow of the saddle and over the top, then crossed and the ends passed down over the side loads, under the horse and tied to steady all. One took a slasher, another an axe. We all mounted, and Peta Tahatika taking the lead, we started along the waggon track at the bottom side of the low foothills on our right hand.

Soon we came to a swamp. Peta's horse wallowed in, next the pack horse on a flax rope, and one by one we all filed after. It was a still day and as I puffed my pipe in the warm sunlight, I felt cheerful. At least we were on the move again, only at a walk it is true; but we were under way. On our left we passed two native whares with punga sides and thatched raupo roof, from which an old man, and two withered old wahines emerged to smile and wave to us as we passed on. Somehow their presence as they stood under a yellowing poplar tree made me feel I was near a friendly people and my mind felt more at ease than it had done for over twenty-four hours.

The track led us now over another small water course on to a shingle flat through some more tall manuka to the river's edge where it flowed wide and smooth. We crossed and turned right up another flat with "fern above the saddle bow". High above us was a steep hill face, with deep entrenchments on the top. I enquired of Waho if he knew about them.

"Oh, Te Kooti lived here one time," said he. I knew enough of that free-booter to wonder when; but Waho knew little more.

Again we crossed a wide ford and on another fern-covered flat rode under some high cherry trees, bare now of leaf, beside some native graves. The next ford took us in under a high bush-covered hill on our left on to a narrow spit of shingle which led in turn to a flat, with fern and bush alternating, whilst to our right over the river was a large grove of magnificent kahikateas in boggy ground which had thrown us over to this side of the river in observance of the native custom to avoid obstacles by going round rather than through them. This might be said to characterise their lives in general at this time; with life secure, plenty of potatoes to fill the stomach, and time no worry, why bother to surmount anything if you can go round it?

A quarter of a mile brought us once more to a ford with high banks this time, and the river narrow, smooth and deep. Along the flat, fern again, with one tall kahikatea in the centre and steep bush-clad slopes now closing in on us. Another deep ford and we were riding through a grove of tree ferns called pungas, lovely I thought; but nothing to what I was to see later on. As we splashed into the next ford a flight of wild duck took the wing and circled away above us. We now trailed up the shingle bed of the river which we presently turned from, to avoid a swampy place on our right and continued up the flat towards another great grove of kahikatea where the tuis were calling the news of our approach.

Leaving these on our right front we crossed a swiftly flowing ford — how many is that? — on to a grassy patch with a may tree in the centre and a shingle-bottomed creek on the left flowing into the Waipa on our right. This, I was told, was the Waimahora. A cock pheasant swaggered in front of us deliberately raising his feet as we came on. We watched his flight as he went two hundred yards to descend into the tall scrub which clothed the flat ahead and the low hills into which for the next three miles or so the country now opened. We followed the flat and the stream. It was smaller and shallower than the Waipa of which it was a tributary. We crossed and recrossed it every few chains, the track, just wide enough for a single horseman to ride, passing through manuka high above our heads.

To our left there was a gap in the hills indicating a wide flat.

"Pakeha he live there," said Peta waving his hand. I stood in my stirrups to crane as I rode, feeling a great interest, for this was the first European I had heard of since leaving Otorohanga the day before. A stream, the Tauraroa, flowed into the Waimahora here. But I could see no sign of habitation.

Sometimes we came to an obstruction of fallen manuka when the leading men would dismount and cut a passage with a slasher. More than once the track climbed a high bank, and at one point the pack horse at a steep pinch scrambled with his feet, slipped, and fell over into the scrub. The natives were not the least flurried though he remained down on his back and side, nor did the horse, after a kick or two, seem to trouble much; but lay still whilst they untied the pack saddle and cut the scrub around him. When they had cleared enough, Peta gave a tug on the head rope, the animal got up and shook himself. He was reloaded and on we went again for perhaps another two miles when two more crossings of the creek brought us to where the hills, bush-clad, high and steep again, narrowed in on either side and we came to what looked like a wall of bush in front of us.

Here we drew rein. There was a little grass interspersed amid high fern, an easy bank rising about six feet above the stream level and a small grassy space about ten yards square. We decided to halt and pitch the tent here for the night whilst the light was with us. Waho tied his horse and went into the bush to cut tent poles. Peta unloaded the pack horse. I got out the billy, filled it with water, and put it on the fire that Stanley was starting — we were already learning the routine of bivouac — and Mr Cashel gathered wood. Waho bringing stout poles, up went the tent, and galley in front, for which we brought an extra fly; Peta, having tethered the horses, helped him as did Mr Cashel and I after tethering both of ours. We then got out the food and assisted Brittan to prepare the meal, when, satisfied we could do no more in that line, and that an ample supply of firewood was to hand, we unrolled our blankets in the tent for the night.

Now we were, I felt, making progress. The bush crowded in on us on three sides. My place was only a little over two miles away. It was very cold this night away from a fire as the sun did not reach this spot until late in the morning in winter and soon lost it at night.

The tent felt like an ice vault. The two Maoris shared their blankets just inside the door and we lay side by side on the ground at the back. We shared our blankets too, Brittan lying between Mr Cashel and me. We soon turned in and lay smoking by candlelight. I said what a wonderful thing was tobacco.

"Yes," said Mr Cashel, "but the effect is largely imaginary. I believe blind men do not smoke, and no one wants to do so in the dark unless he can see his smoke." We tried it and it appeared to be true.

Next morning we decided, before proceeding further, to make a block for the horses about half a mile behind us where there was some tall manuka, to enable them to have a run and pick what grass there was along the stream. We went down with axes and slashers and finding a deep cut washed by a small stream from a gully to the east, which horses could not cross, we started to continue this by erecting a log fence, called a dog leg, from the end of the cut and across the Waimahora. Whilst doing this I was surprised by a white man greeting me. He said he lived on the Tauraroa about two miles off and had come to see what we were doing. He had seen our tracks, he told me, and came hot foot to join us and hear the news. He seemed to my eye a queer specimen, strong as a horse obviously, clad in an old sleeveless flannel which hung outside his tattered dungaree trousers, and broken boots with no socks.

He talked with little pause, giving us his advice and information about the country. I presently turned back to work, falling a manuka about six inches thick.

"I have not done much of this work," said I.

"I can see that," said he watching; and presently, "Here, gimme the axe," and he did a bit of showing off, cutting one clean scarf very quickly till the tree fell. He continued to help till we finished and then followed us to camp, joined us at lunch and went on talking all the time.

Leaving one man in camp, the rest of us entered the bush in the afternoon, the stranger coming too. It was very thick, chiefly konini and mahoe, interlaced with supplejacks and lawyers closely tangled. Fortunately there was an ancient track to follow, just wide enough for single file; but it was badly blocked by windfalls. If the latter were large we went round them. If they were small we cleared them sufficiently with a slasher to let us creep through. We crossed the running Waimahora eight times. The bottom of it was shingle, the water clear and icy cold. The bush overhung the stream, but did not completely block out the sky.

At the end of about an hour and a half we saw a large slip to our right on the steep hillside which ran right to the top and had carried down several acres of ground. The opening it made in the

33

bush showed the height of the ridge and the nature of the soil composing it, a reddish yellow clay. It was different from any I had seen in the South Island, and I was not qualified to judge its fertility. We continued to feel our way forward, our strange visitor, whose name proved to be Macfarlane, up near the van using the slasher when necessary like a paid hand and talking all the time. Eager as I was to see what was before us, I found myself compelled owing to my lack of bushcraft to follow in the rear with Stanley Brittan who showed unusual animation and more than once said, "'This is interesting, Spen. It is very interesting. Who does this land belong to?" A question I could not answer, as we once more entered the semi-twilight of the bush.

A slight rise from a creek crossing showed light ahead and in less than fifty yards we emerged on a beautiful flat of nearly an acre with a natural sole of good grass about six inches high. It seemed a perfect oasis in a deserted land of dense trackless forest. We paused and as we each in turn stood forward we formed a silent group entranced by some fascination of the beauty of the scene, accentuated manyfold in my own and Brittan's case by the discomfort of the struggle, which, though neither would confess to it, the journey through had been to us. Even Macfarlane ceased to chatter.

Had we ever doubted the capacity of the land to grow grass, here was its proof before us. This was no catch crop on the humus of recently felled forest; but a close sward obviously many years old.

What had caused it? Why was it here? When at last I spoke, these were the questions I asked. Waho pointed before him to a cone-shaped hill rising straight up from the other side of the little clearing, its summit some feet above the light bush with which the hillside was covered.

"The old people lived there," said he, "many years. Long before my grandfather. There was a pa. They called it Taitoki. You see the line of the trench at the top? Yes? Gone away a good while, before I am born." This was as interesting as it was unexpected, for I had seen no sign of any human activity on my journey at the other side of the mountain with Hughes, nothing but the forest, primeval and undisturbed, till the coming of the surveyor.

Rangitoto itself, I now observed to the south about a mile, rising steeply and overshadowing Taitoki which was south-east of us.

"Well," said Cashel breaking in on my reflection, "if we are to sleep in camp we had better start back. This 'grass patch' will be useful to us as a camp site."

I agreed, and the place became from then on known as the "grass patch".

We returned as usual quicker than we came. As we went I was worried about Macfarlane and how he was to get home. In those days I liked to offer food and lodging to anyone who was at my place at nightfall; but though food was available, space in our little tent was limited, and the previous night had proved we had no spare blankets. I tried to say something of this to him, apologising that I could not ask him to stay; but he cut me short saying, "Oh, that is all right. I'm not particular and I need no blankets. I can lie down anywhere, and I sleep sound at once. I don't want the things other men need. You will never be as tough as I am."

So he stayed. He might not need what other men needed; but he ate twice as much as any of us that night, tinned meat and potatoes, tea and rice, topping off with large slices of thickly buttered and jammed bread from a store that I now saw could not outlast the journey.

"I like this baker's bread," said he, "I always bake me own. It is better than this for stickin' to yer. But for a change, a slice of baker's bread goes all right. Now soda bread. It ain't any good if a man has to work. Leaves him all weak like, no go in him. I wouldn't eat it if you asked me to." We hadn't but still I felt guilty about it. "Give me plenty of meat and spuds I say, and I'm all right. Wild pork now. I ask nothing better; but the wild beef from the cattle up here, if you kill one of them you're all right. You can eat all you want and there is plenty over. I like good food. Give me that and I can go all day. I don't want nothing else."

Before turning in we made plans for the morrow, to strike camp after breakfast when the horses had been caught and saddled, load up, and taking them through with us, make our camp on the "grass patch" preparatory to finding the peg and starting work the day following.

The night was cold again to begin with and I had not been asleep long when I found our unbidden guest who was lying beside me trying to filch a bit of blanket despite his hard constitution. I was inclined to let him have it; but the other edge covered Mr Cashel and he was not letting go of any of it though he never woke up. The cold moderated towards morning and it commenced to rain in showers. After day-break we went down to the creek to wash. As always I pulled off my shirt, and lying on the bank, plunged my head, bare shoulders and arms into the water as far as I could go without wetting the top of my trousers.

"Hell," said Macfarlane, "that is hot stuff." For the first time there was a respectful note in his voice. Not for long though. At breakfast he was telling me once more how to manage my affairs. We had a billyful of porridge.

"Porridge ain't much good to yer to work on," said he. "It don't stick to yer. You are hungry in half an hour," quickly finishing his tin plateful. "Is there any more in that billy? Thank yer," emptying

35

what was left. "Give us some butter. It goes better to mix it in the porridge. Now some of that condensed milk. Throw us the sugar, will yer. Sugar is supposed to be good for a man. I don't go much on it meself," taking about four spoonfuls nevertheless. "What's that tinned meat yer eatin'? Beef? Well it's all right for a change," digging out half the tin, "but meself I prefer fresh beef, though a bit o' corned is not so bad. You ought to get some, it'll keep well. Spuds? All right. Ain't yer got some onions? They are good for yer when yer can't get other vegetables. I can eat lots of onions. Some more tea? What about a bit of bread and jam? Even if yer haven't time to cook 'em, a raw onion will do all right."

We failed him there though. After breakfast he "reckoned" he'd be going, with some reluctance. No one argued the point and he accompanied us down the creek as we went for the horses. One of these was on the wrong side of our very makeshift fence. He was easily caught as he would not leave the vicinity of the others; but we felt we must see where he got out, and finding no break, had to raise the obstruction at its lowest points. This meant sending back for axe and slasher, and though it did not seem to take long it was nearly eleven before we were back at camp, so we decided to boil up, have some tea and bread and butter and then go right through to the grass patch without stopping for lunch. I was a source of amazement to the natives that I drank no tea, under the impression the tea habit was bad one. The wai matau, cold water, from the stream, was the best and purest I ever tasted anywhere.

Tandem-at-length — we started, the two natives leading, axe and slasher in hand, each leading a horse, then Bob Cashel whom I still addressed as "Mister" though the natives more than once called him by his Christian name, which as yet scandalised me, and after them Stanley and I followed with our horses, the pack horse being in front of us. We were constantly stopping whilst the overhanging supplejacks and lawyers were cut to enable the animals to get through, and from time to time a fallen tree blocked the way. They said a bad gale had brought them down the previous summer. If they were small and low, we made the horses step over them. If they were waist-high they had to be cut. The larger trees necessitated cutting a track round them. During these halts the animals grazed on the coarse bush grass, on the leaves of the mahoe, and shrubs.

The rain settled into a steady downpour. We were soon all wet through; but not cold, and when at last, late in the afternoon we reached the grass patch, the mists were rising from the gullies and shrouding Rangitoto. The horses got their heads down to the thick grass straight away. The natives made a block across the track to keep them there, we unrolled the tentage and soon had the camp erected above a floor of wet grass; but never minded that. Waho got water, Peta kindled a fire. We unpacked the blankets and stores and got them and the saddlery under cover. Then, Waho supervising the cooking, Brittan and I accompanied Peta to cut and carry firewood, of which an ample supply lay within a chain at the edge of the bush.

Mr Cashel by virtue of his age and standing was not called upon to perform these duties, though he was still as good at them as any of us. We were acting in the role of a survey party. These parties were organised and ordered much as is a military unit. The surveyor and his cadet, if he had one, had the standing of the officer class. The chainman was the N.C.O. and the rest the other ranks. I shall say more of this later on. Though, to all appearance equal in mode of living, the Surveyor was the educated man, and his word was as much law as that of a ship's captain. He roughed it with the rest; but the men recognised his position by calling him "Mister". Bob Cashel then, whilst we hewed the wood and drew the water, consulted his maps, and taking compass shots at the mountain, tried to fix our present position.

A good evening meal and a roaring fire thereafter cheered us inwardly, and outwardly dried us sufficiently to send us into our blankets full of cheerful expectancy for the morrow. Our stores would need replenishment so it was decided that Peta was to go into town after breakfast and get the stuff required, taking the pack horse and the signed order from me. He might not be back for several days. We had enough till then, though not to see the job out. I was awake before dawn and went out to see a bright starlit sky. All promised well, things seemed to go easier the further we went.

An hour later it was pouring again, a blue lookout; but during breakfast it cleared. Bob got out the plan whilst the men were tidying up the utensils, and pointing with a pencil explained to me, "The map shows a line cut to the nor'-west corner peg of your section, somewhere to the east of us, but as I have not been able to get a shot on to the top of the mountain where the trig is, I cannot tell its position with any certainty. It may be only a few chains off, or a mile away. Further, it was cut some years ago, and may have since become too over-grown for us to find easily. Had we had that scoundrel Waiotapu with us he could have told us these things, taken us straight to it, and saved us much trouble, for the peg cannot be much more than half a mile from here. A continuance of this line cut through the bush is your western boundary. We might easily waste a day looking for it".

On the other hand, this native Waho was employed more recently, cutting a parallel line about two miles to the west of it. This line terminates in the bush; but another running from it eastward goes in a straight line direct to the peg. It seems an old track up the mountain, which he can find, crosses the west-east line. I therefore suggest we use this track till we come to the line and then follow along it until we strike the peg. It will take several hours, and entail a fairly long journey round; but we shall have the advantage of being certain where we are going. What do you say?"

"I say we will follow your suggestion," said I. "When can we start?"

"Now," said he.

Waho had put a billy, some tea and sugar, a loaf of bread and some butter into a sugar bag which with the two pieces of flax tied to the bottom corners and round the top made an excellent little haversack to carry on his back. With this on he now stood ready, slasher in hand, to go. He wore dungaree trousers, boots on his feet and a blue flannel open at the neck, and on his head a handkerchief knotted at the corners to form a sort of cap. This I found was not to keep his head dry; but to keep the twigs and pieces of dust and bark out of his hair. Mr Cashel wore a waistcoat and short leggings, otherwise was similarly dressed. Brittan had copied Waho. I, having heard that the troops fighting in the bush had discarded trousers in the early days, did the same, having a long shirt on. Years before Hegarty had told me, "The boss should not take his coat off." I took him literally and wore mine.

Brittan was amused at my dress. Mr Cashel was polite about it; but said, "They used to dress like that years ago in imitation of the Maoris; but unless you are used to it, you will find the sand flies trying." For the moment it seemed cool and ideal to walk in, and I continued it; but I found in the long run that Bob was right and seldom repeated it.

Away we went and in a minute or two were walking through the stream. I had already discarded socks, as I found it hopeless to try and keep feet dry. To our left the valley was covered by tall tawa bush. They said it was flat. I took their word for it. To me it seemed we were constantly going up and down. We crossed another small stream about a hundred yards on. I had not the remotest idea of which direction we were going at any given time, as the sun, when it did show, was completely hidden by the foliage. Cashel and Waho said the track was good; but half the time I could not see one at all, and still stumbled over roots if we went at any pace. We climbed a clay bank, deeply worn by the feet of cattle and pigs, passed through another grove of tawa and again climbed up on the clay, the track following a sideways route round the hill; but always rising sufficiently to affect the breathing.

The going got a bit easier two or three hundred yards up and when we paused to relieve our lungs my attention was drawn to the fact we were passing through big manuka up to twenty feet high. My eye was too unpractised to note this or the deep pig rootings that ran everywhere over the hilltop. I was too busy when walking to watch for anything but the roots which might throw me down. On we went again and breathing more easily made me realise we were going on the level till we came to another tawa grove which they again called a flat. Emerging from this after about a quarter of a mile we began to ascend a steep slope through light bush of tawhero, which I was disappointed to see, as it was said to be a bad indication. The track was well enough defined, being deeply enough worn in the hill for even me to see it. Both Brittan and I felt the going so much there were frequent halts in which I was pleased to note even Cashel and Waho were glad to pause for breath.

One of these pauses came in a glade with some grass on which the sun was now shining. We could glimpse the way we had come, beneath us, and saw a wide, level-topped ridge north-east, and to our right a wide pleasant-looking easy valley with a raupo swamp which we had headed in our walk. Cashel said the track led right over Rangitoto and was an old native thoroughfare, now disused; but in centuries past a route to the Taupo plain. The manuka on the flat top ridge was second growth. It seemed the people in the Taitoki pa must have cultivated there, and having left it, the forest had once more claimed its own. Such big manuka could be no recent growth; but must be thirty or forty years old at least.

Steadily we climbed again and then more easily along a level enough ridge for about a hundred yards when Waho stopped and, grounding the end of his slasher, pointed to the bush on our left. I could see nothing except the broad leaves of the rangiora scrub, of which there was much hereabouts, with their white undersides. Mr Cashel gave one glance and said, "Here we are," to which I could only ask, "Where are we?"

"Why, we are on the line," said he. "Don't you see it?" I had to confess I saw no indication of it till he pointed, and I could see a very slight opening in the tops of the trees left and right which I would never have noticed myself, and closer at hand here and there the cut branch of a shrub.

"Well, we've got to follow this," said he turning to the left. "Lead on, Waho," and we filed after him down the hill. For Stanley and me the next two hours were torture. We were on a sidling at first and the supplejacks and undergrowth were the thickest I had ever seen. The line, cut two or three years before, was overgrown and the vines overhung it like a net of tangled ropes. Here and there Waho cut a sapling. For the rest we hung on by our hands and followed in silence and determination. Presently we dropped steeply to a small stream across our path, and then we climbed out of it as high again. When we slipped on the hillside, which we did frequently, we fell on the points of cut supplejacks. We climbed over one ridge after another. I was too occupied keeping up to count them and it seemed hours ere at last Waho once more stopped and clearing away a few branches of fern pointed in silence to the ground with his slasher.

"And what's that?" said I.

"That," said Mr Cashel, "is the peg we have come out to find."

Despite our long struggle to get here I cannot say I was thrilled at the sight of the first indication of the property of which we had become the lessees. The peg was a totara stake, about three inches square on the top, with a tin tack hammered into it. It stuck about three inches out of the ground and was weather-worn. Just that. I walked round it to feel sure I had been on my own property and then enquired, "What next?"

"Now we start work," said Mr Cashel. I saw Waho's face fall. He looked exhausted and white, notwithstanding his brown skin. He had been setting a stiff pace in all eagerness and now there was a visible reaction. I felt done up; but then I usually did before I had gone far in the bush, and miserable though I might be inside, just knew I must keep on while the others did, and try to look as if I liked it.

"Anyway, let's have something to eat," I said, and we started on the bread and butter. We discovered it was three o'clock. We did not know how far from our camp we were, nor what the going might be like to reach it. We decided to call it a day and go home. I think everyone was relieved as we dropped down the hill and striking the water, reached our camp in half a mile.

*   *   *

Next day we climbed the steep slope from the creek to the peg and started work. I acted as chainsman. Mr Cashel set up his compass on a flat-topped stick above the peg and taking a sight on the bearing of the line shown on the map, we aligned ourselves at intervals of about ten yards or more, and started cutting the undergrowth with slashers to stretch the chain along it on a straight line. As each man cleared his own piece he moved up beyond the furthest man and continued on the same alignment. When a chain length was cleared, I went forward and Cashel, looking through the compass, directed me where to stop, then he called, "Pull tight and mark," when I would cut a short stake of green sapling and drive it into the ground. He kept a record of the number of chains in his note book. In this way we climbed steadily, leaving a clearly marked line all the way.

This was called a rough survey. Had we been doing an official survey I learned we would have used a theodolite and much longer chain whilst clearing all obstruction on the line, even large trees. When we came to one of these, we offset it by taking a compass shot to its base, then measuring far enough to the right or left to get round it, measuring similarly past it, and back on to our original line on the far side, blazing the tree so as to mark it well. Up and up we went, though our progress was slow owing to the density of the undergrowth of which the supplejacks, thick as a man's thumb very often, and very tough and strong, were the worst. I found the cutting difficult at first. The vines were so resilient, they bent before the slasher and sprang back into place.

Brittan, I noted, took readily to the work in a quiet efficient way. He seemed to do nearly as well as Waho who was bred to it. He would finish his length, move up into line without haste or scrambling, look back for the direction of the line and commence cutting on, as Waho did.

I envied him, until presently Bob Cashel said to me, "I think I can show you how to cut more easily. You are cutting high up and straight across the vine. That makes hard work of it. Now cut low, and try to do it on the slant, not more than a foot from the ground. If it is stretched across the line higher than that, then take a good slanting cut at it. If above your head, hold it in one hand and slash upwards; but remember, the more slant the easier the cut." I heeded what he told me and did better.

The bush was in subdued light; but this I was getting used to. I still found the work and conditions grimly uncomfortable; but by comparison with my beginning it seemed certainly easier, and there was a very real interest in it to note the growth about me and the quality of the soil under foot. Even the smell seemed to have a warm humid richness about it, and as we worked we were accompanied by a fantail fluttering so close that one felt one could reach out and catch him. We discussed him and liked to believe he was there out of pure friendliness. It was said he came along for the insects we disturbed. If so, they were too minute for us to see. No, we refused to believe it was for any other reason but his preference for human society, and when another bird intruded and he drove him off with much twittering, we thoroughly approved.

All the same it was arduous going. A glimpse of light ahead would delude us into the belief that we were approaching a ridge top only to find when we got there that the steep hillside went up higher and higher. It was a relief to us all when after crossing a small mountain trickle which went leaping down the hill, Bob said it was twelve o'clock and time to boil the billy. As we sat round

41

having lunch and drinking the hot tea we felt thankful for it, and grateful for a short spell thereafter in which to lie back on the warm soft earth and smoke our pipes.

Said Bob Cashel reflectively, " 'There is pleasure in the pathless wood'," and paused for our comment.

"And I wonder what ass of a poet wrote that," said Brittan. I recalled that I had been told that Anthony Trollope when visiting Australia had written: "Life in the bush is one prolonged picnic."

"Oh yes?" said Stanley. "I'll bet the Australians saw to it he only stayed at the best squattages, with a nicely cut lunch when they drove him out to hear the kookaburras, a case of champagne under the seat of the buggy, and a nice hot bath when he got back to the homestead before he changed for dinner. That is the kind of bush life that the distinguished stranger from overseas is shown."

We all laughed including the Maori who only half understood what we talked about.

" 'We poor sailor boys is scuttlin' up aloft, with the landlubber lyin' down below' " — I hummed a snatch of an old sea song of my father's. Bob looked interested and reminisced.

"Yes. If they knew what it meant to reef top sails in a southerly off the Horn, many more people would feel grateful for small mercies. What a curious lot of unpleasant things there are to do in this world, just to make life comfortable for the people who won't leave the cities. Well I suppose we must get on with our little part of it."

We worked on till well after four o'clock before knocking off to slip and slide down the hill whilst the sharp points of the newly cut supplejacks stabbed the softer parts of our bodies. For the second time in the day we waded knee-deep in the cold stream as we made our way back to camp and bed.

Next day was a repetition of the one before; but as the afternoon wore on, it became evident we were getting near the top of the ridge which we knew was a spur leading up to the mountain top. The bush became thinner and the light was better. There were fewer supplejacks. As we went up, so did our spirits. We hoped to get the line over the ridge that night; but by four o'clock we were still some distance from the top. Brittan wanted to get there in the hope of getting a general view of the country. If it satisfied him, he meant to obtain a block of it. He wanted to go back to town next day, so we decided that he and I would climb up the ridge, the other two waiting for us at the top of the line. Bob Cashel considered we should always leave ourselves a clear hour of daylight in which to get home to camp, in case of any mishap on the way down.

We decided not to make the long climb up the mountain next day, to finish the short distance necessary to take us to the ridge; but to work round to it, when we had completed the other three sides of the block.

Brittan and I climbed up through the undergrowth and at the end of perhaps three chains, found ourselves on the track leading along the ridge to the top. It was steep; but could be opened up where we were, sufficiently to enable horses to come up, though the work would take a day or two. A tree had fallen across it near us making an opening towards the south west. We climbed on this and looked out. For miles richly timbered bush lay before us. After a pause I asked. "Well, what do you think of it?"

"I think," he replied, "that at a rent of a shilling an acre, a man should take up as much of this country as he can. I will go straight to Te Kuiti and take up this block to begin with as soon as I can get it."

Naturally I was elated. I valued his opinion and was glad to think I would have a neighbour whom I knew. It confirmed my own judgment, and strengthened my confidence in the future. We were a cheerful camp that night. I remarked jokingly that we had missed the voice of our new friend Macfarlane since he left.

"Yes." said Mr Cashel, "I think he is one of these bush diamonds, rough on the outside."

"He is the funny man that," said Waho, "Maori call him 'Hongi Porka' — smell the pig. Why? Because one day some of the Otewa men go hunting. They see him. They ask if he know where any pig are. He say 'Yes. Up the valley there in the fern.' They ask 'Have you seen them there?' 'No,' he say, 'I have not seen them; but I smell them as I came along.' Werry funny man they call that. Tito — liar — they think, so now they call him Hongi Pork because he smell the pig." And from then on to all of us he became known as Hongi Pork for evermore.

*   *   *

Up early as usual, my pony was saddled before breakfast. Brittan was to ride him and Peta bring him back when he returned with the stores. As we ate breakfast a gloom settled on me that I was going to lose the one man of the party that I had known since boyhood. It seemed absurd, for he was not going far. Still, as clad in his civilised clothes and waterproof coat he said "Goodbye" to the others and turned to me, I said lightly, "Oh, I will come with you and put the rails up after you," which he could have done himself. I went down the narrow track with him until the first crossing of the creek deprived me of excuse to go further, and stood waiting as he splashed across and the bush on the far side swallowed him up.

As I turned back to the camp I felt that such a forlorn loneliness had never been my lot before. Here I was left, not only alone

43

with strangers, that did not worry me; but I felt Brittan was able to go off to town. He could pack his things there and go off to South Canterbury if he so listed, and it would not matter; but I was anchored here. Whatever happened now, the die was cast for me. Here I must stay and work out my own destiny by myself with the thought that if I went wrong, my father and his family would be the losers. I could never now leave while the place was in our hands and undeveloped. To do so would be desertion. I did not of course cry; but I felt that it was the one thing that would ease my feelings.

Cashel and Waho stood awaiting my return and once more we filed out into the bush and up the cold stream. A blue mountain duck, as we crossed at the track ford, fluttered up the surface of the water a few yards from us with whistling cries of alarm. It seemed we might have killed it easily as it did not rise upon the wing. It was the first I had seen and is of a rare species that will always bring the memory of sad thoughts to my mind. I could not yet trust myself to speak, and we all proceeded in silence. When we got to the peg and took a breather, I saw we must now go east and that to begin with, our way lay downhill. I had a plug of torori, strong, black, native-grown tobacco and it seemed suitable to fill my pipe and light it. For the first time I would smoke at work.

The going this morning was surprisingly easy. For the first chain or two it lay downhill and though the supplejacks were thick, we made great progress and were well up the next spur by lunchtime. As we boiled the billy I found I was still smoking the pipeful of torori I had started with. It had often gone out and been relighted though. It was powerful stuff. I believe if I wished to cure myself of smoking I would try torori, if my friends would live under the same roof with me, which I doubt. My depression had been slowly going as I tended the duties of cutting and measuring the line. Work will cure most things in time; but that even my companions had shared my feelings I learned, when Bob lying back against a puketea said, as he lit his pipe, "Always a depressing thing when anyone leaves camp. It is hard to start work again; but the feeling passes"; and so I have found it, often in later days and more distant lands. Nothing is intolerable in this world if one sticks it long enough.

Our line carried us over the spur and along a sidling downhill. The three of us had done over thirty chains by the time we stopped work.

All the same, the country was so steep and the going so arduous, I had begun to realise the task we had set ourselves was not going to be as easy as I had thought. My father's idea was to fall a thousand acres of bush; but to do that, I saw we should have started earlier in the year. Further was the problem of transport. All gear, stores and food, would have to be packed. To do this tracks must be opened to the bushmen's camps wherever they might be, right over Rangitoto. A large number of pack horses would be necessary and they again would need oats and chaff and there was not enough grass to last more than a day or two. I discussed these things with Mr Cashel and the upshot was that I decided to lay off only 400 acres this year, which would be a good beginning, and provide grass on the mountain for pack horses the year following. It is a curious commentary on our inexperience of bush farming that we had not taken the cost of packing, nor making tracks, into our calculations at all.

Peta had arrived with horses and stores when we got back to camp that night. He was a very pleasant brown man, a full-blooded Maori with a smile that would not come off. He was keen to go on with the job with us, and we were glad to have him. Brittan had met him on the way down and it seemed that Peta had amused him immensely by his enquiries as to whether I was not "a very big rangatira — kanui te utu eh?", in other words, a great chieftain with plenty of money. This reputation stuck to me long.

Brittan had had a trying ride out, I learned. The river had been high and the track being new to him, the fords were hard to find. After several mistakes when the pony would decline to go on, he decided to give him his head, and found he walked unerringly into the river, took a slanting course down the current and leaning against the water kept his foothold to the other side. The rider sat coolly on top of the saddle and put his legs along his horse's neck. He was full of Jeff's praises when next I met him.

Our line now continued easily down to a creek, the Waimahora, leaping down over huge boulders from the mountain. Just before we reached it, a dog Peta had brought got on to a pig which charged down the hill nearly on top of him. He clove it with his slasher to the brain. It proved a nice sow about eighteen months old and brought the work to a temporary standstill, whilst the natives lit a fire and singed the body, scraping off the bristles with their knives. During this process Peta's look of satisfaction reminded me of a cat purring over a mouse.

The west-east line ended about a chain over the stream. We were due to turn, so we lunched and decided that to carry the next line south we would save time if we slept closer to our work. We could not bring a pack horse here, so must carry what we wanted up the stream and make a flying camp beside it at this point where the line crossed. We went back along the line and rolled up our swags, dividing the food and utensils necessary amongst us. The pig would provide us with good fresh meat for days to come, so our most bulky rations were bread and potatoes.

The journey up, loaded as we were, was no fun. There was nothing for it but to get into the creek and follow it up as the hills closed in on either side into a gorge in which the foliage went over the water, and the supplejacks equalled anything yet encountered. The sun never entered that awesome watercourse and the leaves everywhere were dripping with moisture. The water rushed round and over large boulders two and three feet high, slippery smooth as ice, and as cold, with the uninterrupted wash of centuries. On the lower sides were pools often waist-deep. The distance was only a little over a mile; but we were scrambling and climbing all the way, and it must have taken over two hours; but our attention was so occupied with the toil of keeping on that I was gladly surprised to find on following the others out of the water at a bend that we had reached our camping place.

What a camping place it was though! Never have I known a worse. That everything was dripping seemed a minor drawback, for there was not a flat yard of ground. Having built a fire we had to fell a tawa six inches in diameter to prevent ourselves slipping into it. Above this we spread our blankets and over these we erected the fly, open on the side facing the fire. The pork, potatoes and onions that we had for tea were good though, and we slept well enough despite the fact we all slipped down against the log and lay curled like dogs, together, until morning and the tui high above us in the treetops on the mountain, woke us to the day's work.

Two days we ran the line south from here, parallel with our first one and in the afternoon of the second had turned west. The bush was getting lighter. We were eating well and sleeping well, and the weather had turned cold and fine. We called this uncomfortable bivouac the "flying camp". Had we brought up a spade we might have at least had a level place on which to lie; but we were just as glad to return to it each night for food and sleep, as I have been at the Grand Hotel, Auckland, and we earned our rest.

The scramble along the cut line each morning and the return at evening by the same route, were to me the most painful part of the day's work. Falling on the sharp point of a supplejack which one often did on that steep hillside, tore the clothing and more than once brought blood from the skin. On the other hand, the flying camp being higher, we did not have to climb so far each day as on the first line.

As we drove on, the day after we had turned west the upward slope became more gradual, and the bush itself lighter. There was not the tangled undergrowth to contend with, the trees were straighter and smaller for the most part, and there was much mountain totara. So favourable had become the going that we had measured over forty chains on this line by the time we boiled the billy for lunch. To complete this line to the other side we had to go between twenty and thirty chains. We were eager to do this and get out. On the other hand to go too far meant a much longer walk back to the flying camp than we had hitherto done. We might be forced to sleep in the bush, as one cannot move in it after darkness falls.

"What about it? Shall we finish the line and risk not being able to get back to camp?" That was the question I put to the little party who had listened to me discussing it with Mr Cashel. The natives smiled and said, "Kapai — it is good, whatever you say." Cashel was willing enough. The decision seemed to lie with me.

"Very well then, we go on the the end," said I.

Between three and four hours' work brought us to the hilltop where we expected to find the trig station, and here I must confess to a fault in my draftsmanship that taught me a lesson I never forgot. In tracing the plan in Cheal's office I had ruled the lines all right; but had dotted in the trig station rather carelessly, on looking it over afterwards, not realising its significance to Mr Cashel. We cast round and round for it. Had I been correct, we should soon have found it as it was on the highest point, a prominent feature. Bob Cashel had been with the party that erected it in 1879, thirty-one years before.

He now said, "If I remember right, it was further to the south. If we leave our line and follow this ridge I think we might find it."

So we set off and after travelling what later proved to be about fifteen chains we came to a patch of grass a few yards square and the trig itself, a small mound with a two-inch pipe in the centre.

From it we had a glorious view. The sun was setting over the ridge twenty-five miles away. North-west was the bush-clad sacred mountain of Pirongia. The sky was a rich red. The intervening country lay in a half light, the ridges standing up, the valleys in shadow. Northward, the nearer view hidden by the bush ridge up which we had come, the distant gaze showed us the valley of the Waipa and beyond of the plain of Waikato stretching to a further dim and distant range now becoming hazy. We stood entranced, but not too long; a cold wind came gently enough from the south to remind us we had rashly decided to sleep out, and we must now keep our resolution. We were over 2,800 feet above sea level. The time was mid winter. The nights were at their longest.

A long since dead and prostrate matai log lay beside the trig on the south side. Sheltered by this, to some extent, from the cold southerly air we decided to sleep and immediately built a fire for warmth, gathering ample wood for the purpose, as there was plenty on the ground. The best was a timber the natives call papamu, a large but stunted twisted tree which grew along the mountain top. I have seldom seen it in the north; but in Southland it is well known as broad-leaf and used for posts. Its lasting qualities were shown by the fact that it had lain, exposed to all weathers, on top of the

47

ground, since the surveyors felled it to get a sight in 1879, thirty-one years before.

Our clothing was hardly suitable for sleeping in the open. Mr Cashel wore a waistcoat, otherwise we were all dressed in short-sleeved flannel singlets and dungaree trousers. I carried a jacket strapped to my waist which I now put on. The Maoris made themselves short capes of a mountain flax-like leaf, rather like a cabbage tree, and we spread a lot of this on the ground to lie on. For the first hour or two of darkness we smoked our pipes, tried to delude ourselves that these took the place of food, and talked.

Though the track which we had again struck on the mountain top was overgrown, it was well defined and worn into the ground well over a foot wide. Why was this? I asked Bob Cashel. He said, "It was probably a well-used thoroughfare in ancient times. The natives always walked in single file, headed the springs and creeks if they could, and therefore followed the ridges. Down on the lower levels they followed the water-ways in their canoes. The coming of roads and railways has of course changed their method of travel. Many of the old tracks have fallen into disuse, and canoes are rarely to be seen anywhere. In the lifetime of men still living they came up all the rivers and streams with more than a foot of water, right up the Waipa past the point where we left it.

"The river flats up which we rode were cultivated and there were still settlements all the way, right up into the bush as the pa on Taitoki above the grass patch indicates. When they learned the purchasing power of money they naturally tended to go towards the railway where they could obtain a share of it. When trade first began it was largely by barter. They used to grow corn after the missionaries arrived and taught them how, taking it down the Waipa to Te Awamutu together with pigs and potatoes and exchanging it for clothing and anything else they fancied. In that way they came to give up dressing the flax with the care and pains they once took when they made the fine mats they used to wear in the daytime and sleep under at night. I wish we had one now."

The last remark was one we all echoed when at last we stretched ourselves out to sleep. At first this came easily enough to me; but not for long. With my face to the fire one side of me was warm; but in half an hour I awoke with the cold at my back. Invariably I found one or more of my companions awake in like case, usually putting more fuel on the fire to make it blaze. I turned my back to it, went off again, only to wake once more and thaw out the other side. It was freezing hard. The stars sprinkled the sky coldly above us. We made a joke of our plight; but inwardly longed for daylight. The natives were restless and really nervy thinking of evil spirits, especially Tara-pikau. Only the presence of us two Europeans had brought them so far. This may seem curious in Waho's case as his great-grandfather Emery, had been a Welshman; but like most of his breed in the King Country, he had been reared a native and was Maori in outlook.

The darkness lasted a full twelve hours, the longest I had ever known. My relief was intense when at last the eastern sky began to pale. I came of a soft generation, was used to a spring mattress, sheets and as many warm blankets as I could need. At the first light we were all stirring, standing up to ease our joints and stamping to restore the circulation. The frost lay white on the ground around us. The view was again superb; but I derived little pleasure from it, nor indeed from anything else until the sun shone and warmed the blood.

Hunger is no joke though, and by now we were ravenous. We drank water, for we had not even tea with us, having left the billy at the spot where we had lunched the day before. Peta and Waho were busy with their slashers on the matai log and presently brought eight large huhus, juicy white grubs that they had dug out of it. They pulled the heads off and setting them in a cleft green stick, toasted them brown at the fire, and when finished placed two before each of us. I asked Cashel if he intended to eat them. Most emphatically he said he did, suiting the action of the word. I did the same. They tasted very good to all of us; but were not at all filling. That was our breakfast. We were ready for the day's work.

First we had to find the line where it had ended on the hillside the last day Brittan was with us. We had to continue it on and then connect with the one we had left the previous day. To do this did not mean much length to cut, perhaps fifteen chains in all, and the bush was light; this done, the work was completed, we could then go out to civilisation, collect bushmen and start the felling.

Down the track we filed and soon passed the end of our line where we had left the previous evening. Our route lay over a small knob and soon Mr Cashel judged the line could not be far below us. We sent the natives down to locate it, widely separated to swing along the hillside and shout when it was found. Peta went first then Waho. I was relieved to be told to wait where I was and listen whilst Mr Cashel went a little to the left to try and get a look out. The wait seemed interminable, my stomach felt weak, I had no kick in me, and the silence grew oppressive. At last I shouted. A reply came from the bush below me, perhaps a chain away.

"Have you found the line?" I called.

"No" was the reply. Bob Cashel joined me. He called again. We found the man near us was Waho who said Peta was below him equally unsuccessful. Bob went down a little way to see, not very far, and returned to say, "It is harder than I thought and the natives

49

seem done already. I do not think they can work until they have had something to eat."

That was how I felt and said so. He said he was that way too. We decided to call in the men and find our way back to the flying camp. As they trailed up they looked relieved at this decision and were glad to file away along the ridge. It was a trying couple of hours that followed and we moved in silence until we reached the flying camp where Waho started the fire, Peta cut up the pork and prepared the food and Bob examined his map and notes. I had been doing some selfish thinking and took the plates and mugs to the stream to wash them. I also took the porridge billy which had had water standing in it since breakfast the day before. Pouring the water away I was pleased to find as I expected a residue of cold porridge. Usually it would be a revolting thought to eat it; but I found it very good indeed before I scraped out and cleaned the utensil. I am not proud to think of this; but I tell it to show the depth of depravity to which hunger can reduce us, and it did not diminish the gusto with which I fell upon the pork and potatoes, the bread the butter and the tea which we had when all was ready.

Even the flying camp seemed a good spot when, fully fed, we allowed ourselves the relaxation in which to stretch our limbs a bit and smoke a pipe. We decided to return to camp and complete the work next day. It did not take us long to roll up the gear and presently we took to the stream once more. Arriving at the grass patch after four nights away from it was like getting home again.

*   *   *

The next day's work proved an easy one, but for the climbing, and saw the job completed. We had laid off 400 acres ready to start work on; but it was all steep mountain face until one reached the top where it was easier. As grazing for sheep it was as good, we thought, as any hill country bush in the North Island; but it presented a problem as to where we could erect homestead and woolshed. I decided that for this year I must camp on the mountain top; but to shear up there would mean packing the wool right down the track which was a steep one in many parts. The grass patch was an ideal spot for a woolshed, a good flat, and there was an obvious route for a waggon track to it which could be cleared in the course of time. I made up my mind to acquire it if I could.

It was on Crown land, a block of over 1100 acres of comparatively easy country including the valley we had headed the day we found the corner peg. It had been acquired by the Crown as a survey lien. The system was, when surveying native land, to charge the owners for the cost; if they chose to pay cash they could do so. If on the other hand they were satisfied to make the payment in the form of land, of which they had far more than they cared to use, the equivalent value was laid off and became the property of the Government, with a view to future settlement. The surveyors in their zeal took care to see that some of the most desirable land was set aside in this way. Its advantages to us were obvious as soon as we looked down upon it. I only wished it might be already ours.

Wednesday, two weeks from the day we set out, saw us jogging along the track for Otewa and Otorohanga, where Mr Cashel and I caught the train for Te Kuiti. Peta stayed with his family at Otewa. Waho at Otorohanga bought a bottle of whiskey from a sly grogger and poured half of it neat down his throat behind a building before he paused for breath, and from a rather woebegone figure he became a formidable fighting man once more, a king amongst his fellows. Aha, the blessings of civilisation!

I had not shaved since I left there and was in rags to the waist. It suddenly dawned on me what a disreputable figure I had become when I noticed the look of amused surprise on the face of a friend whom I met outside the Post Office.

Later that evening a venerable gentleman with greying pointed beard was noted sitting at the bottom of a dry ditch in a back street in Te Kuiti. By his side was a bottle of whiskey half consumed. In response to a solicitous enquiry he stated that he stood in no need of assistance, that he had been dining with his friend Mr John Tammadge, that whilst the company had been good, the wine had left something to be desired, that in fact there was not any, and that the crude spirit of whiskey had had to suffice. Only that had raised a doubt in his mind as to whether he should put on dress clothes, and white waistcoat, and proceed to the opera; that and the fact that he believed Madame Patti would not be singing tonight had decided him to go to bed early. In the mean time he was very comfortable where he was, and desired no better company than his own, thank you.

PART TWO

BREAKING IN THE BUSH

*Now the girths and ropes are tested; now they pack
their last supplies.*

PART TWO

BREAKING IN THE BUSH

TE KUITI HAD for me at this time a homely feeling. My headquarters were at the Grand Hotel. Mrs King, the wife of the proprietor, put me in an upstairs room with two beds, that she said was kept for Mr Pettit. He kept his town clothes in a chest of drawers in it. I had met Mr Pettit and thought he might demur at this arrangement, but found he was quite pleased. Most of the upstairs rooms had two beds, and these were allotted as often as not to men who were complete strangers travelling through. Price of bed and meals was 6s a day; but if you were a "regular" you were charged at the rate of 25s a week. The food was plentiful and good, commencing with a cup of tea and bread and butter in the bedroom in the early morning. Boots put outside the door at night were cleaned. There was an annexe at the back, on the ground level, with windows against the street, where one was sometimes given a bed in a single room if the rest of the house was full. Most of the regulars, the men who worked in the township, lived here and paid 17/6 a week for it. I believe the Grand Hotel paid its proprietor as well as any other kind of business in the King Country. People were always coming and going and the house was always full.

There was talk of building a club, and our names were put down for it as prospective members. Existence was rather aimless at the moment, but I had to endure it until I got replies to an advertisement for bushmen that I had put in the papers, for I hoped to fall 400 acres of bush that year.

To my delight Rowley Hill now arrived and joined me at King's. He was eager and enthusiastic, anxious to go out and see Rangitoto and become a landowner, but this we could not do at once, as I had to interview the prospective bushmen.

Our first requirement was a ranger, that is, a man who could direct the bushmen to the job and see that they performed the requirements of the contract. It was agreed that in this my first year I was quite incompetent to do it and would be imposed upon. Macdonald, the land agent, recommended a man called Mac-Cracken, whom he had employed as a boy. He came in to see me from a place where he was doing day-work on wages as a bushman for some contractors called Woods and Gates who had a number of men felling large areas of bush. He proved to be a tall, fresh-faced fellow, of easy speech, and I engaged him at £3 a week "and found", to go out with me next day, go round the piece we had surveyed, establish a camp at the trig (unless he could suggest somewhere better), show prospective bushmen round the area, and open a track up the mountain. He had lots to do; but he seemed quite cheerful at the prospect.

Rowley was impatient of waiting. He wanted to go out and see the block of bush to the south of me, 1137 acres belonging to my landlord's brother, Wherowhero; but in view of my own rough journeyings, and the fact that the weather had become much worse, I said it was impossible at present.

With Brittan he went to look at a large block of easy fern country close to the railway and very accessible, but I was glad they had the sense to reject it. It was leasehold and held by a speculator. Brittan had not after all bought the 1422 acres next to me, having found over 2000 acres of the country I had traversed adjoining Mac-Luckie's were still open to purchase. It was good bush, and, once there, comparatively easy country. He instructed Falwasser to obtain it for him. At the same time he advised Rowley that he could not go wrong on the 1422 acres adjoining me to the west, so Falwasser was commissioned to get a lease of this for him. The only difficulty about these places was that they had a number of owners, from whom signatures must be obtained, and this always took time. My two friends were full of eagerness to get on with the business of life; but meanwhile must exercise patience in Te Kuiti, it seemed. Both visited Falwasser's office every day; for the rest they loitered, talked land and learned to play billiards in the evenings.

*   *   *

I had cause for uneasiness myself at this time. I had observed things and kept my eyes open, and I did not see that the landowners who were working the land were very prosperous. That, I concluded, was because they were putting all they made into its development; but the men who seemed to be making the money were the men who were selling the land itself. Then, as I used my eyes, I did not see the livestock it was said to carry. A man would tell you a place would carry two sheep to the acre; very well, where were they? In South Canterbury one saw the sheep. Here I saw very few. When I asked about this I was told the best land lay away from the main road. I saw cattle, but they were nothing to enthuse about. I was told that was because they were not well-bred. When good blood was brought into the King Country one would see what it could do.

"Well why did they not bring 'em?" I asked. To this I was told the country was new. The railway had only gone through the year before. A man wanted patience, then he would learn. I was young yet and inexperienced. Wait till I had battled around a bit, worked in the bush and knew something. I would see. I met old Mr Mac-Cullagh, a well-known auctioneer from Hamilton. He had had a drink or two and was accompanied by a young tally-clerk for a sale. They were talkative and to one of my upbringing it seemed very satisfied with themselves. They obviously looked upon me as a simpleton, and joked about my chokebore trousers. I always wore riding breeches. I kept my temper; but they annoyed me without satisfying my curiosity. I thought North Island auctioneers a lot of ignorant vulgar men, and at one or two sales I attended it seemed to me the chief operators were dealers and middle men. Both they and the auctioneers talked of the true settlers as "cockies" and their manner showed a contempt for them, good humoured and bantering; but a contempt none the less. They knew what I did not, how deeply mortgaged the "cockies" were.

All this made me cautious, and though I did not then know it, a little hard too. I was more resolved than ever that I would not fail through carelessness or giving any points away. I shuddered to think what would happen to my father, my mother and my sister if I failed at all. So it was with the utmost caution that I now prepared to close arrangements with the bushmen.

Macdonald helped me in this. He had been a bush farmer in the Marakopa, and knew every pitfall into which the landowner might fall if he had not a cast-iron agreement on paper, and someone to see that it was carried out. He had drawn up a form of agreement that left no loophole for evasion. To make doubly sure we showed it to Finlay, to make certain it was good law. Finlay laughed at the form of it, reluctant to admit that anyone but a lawyer could draw up such a workable set of stipulations. All the same he had a copy of it taken in his office, and I believe did not alter a word of it, and that if today anyone wanted a bush-falling contract from him, the terms of that one would apply.

Firstly the bush was all to be gone through, and the scrub, up to an inch in diameter, cut with slashers to the satisfaction of the owner or his ranger before an axe was laid to a tree. This was to prevent the heavier timber being felled on to uncut scrub, as it was well known many sharp bushmen could do this, trusting that the subsequent fire would destroy everything. It might in a dry season when it was said, "Many a good fire covers a bad piece of felling." On the other hand bad scrubbing had often caused bad burns, or no burn at all in shady places, leaving the unfortunate farmer with harbours for all kinds of weeds and second growth, impenetrable gullies and less grassland than he had paid for. The bigger trees were to be felled up to a diameter of three

57

feet, and all tawa, that being a good tree to burn and carry a fire, especially through its dead dry leaves.

The owner undertook to pay a price fixed at so much an acre. As the men had to be insured, and the figure for this was a high one of over four pounds in every hundred paid to the men, the owner undertook to do this, charging it against the contract, otherwise he might find himself liable for compensation — and risks were greater in bush felling than any other form of work. Sometimes he might have to guarantee the cost of the men's camp equipment at the local store. It was laid down in our contract that we did not do this, but were to make progress payments from time to time. If any man left before completion of the contract, he was to be paid at the rate of a pound a week whilst he had been working. Finally, and a good clause this, any claim against the owner was to be made within twenty-eight days of the completion of the work. The balance owing was to be paid to the men on the completion of the contract.

We met the bushmen in Macdonald's office to settle terms. They asked 32/6 an acre. We had generally understood that 30s was regarded as a fair price, though I recognised that in view of the way land was booming, and the general demand for men, we might have to pay more. It is easy when in funds to give what people ask and earn the reputation of being a good fellow, but to do so tends to make men feel they need not exert themselves, and they get careless. Also, to do so in one thing makes people expect you to do so all round, and thereby a sound enough venture may turn into a financial failure, which, extended over the years may and probably will lead to the ruin of the employer. So I had to haggle. Conceding a shilling on our original estimate, I asked, "Well, I suppose you fellows are willing to take on the job at 31s an acre?"

And the men replied, "Oh, yes," "That's all right," "That'll do me," and so on, thereby showing their eagerness to get the job.

So they signed up, asking for two days to collect their gear and engage a cook. MacCracken went out by the early train next morning to continue opening the track to the top of the mountain, and I was to accompany the men out from Otorohanga.

*   *   *

They were a crowd of men I was disposed to like. Three of them had already made an impression on me. Knap, the leader of the gang, was still in his teens, but strong and sturdy; bred a bushman; of German stock from the Taihape district, and obviously a superior young fellow for him to be acknowledged leader by the rest of them. Another young man, short in stature but with magnificent chest development, came from the same district and was said to be a son of Captain Tegner of the Fusiliers. No one seemed to know what fusiliers, but it sounded impressive, and he had a quiet, respectable manner, and looked like work. The third, a man called Flint, was a few years older than the other two, but of the same strong, thickset type, though rather larger. He seemed to do a lot of talking, in a quick, not uneducated voice, and rather dominated the others. The other three, Benner, Wallace and Brown, were quiet, clean-looking fellows. The last-named was of slighter mould than the others, good-looking and of delicate features. On the whole they seemed a superior lot who might have done well in other walks of life but wanted to lead an independent life in the open, and followed bush felling because of the big money earned at it. I had been warned to expect that all bushmen would take their employer down when they could, and was on my guard against it, but I was pleased with this lot on the whole and determined to carry out my part of the contract. In their attitude towards me there was rather an air of amusement, though they were quite polite, and gave me the impression that they liked to work for me. Was this because they thought me a bit of a fool and an easy mark? I rather thought so, and felt that if I were to get good work from them I must command their respect, even if in doing so they liked me less.

When the party left Otorohanga with their gear in a waggon, they had been promised that pack horses would be ready for them at a place called Mangaorongo. S. W. had arranged this with a Maori named Hika, in Otorohanga. As well as the bushmen, the party included Macfarlane, nicknamed "Hongi Pork", who, without invitation, had decided to join them. They could get no sense out of anyone at Mangaorongo as to whether they could expect the horses or not, but they decided to sleep there in any case.

Next morning there was still no sign of the horses. Knap pointed this out to me. I noted more than one man listening and sensed an atmosphere of doubt abroad. To Knap I said, "If they aren't here by eight, I must do something about it."

"And what do you mean to do, boss?" he asked.

"I shall go and find Hika and if he has not got the horses ready we must do it for him. We have two riding hacks, my own and Macfarlane's. We have four pack saddles. These will not carry all our belongings; but they will take a lot of it. Get the men to make up four pack horse loads of the most important things, and some of the main items of food such as flour and sugar with camp oven and cooking gear. You will know what they require the most. Make up even packages, of from fifty to sixty pounds each, as side and top loads. They can put the sling straps on and have the saddles out ready to put on the horses' backs as soon as they appear."

Knap's face lighted up.

"Right oh, boss," said he, and went amongst the waiting men who soon sprang to action. Half of what I had instructed them to do was already done; but the stuff needed resorting and I stood around close to them whilst they were doing it. There was an air of pleasurable anticipation and slight undercurrent of excitement as men rolled bundles and tightened straps with their heads together. I could not help hearing snatches of low-voiced conversation.

"Something doing now eh?" was the prevalent note, and what was doing? I asked myself. I certainly longed to see Hika and the horses; but they did not appear and as eight o'clock approached I noted that the men with watches looked at them furtively every minute or two. A silence seemed to come over us all, and the men were standing erect showing me, as I looked at mine, that the fateful hour had come. There was nothing for it, I walked across to the pa and my gang came following after.

A little boy ran out of the whare, and before he could dodge back again, I stopped him and said, "Where is Hika?" He looked frightened and in silence pointed to a large whare and then bolted. I walked over and stooping at the low doorway, entered. The windowless place was rather dark; but, their heads to the wall at the end, lay three natives side by side on the usual bed of fern on the floor. One was an old man with a blanket over him. On the other side was a racing gentleman with a check suit wearing field glasses and a homburg hat. In the centre covered by a magnificent brown oppossum rug was Hika, who now sat up.

"Hika," said I sternly, "where are the pack horses?"

He mumbled something to his companions and looked away from me. I could now scarcely repress my temper.

"Now then, Hika," said I, "you promised me in Otorohanga to have pack horses here to take my men to Rangitoto. You gave your word and I believed I was dealing with an old time Maori who told the truth. Instead you have not brought out the horses and it is eight o'clock. We should have started an hour ago. I find you in bed when you should be doing what you said you would. I expect you to get those horses at once, and if they are not there all saddled up and ready to start, at half past eight, it will be the worse for you."

Whether Hika had any reply to what I said, I know not, for the old man throwing aside his blanket to disclose his long shirt and naked limbs, said, "Yes. Yes. It all right. Hika he get those horses for you."

"Very well," said I, "he'd better be quick about it or there'll be trouble." And as I turned to go out of the door I found that all my bushmen, each with his coat off and arms bared, had crowded in after me. They stood back to let me pass into the sunlight as I strode out in silence.

Knap came up beside me as I walked back to our equipment. He looked at me sideways with a new air of respect as he said, "That's the way to talk to 'em, boss. They can understand you all right if you don't use too many long words."

This was all very cheering and I certainly felt a new man, having got that off my chest. At the same time we were not started yet, and I did not wish to undertake the next step if I could help it, which was to have the bushmen catch every horse in sight, put the saddles on, load them up with everything they could carry and go off with them. I respected the law of the land; but it seemed to me that here it did not help us much and we must be a law unto ourselves if need be. It might mean trouble later. I must risk that and it was not a pleasant thought. I was relieved on looking back to see Hika emerge from the whare and presently a boy and two men joined him, each with a bridle in hand. They all made off in the direction of some grazing horses and very soon came trooping back to us leading half a dozen of them.

On went the saddles, and on top of them went the loads. Everyone worked with a will, Hika and the natives bustling at it with the best of them. Hongi Pork put one saddle on his piebald with an extra heavy load. Two boys, both mounted, rode up and joined us, accompanied by four useful looking pig dogs. The surplus stores were stored in the pataka. As I stood by Jeff, who was saddled with my own swag strapped on the pommel, things took the desired shape before my eyes. The men, swag on back, stood ready, looking at me expectantly.

"All right?" I enquired.

"All set," said they.

Then waving my hand to the hills, I said, "Lead on."

Hongi Pork knew the track. I did not. He went first, riding his bay horse and leading the piebald who, despite his large load, stepped gamely out. The other three pack horses followed, driven by the two native boys who headed them back if they attempted to stray from the route. After these came the bushmen, Knap in front. Each had the traditional swag of the southern hemisphere, the blanket roll with the lighter possessions of the bearer inside it, such things as billies and pannikins being tied on outside to be handy for use. Flint had an enormous roll which made him look like a snail with its shell on. Young Brown carried a shot-gun. I brought up the tail of this little procession. When we started, the men gave a spontaneous cheer in which the natives joined. The others clustered round to look at us and waved as we passed up the grassy flat.

The men broke into chorus as they swung along.

61

Every night I used to hang my trousers
upon the back of the bedroom door.
I rue the day.
I must have been a jay.
I'll never hang them up any more.
For the wife she used to wander through
my pooches
when I was fast asleep. Beneath the
quilt.
In the mornin' when I woke.
I was always stoney broke.
And that's the reason noo I wear a kilt.

As they strode along this very soon died down and as the track
left the grass and began to wind up a low scrub-covered ridge we
moved in silence.

I now had leisure to appreciate that it was a lovely day. On the
hills before us "the morning mist rolled up the glen". I was steeped
in the romanticism of Sir Walter Scott as well as Thackeray, Kipling and the like and was enjoying the gratifying reaction to the
fact that after prolonged hours of anxiety, I had imposed my will on
human obstruction and affairs were moving as I wanted them,
always a pleasing reflection. Yet pleased as I felt, I was puzzled.
Had I been obstructed? All the Maoris at the last, Hika included,
seemed glad to help us. There seemed a mystery about it all. What
was it? I had had to make arrangements with a strange people with
the use of my own tongue, where they had appeared only to understand Maori, yet the boy Jimmy spoke good English. Where was
the hitch? The horses had been so readily forthcoming in the end
after I had spoken with unwanted forcefulness. Were they at first
trying to blackmail me? To make me raise the price? I was inclined
to be suspicious. I had been warned by most Europeans in Te Kuiti
that I had need to be. Many were the stories Macdonald and the
like had told of the trickiness of the natives. Perhaps that was at the
bottom of it. Yet my instinct made me feel they were friendly more
than otherwise. Knap and the bushmen on the other hand were
hostile from the first and mistrusted them in anything. They would,
I felt, set me against them if they could. I was determined not to
allow this to happen at all events. In the end I gave up the riddle
and ceased to worry until another problem should arise. I began to
feel confident I would deal with it all right.

Later, Cheal, the surveyor, partly explained things to me when I
told him of this business. It seemed that Hika was, what he looked,
a descendant of a long line of rangatira. His father and grandfather
were known in recent times as great and powerful chiefs and
fighting men. They were therefore lords of wide lands in the

Mangaorongo district. These, when they were covered with rather worthless-looking scrub, Hika sold to the Government, and thought he had done well, squandering the money on racing and drink. He now had only thoroughbred horses, the oppossum rug and a few worthless odds and ends to show for it all, but still thought he could lord it over his fellows as of yore. He had under-taken my packing in all good faith, expecting to use any horses he pleased, no matter to whom they belonged, and in the end I learned that the horses we had taken were not his.

A very satisfactory feeling came over me as I rode. I thought I was a very fine fellow. I let the reins fall on the pony's neck, lit my pipe and blew a cloud into the still morning air. Life was good. "The after-breakfast cigar lit, the squire trots off to the farm." Well, not quite; but still I enjoyed something akin to the sensation.

The track up the ridge led, after a mile or two, on to rolling ferny uplands and the distant view before us was one of grandeur. Some miles ahead the land rose steeply in ridge after ridge of rich green forest. I scanned the hills ahead and at length distinguished Rangitoto Mountain at the western end and was reminded that my next problem was to get the pack horses to the top of it, where Knap had chosen the camp site. Hitherto we had climbed it afoot and at no point had I seen a place where horses could go without weeks of work and expense in track making. To find a way up was Mac-Cracken's first duty. I hoped he had succeeded; but the outline of the mountain, whilst it showed a long fairly level top, fell away steeply at the western end where we hoped to go, to such a degree that I could not imagine horses climbing up to it. Another problem concerned me. The obstacles of nature might be more difficult to overcome than had been the human element. I reflected ruefully that this long journey round had been caused by one already, the Waipa river.

None of these thoughts showed in my face, I hoped, as about midday we stopped by a stream to boil the billy and have lunch and a spell. The journey was telling on the men. They were all hot and somewhat weary; but they cheered up and started joking again as they put off their swags and lay back in the fern. Flint, whose nickname I had already learned was "Bully", was twitted on the bulk of his belongings which was accounted for by the fact that he was carrying a kapok mattress which he had booked to the general account at the store. He said it was well worth the trouble of carrying to be able to sink into it at night after a day's work in the bush. All the same I noted one of the Maori boys had been carrying it for him on his horse for the last hour. Young Brown had also given up the gun to Jimmy who had proudly carried it, butt on hip, like a dragoon in a picture.

Brown was inclined to complain at the heat and the rise and fall of the track. Not so the others. Beyond a question or two to me as to "How far is it from here, boss?" which I could only answer by pointing out Rangitoto they showed no concern as to where they were going. For the first time in my life it had been dawning on me that I was the one they looked to, and that they had complete confidence in my arrangements. A flattering thought perhaps; but also a disturbing one. I was reflecting how slapdash I had been, and what risks I was taking in bringing the men out without even first making sure they could go to their destination. I hoped Mac-Cracken might not have failed me; but realised now that his task might not be an easy one. I did not sufficiently know my own limitations in not having worked in the bush, and that I had perhaps set a man a job too big for him, was only now beginning to dawn upon me. All the same I reflected that to have the bushmen on the spot in the event of meeting with an obstacle, meant that I could use them to clear it, even though it might mean paying them extra to do it.

"Bully" Flint swore, though not ill-temperedly, and Brown complained, when the time came to move on again. Nevertheless though the steady tramp had obviously been telling on them, they were much refreshed by the food and the drink, combined with the short spell they had enjoyed, and everyone shouldered his swag readily enough, moving off this time in silence for the most part: a contrast with the morning when there had been a good deal of talk to begin with. I was beginning to realise by now that our party could not reach our destination, the grass patch, before dark, and that might mean we must spend a night in the open. It might not be a popular thing; but with their swags and plenty of food it could do them no harm, and if they did not like it, they were too far out now to retrace their steps.

The track wound through scrub and fern, which, except in the low-lying places, was nowhere more than waist-high. It was only wide enough for a horse; but quite distinct, and at a spell I took the lead, Hongi Pork telling me it led straight on to the Tauraroa where his whare was. Knap came up with me too and presently we saw we were approaching a wide valley at a lower level than the route we were following. This excited our interest and there was a general improvement in our progress till soon we stopped on a low ridge and looked down on a flat of tall manuka with a stream running down it. About thirty acres of the scrub had been cleared and was grassed and in this clearing was a shingle whare about a hundred yards away below across the stream.

In front of the whare on a log sat a man drying his feet. He rose and waving his hat cheered to us. I rode on down, followed, at intervals, by the others. The pony crossed the stream and all hands followed suit, regardless of wet boots and socks. The stranger was MacCracken, who greeted us with an effusion of warmth after his period of loneliness. He said that as the days rolled on without our arrival he had made up his mind to go to Otorohanga and see what had happened. He was about to continue his journey and had we not arrived when we did would have been down the Waipa and we would not have seen him. To my questions, he replied that all had been well. He had opened a track up a leading spur to the top of the mountain. It was steep; but horses could get up it. He looked the bushmen over and asked how far they meant to go that night. I told him we had hoped to reach the grass patch. He shook his head.

"They don't look like doing it, skipper," he said.

They certainly did not. Most of them were sprawled out on the ground. Brown was complaining in an aggrieved tone and "Bully" Flint was enquiring audibly where was the sense of going any further. Hongi Pork, who had dismounted, was saying there was plenty of room for a dozen men in his whare that I saw had a sack hung over the entrance as a door and an earthen floor. The native boys were sitting on their horses. They were the only ones who looked as if they had enjoyed every minute of the outing and were still eager for more. Only a quiet man called Benner, and Knap, remained on their feet. I called Knap over and had a short conference.

MacCracken, in response to my enquiry, said he thought it might be another five or six miles to the grass patch. I asked Knap if he thought the men could do it before dark. He said he could; but doubted the others. I did too. I was eager to get on myself; but then I had a horse. We discussed the pros and cons. Knap wished to get ahead of the men and clear the tent site before they arrived. We decided that he, MacCracken and I should go to the grass patch leaving the others to come on in the morning after a night's rest.

This suggestion when put to the men was a popular one. We impressed upon them to turn into their blankets early and rest, and that it was important to get off as soon after dawn as possible so as to have time, after arrival at the mountain top, to erect their tents and make things comfortable for the night. They all agreed. There was plenty of grass here for the pack horses. Hongi Pork said he would tether the piebald and he and the Maori boys would see that the others did not stray. Flint speaking for the others said they would carry out these instructions to the letter, the cook started a fire to get the meal ready and, seeing all in order, we left them.

MacCracken led the way. He was a hard man to follow at all times, as he was as footsure as a goat, on the roughest track, almost going at a jog trot. Knap was smaller; but he too was bush-bred

65

with the heart of a lion. He kept up; but I saw his swag would weigh him down and I took it on the pony in addition to my own. All the same we were well over two hours on this part of the journey and darkness was closing down as we reached the tent on the grass patch.

The worries S. W. had felt on this trip were justified. In the event, Knap proved unable to manage the gang, and many episodes showed that they were not working hard enough to have any hope of finishing the contract by Christmas. MacCracken watched developments for some time before he made any comment.

During these first days I began to know my ranger, MacCracken. He was about eight years older than I, but youthful and happy in his ways in camp, and therefore good to live with. He was a son of one of those magnificent soldiers who came out with the 65th regiment, had taken up a soldier's farm at Te Mata, near Raglan, and there raised a family of five children. The name of Mac-Cracken was, I found, well known in the King Country for work and reliability. My ranger was known as "Jack" MacCracken. He always looked fresh and clean, and the camp was spotless. I was prone to be too fond of my bed in the mornings, unless there was something special to be done, but MacCracken was up early, and too often I awoke to be told, "Breakfast will be ready as soon as you are, skipper," and would find the porridge dished out when I returned from a hurried wash.

The camp was really a model, and a great testimony to his bushcraft. The slab fireplace almost filled the southern end. The six feet high walls were made of extra calico, nailed onto poles upright and crossed. A high ridgepole ran from end to end. There was a galley sixteen feet long, covered by a canvas fly sixteen feet by twelve, and a sleeping apartment opening off it in which were five bunks, two being set above the others. The actual beds were made of long straight saplings about an inch thick, on top of which was spread soft fern and feathery bush creeper, making a sleeping place on which to spread one's blankets, soft as any mattress. A properly swung door of sacking on a frame of poles gave entrance to the gallery from outside, and a table of hewn and dressed slabs ran along one side of the galley, with a round rail to sit upon for our meals.

The men arrived and settled into this camp, and began their work, but I could see that MacCracken was not satisfied with their progress. In camp one night he said things were not going too well with the men. They were prone to knock off work if it rained, and not to leave camp if they thought it was going to. "Bully" Flint had too much to say. Knap was not sufficiently forceful as a leader. "Stumpy" Tegner was too slow. He was a sawmill bushman; they did not have to use their heads like contract men. Flint was another. That was why he had brought a kapok mattress. Sawmill bushmen all had them; but they lived in huts, not in camp, and did not have to move about. Brown would never make a bushman. It took time to learn; many did that, but Brown had little heart. If he got a cold he said he was "crook" and stayed in bed. If a man got a cold the best way to get rid of it was to work, wet or fine, and sweat it out.

Wallace, the tall man of the party, should be able to chop all right. He was strong, but he had a great deal too much to say. For that matter, that was the trouble with the rest of the gang — too much to say when they ought to be working. Knap was a good bushman all right, but the wrong man to be in the lead. Instead of keeping things under his hat he blurted them out regardless. The head of a gang should see he got his own way. Such a position needed a good man with sense. Benner, the Tasmanian? Ah, he was a fine young fellow, a good axeman, and you never heard him open his mouth. If they all kept steadily on, like him, the job would be cleared up in no time. Before all was over Benner would be the best man of the lot.

I was advised to speak to them myself, and when two came in one evening I did so, reminding them that it was in their own interest to keep on the job, and that if they did not finish to time I could enforce a penalty. I could also put on wages men at their expense; but, as I emphasised, I did not want to do either of these things. It was very unpleasant, the more so as they admitted my criticism and were contrite, promising better work. I had to remind them that their bill at the Trading Company in Otorohanga was growing out of proportion to the work done. All this worried me a lot. To get a good burn they must cut out by Christmas. They asked me to bring in any good wages men I might be able to find when next I went to Te Kuiti.

With MacCracken I did some track-cutting. His skill with axe and slasher always made me feel my own awkwardness, though I was improving in being able to find my way about in the bush and could now go and visit the bushmen at work without MacCracken to show the way. Pay and commissariat were my function, and there were soon things needed. I was to go out and order them, and I found I was all too ready to do this. I wanted to see Rowley and Brittan and find out how they were progressing. Also, truth to tell, I liked the idea of going to a dance if there were one, though I was not sufficiently honest to admit this, even to myself.

At this time S. W. made regular expeditions to Te Kuiti, and sometimes Hill and Brittan, who were now completing their own purchases of land in the Rangitoto, would ride back with him to his camp. Sometimes all three would spend the night at Otewa Pa, where S. W. was on excellent terms with the Maoris, who did the packing-out of his stores for him. He became especially friendly with Te Ngoi, the headman at the pa, and with Peta, who organised the packing.

On one such occasion Brittan was made an attractive offer.

At Otewa our reception was a warm one. We were given quarters in a pataka where our evening meal was set out on a box that was covered with a white sheet for a tablecloth in European style, the food being carried in by two shy girls. All this was Te Ngoi's arrangement. He had, as a boy, spent a year at St Stephen's College and had never forgotten what he had learned. He ruled Otewa by the common consent of the people there, and it was a model pa, honest, sober and industrious. From my point of view the fact that he spoke good English was invaluable. I had already learned how disconcerting it could be to talk to a circle of natives in English and hear them start a discussion in their language before anyone answered me. On this evening I went with Ngoi into the wharepuni or meeting house to discuss my affairs with Peta Tahatika.

We entered a large dark and windowless building with a high pitched roof supported in the top by a centre pole. The side walls were low. The floor was of earth with fern and mats for the people to sleep on at each side. A kind of passageway was left up the centre and a charcoal fire half way up this on the bare floor glowed and warmed up the semi-darkness of a heavy atmosphere, which after the freezing cold of the night outside, I found quite pleasant. Peta talked as he knelt by the fire and kept pushing the red sticks together.

"When I hear you been to Mangaorongo that time I am very sorry. I think you friend for Hika. I say 'No good that man'; then I think Hika do the pack for you. That is not good at all."

I found it a little hard to follow his drift, and was not sure whether I was being censured. Brittan and Rowley came in. We had agreed amongst ourselves always to address, or speak of, each other by surnames, as everyone in the King Country seemed to Christian-name you before they had known you five minutes. We did not like this, as Christian names in Canterbury were regarded as a sign of old acquaintance, intimacy and equality. Maoris from the beginning of their intercourse with Europeans used the first name they caught. Amongst them were no prefixes. Even the King would be addressed as Mahuta. The natives took an immediate liking to Stanley wherever he went. Now Peta spoke to him.

"Ah haeremai — welcome. You come here. Long times since I

68

seen you, before, the other day, when we go Rangitoto, eh?" He found the name Brittan too much for him; but he made a good shot at it. "Britts, eh? Kapai. We all go tomorrow. You live there too, eh?" He made a sign to a shyly smiling girl sitting back in the shadow. "This my eldest torter. You take her for house-keeper, eh? Werry good the cook. Do everything you want."

This conversation gave us much entertainment and from that day forth Stanley became Brintz or Britts to us for evermore. We three slept on the pataka with a folded tent fly under us as a mattress, very comfortable.

The rain poured down as we moved up the Waipa valley next day, and we all wore raincoats. By now I had adopted the bushman's winter dress which discarded trousers but used instead thick woollen heather mixture coloured drawers, rather like the ancient trews of a Highland man. Peta followed us with more stores and the camp gear for my main camp. That night we all slept at the grass patch. Next day MacCracken joined us in a great state of indignation. It seemed that on the journey up eight men had accompanied Peta and the horses, more than enough for half a dozen animals.

"You'll have to tell 'em it won't do, skipper. You can't have all these b----s coming up here to eat us out of house and home every time we get a pack horse load."

"I think from what they said they enjoy the hunting," I replied.

"Of course they do," he said, "but you'll have to stop it. The bushmen and ourselves are going to be dependent on the wild cattle for meat all this winter. They are easy enough to get at now. A man can get close enough with a rifle to shoot one whenever he wants it — they are so used to seeing men that they are very quiet and tame. The Maoris have only hunted on the edge of the bush where they have killed everything on sight, but they could not come in here without sleeping in the bush. Now with our track it is quite easy for them to bring horses right up, and they will start in to hunt from there. You must stop them. If you don't, they'll bring all the dogs and guns from the pa and they'll hunt Christ out of the country."

This appalling blasphemy scared me, the more so that, try as I might to dismiss such thoughts from my mind, they conjured up a picture that even to this day makes me smile in spite of myself. All the same it was necessary advice. I have always liked the Maoris. I have found them good natured and easy going. It was pleasant to have smiling fellows about me and I liked their company on the rides up the solitary paths we followed. It is always easy to let people do as they like. I felt too that most of the men of my own race who worked with me were hostile to them, why, I could not fathom, and would like to stir up enmity between myself and the natives. I was determined this should not happen. At the same time

MacCracken's experience of backblocks life provided knowledge of the world in which I was to live, and which I knew myself to lack. The South Island of my boyhood might just as well have been England, for all I could learn there of the conditions in the King Country bush. I saw the sense of MacCracken's advice and knew I must act upon it; but how? To turn any man, white or brown, away from a night's lodging was a repugnant thought, to refuse him a meal or a bed was a thing I had never done. No one in the country districts of the South Island ever did that at any time. On the other hand indiscriminate hunting over one's place was not tolerated there without permission.

How was I to order these people off and remain on good terms with them? How could I set about it? These were my thoughts as I wended my way down the track to the grass patch. I had hardly got under my galley roof when the thing was solved for me by Peta poking his smiling face in saying, "Fine day, eh. Very nice. Plenty good time, now all the horse go Rangitoto. Plenty kai for the bushmens."

"Yes Peta," I said. "I hope we aren't going to have any more worry now, and that you will be able to bring the stores up regularly."

"Oh yes. Plenty horse. Plenty men too, ha ha." He seemed to be appraising me. His voice took on a cautious note. "The men been talk to me. They tell me to talk to you."

"Yes Peta," I said. "What about?"

"All the men he say when he come up with the pack horse, you give him to eat the kai, isn't it?"

"Have they complained that I don't feed them?" I asked.

"No he don't say that. He likit the thing to eat. He likit the beef when he go away."

"Well now Peta, I have never refused any man food when he comes here. All the men had kai today when they got to the camp. They have always had what food they wanted the same as ourselves. What is the trouble?"

"He mean that when you pay for the horse to come, you givit the kai for the man too."

"I give that as a matter of course; but it is not payment for the packing. I give it to anyone. That must be understood; but what do you mean about liking beef?"

"Oh he likit the beef and he likit the wild pork too all same to take down Otewas."

"Oh, yes, I see. He like to take meat home, is that it? Beef or pork?"

"Yes, he say sometimes he very hungry."

70

"Very well; but you had half a bull the last time you came up; where is that?"

"Oh we eat him all, one eat."

"Well now I cannot have the men coming up here hunting more than they did before we came. We want the beef for our own bushmen. Is that clear?"

"Aye that is all right; but what about the mans when he bring the pack horse?"

"When he brings the pack horse, I will feed the men who come, in my own camp, with my own kai, as I have already done; but they cannot hunt. We will do all the hunting on my land."

"Aye, but I think the man he no like to come with the packhorse."

"Very good. Tell the man they need not bother. You can say I thank them for coming before; but now no more. When you come with the pack horses you can bring one man or one boy to help you, and you will both be fed. Tell them I said that. Do you understand?"

"One man for the pack horses? He come with me, eh?"

"Yes, one man or one boy. Quite enough to look after lots of horses."

"Oh yes. Plenty mans. I tell 'em what you say. Kapai."

So it was settled for the time being. But I was always handicapped in these discussions by not knowing the language, and was at that time fearful that I might give offence unwittingly, and find them unwilling to work for me. If that happened it would be doubly difficult to provision the men. Even if I had horses of my own I had little grass for them. The few patches of grass were only just enough for the one or two hacks we needed ourselves, and these had the run from the top of the mountain down the ridge and along the stream to where, two miles below the grass patch, outside the bush, we had put a block across the gully with fallen trees.

Meanwhile MacCracken had brought out two wages men from town, but was still concerned about the gang's performance, and saw little chance of their completing by Christmas. Flint asked to be given a block of his own to fell, on a separate contract. This was agreed, and Flint brought wages men of his own to work with him. Knap's gang continued in a lukewarm fashion, even after the arrival of the new men.

The older man MacCracken had brought out to work on wages had overwalked himself on the tracks. I was not surprised, knowing MacCracken's speed — and he started to go off his head. On one occasion he having fallen behind, they waited for him. He was staggering when he joined them, and though his eyes were staring

71

out of his head, he appeared not to see them; but was muttering deliriously, "He's gone from me, and left me to die alone here. Such a decent-spoken young fellow as he seemed, too."

Not easily perturbed, MacCracken now was frightened he had a madman on his hands, a terrible prospect so far back in the bush. He made the man sit down. After a while he had partially recovered to the extent that he recognised him and in gentle tones reproached him for bringing him into such terrible country to lie unburied near the mountain top. His colour was ghastly but his breath which had been coming in gasps, having resumed its steadiness, MacCracken desired that if he was going to die he should do so in bed and pressed him to start on again, assuring him what was the truth, that they were near the mountain top and the camp not a mile away; but nothing would persuade him to move.

"No my boy," said he, "it is no good. I could never stand on me feet again, nor go another yard; but you need not worry. I seen the world. I been near to death in many places, and if it is coming now, I don't much mind. All I asks yer is to bury me deep by the track here so that the wild pigs don't get me, and if you promise to mark the spot I'll be happy enough."

Thoroughly alarmed, MacCracken, leaving the other man, now nearly in tears, to look after the old one, raced to the camp where he boiled the billy, made tea and taking that and some food went back billy in hand in the dusk and got the sufferer to eat and drink something. He expressed himself more at ease then and at peace with the world; but no power on earth would make him stir from where he was. There was nothing else for it. They unrolled his swag, made a bed for him there and when he expressed himself comfortable, left him for the night on his promise not to leave the spot, nor to die till they returned to him.

Next morning he had so far recovered as to get up when they went to him and he followed MacCracken to our camp. There, after a good breakfast he said he was fit for anything, and went on to the bushmen's camp and took up the duties of cooking, which he did very well, and turned out to be quite a character. He was an old soldier of the gunners. After the men had gone to work he would shave and twirl his large moustaches outward from his face and throwing out his chest would say loudly, "H'attitude is the h'art of gunnery and whiskers makes the man."

He at once began to tyrannise over his employers. When he found the position they were in, he expressed his scorn for them in unmeasured terms, ending up by saying, "And if I had been working in the bush for three months and had not got even with my tucker bill yet, I'd cut my throat from ear to ear."

"How did they take that?" I asked MacCracken.

"Like lambs," said he. "That is the worst of it, skipper. They are all so bloody humble. He would talk away at 'em like that, and not one of 'em would tell him to 'go to Hell'. All the same I really believe he did some good in driving 'em out of camp earlier and making 'em work a bit harder, and they didn't go back for a spot of rain either. They were too scared of the reception they would receive from him when they got there. I really believe you might do some good if you talk to Stumpy yourself. He seems one of those men you have to drive. Wallace is right about him; but if you ask me he himself is no better. He's a big useless man and he was not chopping with any heart in it for some time before he went."

"And how about Flint and his new gang?" I asked.

"They have been working. They are bushmen all right and they know they have to go for it to make their cheques by Christmas; but I have had a bit of trouble with them for they know what they are doing and have tried tricks on us. They started felling the bush at the north-east corner before I had passed the scrubbing. I found they had slummed that and made them climb through it and cut it all. They were at it three days and cursed me all the time; but I think they have learned their lesson and won't try it on me again. Flint can work with the best of 'em. He is doing all right; but be careful with him, Skipper. He speaks well; but he is out to take you down if he can. He thinks he has something coming still on the old contract."

"Thanks for the warning. He won't get it if I can help it. From what you say there will be nothing in the job for anyone if things do not improve. It is all very worrying."

"Worrying," said he, "it's enough to put a man in the booby hatch. When is Mr Cashel coming to lay off the inner boundary of Flint's block? They are working up towards the ridge now and in a couple of weeks ought to have the lines cut or they may run on to the other contract."

"Bob Cashel is doing a small job for MacLuckie now. I saw him last week and he promised to be up next Sunday if the weather holds."

"Good," said MacCracken. We sat by the fire after tea. He advised me to talk to Tegner at the first chance, which presently came when we heard footsteps and the man himself appeared with Benner to get any mail and spend an hour hearing the news. Benner was, as usual, quiet and uncritical of his mates; not so Tegner. He told with satisfaction how Knap and Wallace had returned and gone back to work that day. How at the end of it they had been so tired they had hardly been able to climb the hill back to camp and how when they wanted to rest he had been as fresh as paint and set the example leading on.

73

MacCracken looked at me and nodded. I took his cue and told Tegner what was the general opinion of his own behaviour and that it was considered that he had not worked as he should have done, that he was too ready to stay in bed if he heard it raining in the morning and to come home if there was a shower while at work; that he was strong enough, and could slog if he wished; but that his mates felt he was letting them down and was ready to loaf upon them.

He was silent and subdued as I told him all this, and did not contradict me nor try to. In fact he agreed with all I said, more than once saying, "I'm afraid that's right, Mr Westmacott," or, "I know that, Mr Westmacott. I can see that we all took it too easy at first. I was as bad as any," and seemed utterly contrite, promising I should have no cause to complain in future. All through this Benner sat in admirable silence, giving no sign he so much as heard what I was saying to his colleague. It was an unpleasant thing for me to have to talk like this, and I am afraid that the feeling that I had hurt no feelings made me callous about it. We gave them coffee and biscuits and had quite a pleasant chat before they returned to their camp.

When they were out of earshot I said to MacCracken, "I hope I have done some good. He seemed surprised at first at what I said."

MacCracken answered, "Yes. He did not expect it from you. A bit of plain speaking does do good at times. I hope it isn't too late."

"Do you think he will really try to work properly now?" I asked.

"He may, skipper. It has certainly been a shock to him; but whether he has any proper pride remains to be seen."

"Well," said I, "I was surprised at how quietly he took it. How patient he was and the civil way he replied to what I said. I respected him for that."

"That is the devil of it, skipper. He is too dam' polite with his 'Yes, Mr Westmacott' and 'Quite right, Mr Westmacott'. If he had spoken up for himself and told you to go to Hell, I would have had more hope he would pull up his socks and wade in to show what he could do, and it is a poor business the way he thinks of his mates. Did you notice the satisfaction he showed at their being tired out when coming home, whilst he was fresh? Doesn't that give away the show how easy he has been taking things?"

"That did occur to me," I admitted, and it gave me much food for thought then and later; but I cannot say it kept me awake for long in bed.

Next day I went with MacCracken round the work and the pace at which he led me through the supplejacks from point to point made me realise the strain it was to a beginner to follow him and I sympathised with the old man he had brought to the point of collapse. I was glad to find that, although I could never hope to rival him in the bush and he would always pick the route and lead the way, I could now keep up to him without floundering about and tripping over the vines and with less strain.

Flint's gang were doing well, and sending the timber crashing down in a workmanlike way. Each man seemed the equal of his mates and they were felling the bush steadily up a long comparatively easy ridge with the Waimahora leaping over its stony bed at the bottom of a steep fall below them. Their camp was not well sited for sun, being on the shady side of a ridge; but close to a high tributary of the creek. They took turns to do their own cooking, so were saved the worry and expense, and had had sense enough not to overstock themselves with stores, having on hand about a week's supply. They gave me an order for more when I next went out; but were in no hurry. There was no resentment with MacCracken for giving them the extra work in cleaning up their little attempt to slum the bush. They apparently regarded it as a legitimate try on if they could get away with it; but bore no malice when it was detected. In fact I thought I sensed that they respected him the more. The atmosphere was quiet, confident and businesslike.

The others, five of them, were now chopping well down the forward slope of the mountain. Their wages man was working well enough, Benner doing his usual steady chop, his hands obeying a mind that was always concentrated on his own business. Apart from a straight look in the eye and a quiet "Good morning", he scarcely paused in his work. At no time did he look to be going fast; but he made his cut just at the right place surely and easily and his trees went steadily down as he worked his way uphill. The others were all slogging away hard too; but one sensed an atmosphere of discontent in Wallace and neither Knap nor Tegner looked happy, although to watch them these three appeared to be chopping faster than Benner and I am afraid my presence tended to make them work at a speed they could not maintain and which would ease off when I had gone.

In spite of these things, it was a relief to find the work going well. It was a sunny morning, always a thing to make one cheerful in winter. The falling timber let in the light and from the front face of it one could see out, in the clear air, far over the Waikato beyond the bush. When we got back to camp I said something of these things to MacCracken, especially my feelings about Benner, what a fine young fellow he was.

"You are right, skipper. He has worked like that whether you or I are there or not, ever since he came on the job. Never has he joined in all the silly talk nor said a word about how the others have messed things up. It is a shame to see a good man like that tied up in a contract with such a gang. I'd have got out and left 'em to it long ago."

On the Sunday Bob Cashel arrived in time for lunch having walked up from MacLuckie's. It was a never-ending wonder to us, that a man of fifty-four could get about in the bush as he did. MacCracken had not met him before. Next morning we started to lay off the hundred acres of Flint's contract. I have already described how the men were working in from the north-east corner of it. Our task proved unexpectedly easy. We had the southern and western lines only to cut, and found they nearly followed a ridge in each case, we had no gullies to cross, and only a few bad patches of supplejacks to work through. I did the chaining whilst MacCracken used the slasher and cursed in the thick places, where I felt bad language was permissible. Generally in camp we refrained from it, MacCracken knowing that on general principles I preferred it should not be used in ordinary conversation, but where emphasis was needed or relief of overstrained feelings, it was difficult to forbid it altogether, and I quite saw that many men could not express themselves without the use of it.

My father came up to Te Kuiti to see me and how the work was going. I took him to Otorohanga and we rode out as usual. The weather was fine and we made him comfortable in camp. In fact he found MacCracken's large fire rather oppressive. He could not scramble about the mountainside; but I took him to where he could get a general view of the work in progress. Two of the bushmen came to the camp in the evening and he was struck by their good manners and civility. Going back to town I could only find one horse, Jeff, so had to walk to Otewa where Te Ngoi lent me another one. My father was rather upset that I should walk and he ride. He wanted to take his turn; but I could not permit that. Considering he was then sixty-eight years old, he was a remarkable man to do the journey at all with so little apparent effort or inconvenience. I introduced him to Byrt Jordan, the Crown Lands Ranger, and the leading people in Te Kuiti. He went away feeling that things were going well enough.

*   *   *

The King Country continued to boom. All classes of people poured in, and new shops carried the main street of Te Kuiti further north, towards the football ground and the school. What was so encouraging to us was the interest taken in the district all over New Zealand. Tommy Izard now arrived from Canterbury, bringing Fred Elliott. Tommy had been noted for always keeping an eyeglass in his eye, apparently without effort and without securing it by a string. Generally I think we were regarded by the community as rather an asinine lot; but we were all imagined to have unlimited resources, and therefore welcomed as bringing in new capital of which we might presently be relieved, so were rather encouraged than otherwise to do what we liked.

Whilst we were certainly not making a living, we of course expected soon to do so, and the rise in the price of land ever since our arrival indicated that we were on a pretty good wicket. There were others who came in and started, in business, to make an income at once. Amongst these was a Mr Graham from Palmerston. I suppose he was fifty years old, but that was old to us. He set up an auction mart with a weekly sale where we often went when in town. He was Scotch and respectable, and he looked the part as in neat bowler hat and breeches and gaiters he stood on a box in the open on fine days and sold people anything from cocks and hens to household furniture. He seemed to do a quiet steady trade which was helped by farmers who sold out their places and found themselves in a position to give their wives some money to spend.

Mr Graham proved to have two attractive daughters, the Misses Helen and Ivy, who soon were most popular with us, not only at the monthly dances, but in their own little house, where, Mrs Graham acting as chaperone, they entertained largely in the evenings. Not only did they have a gramophone with all the latest songs and tunes, Harry Lauder included, but Miss Ivy was an accomplished pianist who could play accompaniments at sight. She started at once giving music lessons and the little girls of the town flocked to learn.

A place like Te Kuiti, progressing fast — it had recently become a borough and elected its first Mayor and corporation — where young men of means were to be met in the streets and boarding houses on their way to and from the back country, also attracted others who were on the make and had only their own wits and abilities to do it with. On one occasion on his way up from the south, Rowley had sat next to a decent-looking fellow in the train, who was on the lookout to set himself up in business as a saddler. He got off the train when Rowley did, and next day looked round him to find only one saddler in the town, and rather an easygoing fellow, so he opened a shop of his own. His name was MacCorkindale and he prospered from the start and made enough in a few years to buy a farm of his own. Many started as casually as that and made their own way.

The dances in Te Kuiti I really did enjoy, and they were steadily improving. The hall was convenient; Hetet's hall it was called, and the floor was good. The music, an orchestra of four led by Hetet's grandson, Sonnie, was excellent. As all good orchestras should, they seemed to play for pleasure and would go on as long as people liked to dance. At one time people hardly bothered to dress for these dances, but full evening dress was now becoming the rule, and men dug out their tails and white waistcoats and made special trips to town to attend, which considering the rough lives they led in the backblocks was good for them. I think now that these rare dances were a good thing for lonely country men; then, I had a rather guilty conscience about attending them, feeling that I ought to be working in the bush, and I always had some excuse ready, in consequence, when I came to town, usually making the journey for stores coincide with such an event. What was wrong was that, finding some of our friends in the township, one too often made excuse to idle there together for days. I was glad MacLuckie got his dress clothes out and left them at Dr Paxton's, coming in to attend the dances, for one always felt that a sober-minded Scot like him would never neglect business for pleasure. His presence helped to keep us in countenance.

*   *   *

MacLuckie had just had a dust-up with his bushmen. He was not clearing a large area as his funds were temporarily running a bit short, pending the arrival of a partner from Scotland, who was bringing a wife and family out. He had engaged two Tasmanians, Wilson and Pearson. They knew their business and worked daylight to dark. Mac was delighted with them, but when I told MacCracken about them he smiled, saying, "Well, I hope he is careful. They can chop all right. I knew them in Poverty Bay. They can hardly go back there; they made a reputation for slumming that is hard to beat. They know all the tricks. They chop in a district for a year or two until people get to know them then they move on elsewhere. They are hard to keep to their contract."

So MacLuckie soon found. Dr Paxton from Te Kuiti was spending the weekend with him and strolling in the clearing they came within sound of where the men were chopping. Mac was slightly deaf. He went white and turned to Paxton.

"Do ye hear anything?" he asked.

"Only a big tree crashing down and the sound of chopping" was the answer from Paxton, who saw something was wrong. "Why not?"

"Why not?" said Mac. "Because they aren't supposed to chop down a tree till I have passed the scrubbing and I have not looked at it yet."

He took the doctor back to his camp and left him there, whilst, putting a revolver in his pocket, a fountain pen and a new contract, he went to see the men. He stopped them working and made them follow in silence to their camp. There he produced a statement saying they had broken the contract and making them agree not to cut down another tree till they had cut down all the scrub, even under their fallen timber — a terrible job — until he had approved their work. They refused to sign. He said they would not receive a penny till they did, not until they had done what he told them. They looked on him as a new chum. He was only about two years in New Zealand then. They bluffed. He thought of the loaded revolver in his pocket. He did not draw it; but it comforted him. One said, "I'm goin' out to work again."

"You aren't," said Mac. "Not another stroke till you sign this paper." He said he thought they must have sat there facing each other in silence for an hour. It seemed like that, till at last Wilson, the toughest of the two, said he would sign. After that they were model bushmen. When they finished the work, as they did, to his satisfaction, and came into town, they said Mr MacLuckie was the finest boss they ever worked for.

*   *   *

Brittan was able to start a gang of bushmen. His nearest section, a small one, had been surveyed by Cheal. The title was approved and sealed and he got four good men. One was married with a pleasant-looking young wife who went into camp with them and did the cooking, winning golden opinions. Everyone's manners and language seemed to improve when they heard she was there. The men of a survey party in that vicinity all went calling on Sundays. Their cook excelled them all by digging out from his swag a blue serge suit, bowler hat, white collar and tie, an unheard-of thing. Local opinion was in agreement for once that what the country really needed was women to humanise and civilise it.

John Rolleston had also arrived on the lookout for land. I was hopeful he might settle in our Rangitoto; but first like everyone else he had a good look round, riding out with Byrt Jordan. We had known him in Canterbury where he always went up to the Grand National. Rowley was at first rather awed by him; though this did not last long. He was eight years or so older than we were, and I suppose had left Christ's College before Rowley went there as a small boy. John too had been a boarder and Rowley had not.

Having been a boarder at Waitaki amongst the Scots I was free of any feeling of that kind towards older boys of my own or other schools; but John's father had been a big man in colonial politics. Educated at the same school, Rossall, that my father had been to, though some years older, he had been a cautious conservative, yet by no means an adherent of the squatting interest whom in provincial days he had opposed, believing that the strength of a country lay in a prosperous yeomanry making its homes on the land. Consequently he had been trusted, supported and respected, if not beloved, by the small man. It had been a grief to our fathers when he ended his political career. I had felt that, and to have his son with us now seemed an attractive idea.

John Rolleston joined me at Otorohanga on a hired horse at the end of his trip with Byrt Jordan, who was now on his way out to Otewa to inspect the settlement established in the scrub and fern a year before. He led us by a route I had not known of before, on a new road past Symes' farm, just made; but on which as yet the culverts had not been completed. He branched off along the ridge at Emery's farm where the grape vine grew, directing us to follow the new formation, which we did until we came to a gap in the filling across the swamp perhaps six foot wide which we endeavoured to jump. John's larger stable horse got over. My smaller pony just failed, slipping into a muddy-bottomed drain with his hind legs.

Jeff was used to bad tracks and soft places. He kept his front feet on the bank which was fascined and clung on, obviously knowing his danger if he went right in. At first much worried at his situation, we pulled his head. He seemed unable to move. Fortunately he had sense enough not to flounder; but lay quiet. I got a long branch of manuka from the road. John took told of his reins. I laid into him with the brushwood. He struggled with his forefeet and digging his hind ones in, succeeded in climbing on to the bank and was safe; but it had been a nasty moment.

Afterwards Jordan told us he and a settler called Hewer had seen the incident from the latter's house on a hill a quarter of a mile away. They had been about to come down with a horse and chains to pull my little fellow out; but decided to see if we could get him moved ourselves first. Byrt Jordan always considered Jeff too small for me and that other native ponies I rode were quite unsuitable; but my first requirement in any horse was that he must be able to keep his condition on rough grazing and be easy to catch. Later he sold me a bigger grey horse for £10, more up to my weight.

The road we followed led on to the pa at Otewa, joining the track which I had hitherto approached from the other side of the river. It was curious I had not heard of it before, nor realised the number of white settlers in the vicinity; but at that time their small new homesteads, little more than hutments, were half hidden in the scrub. The people had as yet no grass. There was no stock to be seen on the little patches they had cleared and sown; but they were brave hopeful folk and had earned enough to keep them from want this first year by working for the government on the new road. They were fulfilling the late Hon. William Rolleston's first requirement for lasting settlement by making homes, for all were married family men; but the country looked poor, the growth on it was scrubby, the land seemed hungry to a southern eye, and we thought it a scandal for any government to settle people on hundred-acre sections of such barren-looking landscape. We believed ourselves right in taking up bush which we did at least know would grow good grass within its first year of clearing, and gladly rode the extra miles to reach it.

What the Otewa settlers were to grow to make a living off such land we could not imagine. In the South Island there was manuka country; but it was known to be poor and where it grew on the larger sheep runs people did not bother to go to the expense of clearing it. There was fern growing along the low hills here too; but what fern it was. Only about a foot to eighteen inches high and very light and thin. We could not imagine livestock doing well here. There was no trace of wild pigs, and as we came out on the flat behind Otewa pa where there was some grey-looking wiry short-cropped grass, the presence of swarms of rabbits was by no means reassuring. To suggest that anyone could profitably milk cows on such land, would have seemed ridiculous. No one ever expressed such a flight of fancy.

Rowley joined us. We heard him singing in the bush below us when we were half way up Rangitoto. The situation with the first gang had got worse, and crowning all, the brave silent Benner had, without a word to anyone, walked out past my camp at dawn the previous day. Another wages man had come in; but the moral effect of this walking off had put everyone's tail down. Tegner and Knap came up to discuss the matter that evening. I did not mince matters with them as to their own shortcomings; but I felt afterwards I might as well have left that alone. They were pathetically penitent and the time for censure was past. Though outwardly I was hard and practical, inwardly I was intensely worried, not only that these men had got so far behind with my work; but that they should have got into a position where they had little to come to them at the end of it. I felt that I must not let such feelings show in any way; to weaken would not help.

MacCracken now gave voice to an idea he had broached to me before; but that I had been reluctant to agree to. He said, "I see only one thing for it, skipper. Tomorrow I shift down to the camp and go on the axe with them myself until the contract is cut out. I will work on wages to finish it."

It seemed the only thing to give them a lead and as I did not like the idea of letting anyone do what I did not do myself, I said I would go and do the same. I felt an atmosphere of astonishment at this; but I meant it, and there seemed nothing more to be said.

All the same I thought MacCracken's offer a most generous one and later tried rather awkwardly to say so. It would mean rougher living and harder work than he had engaged for with me. He laughed at that aspect saying, "Don't worry about that, skipper. It is time I worked a bit harder and I have felt for some time I ought to get up earlier. I can't stay in bed here now. If I don't get up bright and early, there is a darned quail gets up on that log outside and starts calling 'MacCracken — MacCracken' till a man just has to turn out for shame of that damn bird."

Next morning we started out to work; but as soon as we were out of earshot of the camp MacCracken told me, hesitantly at first, that it was a mistake for me to think of trying to chop bush with my men. The gist of it, said very tactfully, was that I was not a bushman, that I could not hold my own chopping with men who were. This was rather hard hearing to a youth who thought a lot of himself. To my argument that I could learn, he agreed; but said that to reach the standard of an average bushman I should either have been bred to it, or work for a couple of years at it. To come in now on a contract that was aiming to be finished by Christmas might only have the effect of slowing up the others when they found I could not chop as they could.

What was I to do then? I had already rashly announced my intention. He said the best real help I could give was to go out again and get in more wages men, three or four if they could be found. In the meantime if I came and chopped today, he would tell the others I was only doing it in order to get a notion of what it was like and I could return to my camp that night, going out the following day to find new men. I felt rather deflated at all this; but could not deny the soundness of his advice, and later came to be very grateful for it. I was not an axeman and never became one; nevertheless I worked with the men that day and returned to camp that night.

*   *   *

About this time, Rowley, John Rolleston and I, with MacLuckie's man, Hughes, went off into the bush for several days. Rowley was anxious to see the section he had bought with such eager optimism some months before. John was beginning to think that the Rangitoto offered the best prospects of settlement of any land he had seen in the King Country, and I was interested in my own country south of Rangitoto, and whatever lay adjacent to it.

We made good going on the first day, and slept in the open close to the Tunawaia where Hughes and I had been on our very first trip. The weather was fine now. Hughes shot a bull here and we slept under a fly in the open. The blow flies were bad and the dead bull attracted them. We wondered what they had lived on before we arrived.

Next day we climbed up a long sunny face in the bush and along where we imagined Rowley's section was. Here we believed we were in country where man had never set foot before. As Rowley carried a camera, we had our photographs taken at the foot of an uprooted tree, to celebrate the event. From there, gazing north, we saw about four miles off the smoke of a burning rata. That was a sign of humanity, and we started to make for it. Hughes leading, we plunged into the bush, again losing sight of any landmark, and followed our guide blind. After nearly four hours Hughes said, "That tree should be handy to where we are now."

We others had lost all sense of direction by this time, but sure enough, after casting around we found a large rata burning steadily, as such trees do, sometimes for weeks. More than that, we soon found traces of a man having followed a cattle-track and then, in a few minutes more, the dead embers of a fire. We lost further trace and camped where we were.

Next day we walked all morning, and in the afternoon we reached MacLuckie's camp, where we spent that night, and on the following day arrived at my own camp on the grass patch. Leaving the swags there, we toured through the country to the north-east, until we could see the headwaters of the Mangatutu. From the grass patch John and Rowley rode to Otorohanga. Hughes and I, taking the remainder of the things on our backs, climbed the mountain on foot and in silence, and nearly reached the limit of our endurance; but after a good hot meal were not too tired to sit up by the fire for two hours, while Hughes talked interestingly as usual.

*　　　*　　　*

The following week Flint's gang cut out satisfactorily. I passed their work, which thanks to MacCracken's firmness with them in the first place was in good order. They were walking out carrying their swags of clothing only. Following the usual practice of bushmen with good cheques to come to them, they left their tent, galley, camp oven and cooking gear, together with axes, slashers and grindstone behind them for me to do as I liked with. Even the famous kapok mattress Flint had been so proud of months before, remained in his bunk. I thought I might use it, as the fernleaf padding on my own bed had worn away. I had never bothered to replace it, and lay on my blankets with the bare saplings under me. MacCracken had pointed this out to my father when he stayed with us, saying, "Your son, Mr Westmacott, sleeps on the hardest bed I ever saw any man lie on."

It was no fault of his; I had ceased to notice my discomfort in it.

As Flint's gang owed for their stores, I went out and met them in Otorohanga so as to get the account and make all deductions for settling outstanding accounts before paying them off. I also expected a dispute with Flint.

They met me by arrangement in the front sitting room of Clayton's in the township. There was an air of pleased expectancy as they sat round the table. They had been working about eleven weeks and when all expenses were paid would clear a fraction over £2.2s a week each man. No wonder they were pleased with themselves.

Christmas was only nine days away. They did not question the deductions for insurance and for the bill for stores; but when I said I was going to deduct the money I had advanced Flint when he went to Auckland to engage them, he objected strongly. He said that was due to him under the old contract. I would not agree for a moment, pointing out that he had left the others to finish without him and that when the wages were paid it was unlikely there would be anything left under the old contract at all for anyone.

The others listened to this in silence, I could sense that he had their sympathy in getting all he could. He had no doubt talked it over with them. We argued the matter at length; but I preferred to let him do most of the talking as long as I was not bounced into giving way. He still said he would not sign a receipt. At last I said:

"Very well. We do not seem able to come to an agreement. There is a clause in the contract that in the event of a dispute I need not pay out in full; but can hold back 25% of the money for twenty-eight days after the work is finished until all claims are settled. I had intended to waive this and to pay now. Also there is a penalty of a pound a day for every day the work is prolonged after the date named in the contract. You are a week over that time. I had not meant to enforce my rights in this; but I suppose I must if this question is not settled."

There was an immediate chorus from the other men.

"Oh come on. What is the use of arguing?" They said to him, "Sign up, Bully, and don't make all this fuss. Our contract is good. You have got good money. The Boss has been fair enough. Why don't you sign up and have done?"

He hesitated and was lost. I asked if they were agreeable that I make out the cheque to him. They assented. He said he might as well take it. When I had written it out I said;

"Well, you chaps seem better off than I am. I don't expect to have £20 to spend this Christmas."

Flint replied as he read the figures I had written, "Well, I don't know boss, if you can write a cheque like this to be cashed to the bank you have nothing much to complain about."

My next act was to return to Rangitoto to settle up the original contract. They finished three days after Flint, with the assistance of their wages men and the leadership of MacCracken. He returned to my camp that night. To settle the wages men was simple enough. Each knew the amount due to him. Their time had been accurately kept under MacCracken. There were no arguments. I wrote their cheque and they returned to their camp ready to depart early in the morning.

*   *   *

To settle up with Knap and Tegner was not easy. The first thing was to pay for their stores. They had accumulated a bill of £111.16.1d from Greene and Colebrooke. That firm had tried more than once to get me to guarantee their account. I had persistently refused; but of course it must be paid. The figure staggered them. They knew it was heavy; but for long had just ignored the bill. I now said I would pay it for them if they wished. They were glad to agree.

When we worked out insurance and wages to the other men, all of which I had paid, there was nothing left. In fact they owed me a pound or two. I could not have that. They had seen the job through. Even poor little Tegner had worked well in the end. Both he and Knap had chiefly gone wrong through thinking they had too good a thing on from the start.

I did not wish to appear soft. I was my father's agent, in a position of trust, I felt; but I knew he did not expect anyone to work for him at a loss. Knap had had insurances and not done so badly in the past with me; but Tegner, apart from growing fat, had drawn little cash. I bade them sit quiet while I went through the accounts again. I do not know what I missed out; but I worked out that I owed each of them £11.2s. I gave them cheques for that amount. They were delighted. They need not seek work again until after Christmas.

I heard Tegner returned to Taihape, married, and became a successful farmer, working hard to support his wife and children. Knap went on bush falling. I was only sorry Benner had not stayed to receive his share.

When I next met Jack MacCracken in town I confided in him that the first contract had cost us more than the price originally asked for by the men and that I had overpaid Knap and Tegner.

He answered , "I know that, skipper; but it won't do you any harm in the long run. Men like to work for a man they know will treat them fairly. You will never find you have any difficulties in getting labour."

John Rolleston had decided to throw in his lot with the Rangitoto settlers and all going well to take up a block of 3000 acres of bush to the south of Rowley's southern section which he could approach from the sawmilling township of Mangapehi about fifteen miles down the railway from Te Kuiti. This would mean that amongst the five of us, MacLuckie, Brittan, Rowley, Rolleston and myself, we occupied round about 17000 acres east of the Waipa and all adjoining.

Meanwhile, he, Rowley and I were going south to our homes for Christmas. Rowley and I had important business still unsettled, in getting our survey arranged. Cheal had more work than he could perform and would only consider doing ours at a price much above the statutory figure laid down by government. There was no legal objection to paying a premium to a private surveyor ; but old Mr Jordan had undertaken to do it. He was an old surveyor of early days and did not go into the field himself; but his assistant was good in the bush and could run the job well no matter how rough the country. Crawford, like so many, was a hard drinker when he came into civilisation; but this did not affect his work when away from it.

To start however, the work had to be authorised by the Lands and Survey office in Wellington as it all had to be up to Government standard and close with the general scheme of survey throughout the North Island. Application had been made by us through the usual channels, for authority for the work to proceed some time before; but this, though not refused, had not yet been forthcoming. It was suggested to us that whilst passing through Wellington we call at the head office, try to find out if there were any hitch to cause delay, and if possible, get the matter accelerated. It was of the utmost importance to us, as we could not get a sealed title until the work was approved and finished, and to the surveyor himself, with the summer commencing, to take advantage of the longer days and fine weather.

It was with some hilarity that we bade farewell to our friends at 2 a.m. in the morning at Te Kuiti and entered the crowded train. We were in holiday mood. We sat where we could, John and I in the same seat and Rowley beside a kindly stranger on whose shoulder he lay fast asleep when daylight came next morning. We were in a second class carriage. The Christmas spirit was already abroad. At Taihape a bushman in bowler hat and blue serge suit got in and commenced to entertain his fellow passengers. Standing up at the end of the compartment he gave us a tap dance to begin with. Then producing a bottle of whiskey he offered it to those adjacent by drawing the cork and making them drink it neat. He stood over them exhorting them to "Tear it inter yer. Tear it inter yer. Tear it inter yet." After which he had one himself and gave us a song. We were at the other end of the carriage, however, and sitting quiet were not compelled to participate in his generosity.

In the course of many journeys on the main trunk line, I have never known time to pass heavily.

While in Wellington S. W. and Rowley Hill were able to see the Chief Surveyor, Mr Kensington, and obtain official sanction for their surveys to proceed, so they could enjoy the holiday with free minds.

PART THREE

THE CAMP AND THE TOWNSHIP

*Do you know the blackened timber — do you know that
racing stream?*

PART THREE

THE CAMP AND THE TOWNSHIP

OUR CHRISTMAS WAS a happy one. The place at Waikakahi was for sale, and it might therefore be my last at my old home. It was very comfortable. We had a good Christmas dinner, and I departed after the New Year, for I was eager to get back and burn my 400 acres of clearing. I took my dog Fly with me by rail and steamer and lost no time on the journey. Rolleston had preceded me. In a note to the south he gave an account of Te Kuiti in the absence of many of its habitués, saying of his cousin, "Britts, like the poor, is always with us."

Fly was rather a problem on the journey. I was anxious about her and took her in the carriage on the train from Te Kuiti to Otorohanga. A fellow passenger said, "You got more than one dog there."

It seemed he was right. She had eleven puppies in the livery stable within half an hour of our arrival. This was a complication. I could not take this large family out to Rangitoto. Was I to destroy them? Tony Ormsby, at the livery stables would not hear of this. He said, "Leave her here. We will look after her," and gave her a loosebox to herself with lots of clean straw.

In Te Kuiti two big black-haired muscular Sullivan brothers, with MacLuckie's men, Wilson and Pearson, asked for work. I said I could give them none just then, until I had been out to Rangitoto. Rather vaguely I said I might be able to employ them track-cutting and burning for a week or two later on. They were loafing about the township, men of good address. I was vain enough to think they might behave themselves honestly after their experience with MacLuckie.

At Otewa I stopped to lunch with Te Ngoi and arrange about the packing of grass seed and the sowing. I offered 1s an acre. Te Ngoi said he would talk it over with the men. I wanted a few potatoes. He took me out to where some were growing. The other men came too and stood round while he said they wanted 1/3 an acre to sow the burn. I was reluctant to give it. It seemed dangerous always to concede top price, and I stood thinking hard. Te Ngoi watched me, his hands upraised like an auctioneer till at last I said, "All right."

He clapped his hands together saying, "Kapai. Now we give you for nothing all the potatoes you want."

The men dug them quickly and filled a split sack. I asked if he could let me have a boy to go up to the place with me, and a grinning youth was sent racing for his horse and was mounted in no

91

time with a split sack of potatoes behind him on his saddle.

It grew hotter and hotter as we rode up the river. At the last ford before entering the bush, I was so thirsty I got off and drank from the stream; but the native boy looked contemptuous. I saw why when some distance in the bush a little tributary crossed the track. The boy threw himself from his horse and went down to drink at it. I followed suit; the water was nearly ice-cold, never having felt sunlight, where the stream had been lukewarm.

The air grew cooler as we climbed the mountain and reached camp between six and seven on a gorgeous evening. The boy started kindling the fire whilst I went down to where we drew water at a hollow in the top of a gully. It was dry. Here was a bad moment. On top of the mountain, night falling, and nothing to drink. I found a little in the enamel billy and divided it, about half a pannikin each. I told the boy it must last till we went down the mountain to the base camp next day. He grinned. I asked could he play poker. He could. I gave each of us twenty matches and we settled to it for the evening. I lost steadily and he won a boxful. Next morning, just before we were due to start he disappeared. I cursed inwardly all natives. Had he cleared out? He had gone only to reappear in about ten minutes from down the hillside with a billy of fresh water.

We had to go out again that day, the boy and I. I had to complete the arrangements about the seed. I had already got this mixed in 75lb loads for packing, having ordered it before Christmas. It was a considerable amount, about £150 worth. There had been some competition to supply me. Abraham Williams' agent had button-holed me in Te Kuiti, extolling their seed. John Rolleston had been with me and waited patiently until I had heard the man out; he was a fluent advocate. When I rejoined John, he said, "Regular case of Abraham and his seed for ever, eh?"

In the end, after inspecting samples carefully, I bought from Mostyn Jones, who I believe stocked the same seed. He undertook to have it held for me in Palmerston, and not to consign it until I was ready for it as I had nowhere to store it. My present trip out was to arrange with the natives to get it to Otewa and pack it on. I could not find Peta on my way, so ran on to Te Kuiti to see Mostyn Jones about getting it out and hoped to see Peta on the way back. I slept in Te Kuiti.

*　　　*　　　*

The sun was hot as I rode out of Otorohanga; I rolled my jacket up and strapped it on my saddle with my raincoat, my arms bare to the elbows. As I went up the river the heat shimmered above the still places on its course. The natives were bathing in front of the settlements. At Otewa no one was to be seen but old Mrs Te Ngoi and two wahines. When I asked for Peta they directed me on. He inhabited a whare a couple of hundred yards up the track. No one was there. I heard voices at the river and rode over. A crowd of young people in the water ran to shelter as I approached, their naked bodies glistening in the sunlight. I rode up to a clump of bushes behind which some had taken cover. One of Peta's daughters, an elegant girl, stood up, her hands clasped in front of her and enquired what I wanted. Her bearing was natural, modest, and not the least bashful. I said I was looking for her father. She said she did not know where he was. I enquired for Te Ngoi. She pointed out two men in a corn plantation not far off. One was Te Ngoi. I rode over and explained what I wanted, asking him to inform Peta. He said he would have the seed waggoned out to Otewa and packed on to me as soon as I was ready to receive it. I spoke of the sowing. He said he would come up and help me with the sowing himself, bringing the necessary men.

This was a great relief to me as I knew he was most reliable about keeping his word, and doing anything he undertook and I was not sure where I could get the men to do it at this busy time. Hitherto I had not employed more than one or two Maoris except for packing. MacCracken had advised me against it for bush felling, saying, "They can work all right, skipper, on a short job. They'll go like cut cats for a couple of weeks. Then the life goes right out of them." I have since reviewed this judgment. He was prejudiced; but if they went at it the way he described, a gang of them would finish sowing my burn in less than a fortnight.

Alone I went up to camp at the grass patch. I had been told that Hongi Pork had rifled the bushmen's abandoned camp, taking among other things, the camp oven. I went up and took stock of what was missing. Most of the gear had been in the tents, which stood as the men had left them. They would be useful as shelter for the grass seed. As the bushmen had been paid by me, I considered I was entitled to anything left on the ground and resolved to demand their return as soon as I saw Macfarlane.

That afternoon, Crawford, the surveyor, his chainman and a cook, arrived with their gear on the grass patch, to start the survey, the Land Board having at last given its approval to the lease. Crawford was a crotchety fellow, not a bad thing when in charge and as competent as he was; but it made him full of complaints. He said the country looked too steep for survey, and he wanted two linesmen to complete his party. I said the Maoris were to be got, and that I would go on the job when I had time, as surveying had rather a fascination for me.

Just then Macfarlane arrived on horseback, presented me with a bag of peaches he had picked from some trees on the edge of the bush, and asked if I had a job for him. I told him I had not; but that Crawford wanted two men and that I wanted the things he had taken from the bushmen's camp. He took Crawford's job and rode off to get his swag, arriving back next day without malice towards me and with all the missing camp gear.

Crawford got an extra man next day, sent out by Jordan, and started to get his bearings. To my surprise, the Sullivan gang turned up on hired horses, with all their gear, saying they had got tired of loafing and were ready to do any work I put them to. I had plenty, so got them to price a good packing track through the bush, straightening out all curves and bridging the side streams, and corduroying the wet places. They asked 10s a chain. I thought the distance " 'pout a mile", as the Maoris said, and like a fool agreed, without measuring, on condition that they open up a pack track to the lower end of the burn at the corner peg, help me burn the bush when a suitable day arrived, and make pack tracks over the burnt clearing for the grass seed.

*   *   *

As far as the burning was concerned, I believed I had now made every conceivable preparation, even to bringing out a bottle of kerosene to make good inflammable torches to light when we had some favourable wind. The Sullivan gang went to work in a businesslike way, but I found they could not get far round the hillside without striking rock, and had to carry the track down into the creek, mattocking out a siding here and there.

Crawford's gang had a cook whose name was Charles Augustus Fitzpatrick, and who had been at St Patrick's College as a boy. He was an amusing rascal. I enjoyed his stories of how he had set out to get all the fun he could out of life. This was his first job as a cook, and he never seemed to work hard at it, but he got the fire going almost in a flash in the morning. He only stayed a week, which meant that after that the two gangs which were sharing the camp had to do their own cooking. This was a nuisance, and Crawford asked me to get another cook as soon as I went into town.

I was reluctant to go out, as Crawford kept declaring that he was going to write to Mr Jordan and resign, as progress in this mountain country was too slow for them to make money at it. I asked him to wait a bit longer, saying the country grew easier once the first steep slope was finished, but I could see for myself that it was hard in many places to set the theodolite up so as to get a shot. They were not making an average of five chains a day, whereas to pay at all they ought to have been doing twenty.

In any case I meant to burn the bush first, and was only waiting for a day with a favourable wind, and though the weather was hot and dry, it was very still, the air in the grass patch after midday being most oppressive.

At length a slight breeze one afternoon decided me. I told the Sullivan gang to get ready. We tied sacking round sticks as torches, so as to be able to move round the edge of the clearing and get a good wide face on the fire as soon as possible after starting it up. I had the bottle of kerosene to saturate these torches and make a proper blaze, and now went to get it. We found it empty. Jerry Sullivan told me he had seen Charles Augustus Fitzpatrick using it one morning to light his fire. It seemed it must have lasted a week; then he went!

There was not much use cursing our late cook. We made torches as best we could on the spur of the moment with dried leaves tied together, and filed up to the felled bush, taking our station, each with plenty of matches, about a chain apart. They looked to me, at the centre, for the signal.

"Let her go!" I called, seeing they were ready, and, lighting the leaves of a prostrate tawa, prayed now that after all our anxiety and my bushmen's efforts, we would be rewarded with a nice clean burn.

In front of each man rose a straight pillar of smoke; and then the wind dropped. Five cheerful little blazes sprang up — no more. We worked along the edge, lighting as we went, until our torches gave out, one by one, and then we painstakingly used matches. My heart sank. A good burn is of the first importance; a bad one may spell ruin. I took Wilson and Pearson through the bush to the other end of the line to try a fresh start, leaving the Sullivans to continue to do their best where they were.

Never had I gone faster in the forest than I did now. I was by this time fairly used to getting through supplejacks, thanks to my exhausting journeys with MacCracken, and I was surprised to find I could get along so quickly. Wilson and Pearson followed hard. Once more we lined up at the creek and for a disheartening hour kept on lighting along the edge of the felled timber. The fire was alight; that was all one could say for it. It was making no progress.

Depression was deep as we sat at tea. Try as I would not to communicate my thoughts, I knew I was failing; the men shared my feelings. Crawford, who with his party had had a good look at the clearing on his way back from work, seemed to derive a melancholy satisfaction from pointing out the worst effects of a bad burn. I pointed out that as yet this was hardly a burn at all. He agreed, but said it was one that having once started would run in streaks, making it impossible ever to get a real face on it. There would henceforth be no volume in any fire I might light. I would have to patch burn it. That would take weeks and cost a lot of money in wages. We might not be able to sow grass seed on it for months. There would be no proper seed bed of ash when we did. He had seen fortunes lost at bush farming as a result of bad burns. Whatever induced people to take up bush country he never could see.

By the time he had finished in this lugubrious vein I felt inclined to tell him to go to hell; but if he did, who was to finish my survey? Instead we all went early to bed. That was hell for me, too, as I lay and pondered what would happen to my parents if I failed here. It was all a gamble, and I knew that if I made a mess of it they were ruined. It was hard to make decisions as to any course of action either, but I did make up my mind to a course I had already been debating and had discussed with Rowley as, during these last six months, the unforeseen expenses had mounted up. We must take advantage of the rise in the price of land since our arrival, and sell out in whole or part, so as to ensure, that in the event of misfortune dogging our footsteps, financial ruin to our parents would not be complete.

This would of course mean that in the event of success we would not win as much as we had bargained for, and that would be a disappointment, for no one was keener than I to make a fortune as quickly as possible. Also I felt that I would risk all were I alone concerned, as I was confident I could start with nothing again, and win my way, but the thought of those two old people, and my sister too, having nothing to keep them, was too terrible to me. I had not been taught to think out problems, to appreciate situations in the logical manner, as an army officer is, but having worked out, though in a rather incoherent way, alternative courses, I felt relieved, and presently saying my prayers long and silently as I lay in the blankets, my mind became easier and I went to sleep.

When I awoke the day seemed greyer than usual, and as I went out the men were astir. Wilson was starting the fire, and Jerry Sullivan was chopping wood. The air above and around us was full of smoke. A light breeze was blowing. The elder Sullivan, Dick, was standing in the middle of the grass patch in his blue dungarees and light sleeveless flannel. His bare arms were folded as he gazed up the mountain. As I joined him, a rata in the bush about fifty yards off took fire and blazed with a crackle of sparks and flame. Other dry trunks and branches above the green foliage were burning freely. Dick turned to me and said, "The whole bloody country is afire!"

And so it seemed it was. We could not see the mountain for smoke; but speculation as to the the progress of the fire was rife as we sat round at breakfast under the open tent fly over the galley. Of course Crawford said the fire was anywhere but on the clearing. The wind was blowing it westward. The green bush was burning all right. That was just where you did not want it. It would spoil the Crown Land section for anyone who might take it up. No one could fell bush properly at a payable price if it were full of burnt trunks and windfalls.

Never mind; we went up the mountain to see. The fire had caught all right. Immediately before us was a black burn, the ground covered with ash, the bigger logs and branches charred and smouldering. I put the Sullivans to mattock out a track to the corner peg, for pack horses to use, and then to carry it right up the burn to the top of the mountain.

Then I climbed up the main ridge to see the extent of the fire. The going was quite difficult enough, owing to there being no tracks, and in many places big logs and branches lying against each other, over or through which one had to climb, but the long broad main ridge was quite a good burn. When at last I reached the top I had a good idea of the extent of the conflagration. It was still fairly smoky, but I had been able to observe that though the fire had not carried well in the light timber in the gullies, the great majority of it had gone and there was one continuous burn all over the ground that had been cleared. My spirits went up to normal, and I was happy enough when, black with charcoal, I took the long track down the mountain again. We were a cheerful crew in camp that night, in spite of Crawford.

Crawford continued to complain about the problems of his gang, and S. W., Rowley Hill and Ian MacLuckie were sufficiently concerned about getting the surveys of their properties completed to agree to pay an extra £50 each to have the work finished, however slow progress might be.

S. W. and Rowley Hill also discussed further the possibility of selling at least part of their properties, with the idea of putting some of the proceeds aside, and using the rest to buy more bush country. S. W. was particularly interested in the block of Crown Land adjacent to his original purchase.

The Sullivans' tracks had made progress. The one to the corner peg had rather a steep pitch for the last chain up to the burn, but they thought horses could get up it. I tried it with Jeff. He managed the ascent, with rather a scramble it is true; but he was an invincible animal. We could but try it; after all, Maori horses could go almost anywhere. The Sullivans had cleared a track through the logs beyond, and were nearly to the top of the mountain, from which they were to make branch routes over the rest of the burn. After walking over all these I decided to go to Otewa and get the Maoris to come out and start sowing.

On my way out I met MacCracken at the grass patch, come up to look over Rowley's bush, select a camp site, and decide where to start; though he did not mean to commence for some weeks yet, as his three mates were not ready. He brought up a strong lad called Alf Caterer from his own district, who had never been on a contract before and was looking forward to it with youthful keenness. Crawford was glad to employ Caterer meantime. When Mac-Cracken saw my camp and I told him the Sullivan gang were living in it, he said, "Well, aren't they a lot of hard cases? Fancy bushmen like them roughing it like that."

After I had spent a night at the pa, Ngoi, good as his word, mustered his men, seven of them (Peta not present), and it was quite a busy scene as eight pack horses were loaded, each carrying 150lbs. Putting the loads on was easy, thanks to our having had the seed put in bags of 75lbs each. A bag on each side and no top load was what each horse carried.

The river was low. There were no complications and we rode without a care. I went in front with Ngoi. He told me he did not think it was any use for me for Peta to pack any more. It seemed Peta had drawn my cheque for the packing and spent it all on himself. Even the boys who helped did not get a penny. This was not at all in accord with tribal custom, which was communism in practice; but it was not doing the right thing by me either. My only concern was who was to do my packing if I turned him off. Ngoi said he would arrange it, and I could not have been better pleased. From then on I had no trouble. He did not want the money for himself, but had always been the reliable person in the background seeing to it that things were as I wanted them. Now he would be the only person with whom I would deal.

That first night there were nineteen men camped on the grass patch. The bushmen, surveyors and natives sorted themselves into groups round their own camp fires; the pack saddles lay about, the dump of grass seed in its clean new bags was stacked close, the smoke smelt pleasant as it arose in the still air, and the horses grazed outside the circle of firelight. The presence of all these people, each with a definite task to perform, and knowing how to perform it, was reassuring, and sent me to sleep feeling content and confident. Romantic by nature, I imagined myself to feel like the commander of an army in which things were going according to plan.

*   *   *

Next morning the surveyors and bushmen filed off to their tasks. The natives, saddling up early, loaded the seed as soon as breakfast was over, and in due course the train of pack horses was splashing over the stream and following up the trail where Ngoi and I now led the way on foot.

The track was not difficult to the foot of the hill. There it followed an easy gully to the edge of the clearing, where it turned right along the edge of the bush, and the steeply mattocked ascent to the corner peg on the main ridge began. Ngoi and I, well ahead by now, climbed to the top of this pinch and waited to see how the loaded horses fared. The horses closed up, then the leading horse, with an active native at his head, started scrambling up, while another man laid a stick on his rump to encourage him. The animal dug his feet in, and came on in a series of plunges till, a few feet from the top, he started slipping backwards. Making no progress, he reared up, with the native in front holding tight to his head. But the horse had got too near to the perpendicular, the load proved too much for him, and he went over backwards into the supplejacks, pulling the man after him. They went down in a series of audible crashes, the man swearing loudly in Maori, nearly to the track where the men and other horses were waiting below.

Why it should be I do not know, but to many people the sight of mishaps with horses is an excruciatingly funny one. I am one of them. Perhaps because of the element of danger present, the laughter covers our fears. I have never seen a man bucked off without the onlookers enjoying it immensely. So now, though the matter was a serious one for me, I could not restrain my laughter. Not so the owner of the horse who now revealed himself by a stream of pakeha oaths as a rather ugly man called Wao. I immediately went down to see the damage, accompanied by Ngoi.

The natives were already busy with slashers clearing the horse who was tied up in supplejacks. It was amazing that anything could have fallen through such a tangle at all. That the horse had apparently carried his load down with him and was apparently unhurt, was remarkable; but his owner continued to swear at the track in my presence and when I had come within a couple of paces, and this made me angry. I knew I must try not to show temper; but I spoke in a sterner tone of voice than I usually did with the natives. Wao was continuing his tirade when Ngoi quietly said something to him in Maori, and he stopped speaking; but continued glowering at me.

Whilst they were getting the horse on his feet, I was doing some thinking. If this happened here, it seemed we could not get horses up, as there were pinches equally steep on the long climb to the top. To make a proper zigzag track the whole way would entail a lot of labour. There seemed nothing for it but to do what I had wished to avoid, and follow my own long track to the top of the mountain. It would of course, be further, and take more time, about two hours. It also meant passing through what was now Rowley's leasehold, and though I knew he was glad enough I should do so, a track that kept on my own property was desirable. But it would probably be the quickest course in the long run, even though we might have to do some work in widening the way through some lighter growth on each side of the track. I satisfied myself the horse was none the worse. The supplejacks had obviously been a blessing in disguise, breaking his fall, for he could not otherwise have gone down backwards all the distance, without breaking his back with all his load on.

Now I said, "The only thing we can do is to find another way. This is too steep for loaded horses. We will go round by the long track to the mountain top. If it is not clear enough or too steep at any point, we will open it up, and if necessary, I will pay for any time lost in doing so."

This suggestion was received with smiles all round and we started off. As we went up, Ngoi found opportunity to say to me, "I told Wao, when he was speaking to you that time, not to speak that way as you will not like it."

Fortunately the track proved easy to them. We had few delays and were on top of the mountain by midday. The natives decided to camp up there till the work was finished. I directed them to form dumps of seed and cover them with tent flies. The pack horses returned to Otewa that afternoon for the next load of seed and all ran smoothly with the packing till the work was finished.

The Sullivan gang continued on the grass patch as I was able to do without them on the burn soon after, when they continued on the track up the Waimahora.

The survey party moved on up the mountain. I went up each morning to see the progress of the sowing. It was a pleasure to see the Maoris work. Each man split a sack across the middle in front and behind. He then made slits up the sides for his arms. When he put his head through the back slit and through the top he had a sort of coat with a large bag attached in front. A few stitches of flax on each side of the neck to keep the whole in place, and he was ready to go to work, fill the bag in front, and broadcast the seed. The whole gang would fill up and form a line along the hillside returning periodically to the nearest dump for more. They had no idea but to do an honest job and do it well.

Later I heard that Peta's fellow-tribesmen took an opportunity to recoup themselves for the packing money I had paid to him. They bided their time, and presently exposed him for some moral delinquency that normally would have passed unnoticed.

The members of the hapu dwelling at Otewa and all their kith and kin in the vicinity held a meeting and spoke at length on the enormity of his behaviour. Then led by the offended party and his relations they moved in war-like procession towards his dwelling. Loud were the exhortations to strike home and spare not. "Hoo Ha." Tongues lolled out, and the more active of the self-appointed leaders of the "taua" — the old name for a war party — displayed their agility in a highly creditable manner. Peta himself was reared in the ancient customs of his race, having spent his early childhood there, when Te Kooti still lived among them with his warriors, men who had shed much blood in the traditional style.

He waited composedly, regarding it as more of an honour than anything that so great a to-do should be the result of what was after all so small a lapse on his part, a thing that anyone might have done, given the opportunity; but him! he was the big man! Obviously he must be. Were he a person of no consequence, a mean propertyless fellow, did anyone imagine that all these people would go to all this trouble and exertion, all this publicity and advertisement to rob him? Of course not. With an air of guarded indifference, he sat by whilst they plundered the whare of all his belongings, and they made a proper job of it with much grabbing and disputing, all ending in laugher and mutual satisfaction on the part of those who succeeded in retaining the chief articles.

They left him nothing that was movable; blankets, clothes, all went, that he and his family were not wearing. If he had a pang at parting with the beautiful saddle, the nice new shot-gun bought so lately with the ill-gotten gains of his packing, he never showed it, and after all there was not so much to worry about. He and his family would now live on their friends and relatives comfortably enough. They need not go hungry and cold at night, nor would he lack tobacco. He still had his horses, for no one bothered about them, and a dog or two to hunt pigs. These latter were not worth considering either, for when a pig hunt was on, anyone could go, and the numerous curs round the pa always went along as the spirit moved them, much like a trencher-fed pack of old in England. Trencher-fed, did I say? The dogs knew there was no feeding beyond what they could scavenge, and a hunt was their only chance of getting the puku properly filled occasionally.

Life would be by no means hopeless for Peta after this, what to a European would have been a family calamity. He had noted where various items of movable property went, and into whose hands they had fallen. They had better not be careless with them. He might borrow them at a later day when this had all blown over, and anyhow, let them watch their own step in the future. If they became puffed up with vainglory, or too self-satisfied, if they themselves deviated from the strict and narrow path, be sure Peta would notice it, and bring a similar storm about their heads, in which, if he went direct for what he wanted, he might still hope to salvage something of his own.

Te Ngoi played little part in these affairs. He coveted no man's property. His role in the public life of the pa was to hold the scales of justice in which he applied the rules he had learned in his year at St Stephen's College. He regarded it as in the interests of his race that they should work and earn something. It was for their own good, and also meant that they were not sponging on each other and him, and the general wealth was thereby increased. Native custom was too strong for him altogether to dissociate himself from it. His house was always open to any wanting a meal or a place to sleep; but having no vices himself he was always well off and even kept money in the bank.

The humour of this episode came to me by round-about channels; but when the subject was referred to in my presence and I sought to hear more, I found the younger natives like Jimmy Rawiri did not want to discuss it. I am not at all sure they were proud of it though they might have taken part in it. They certainly were sensitive to the possibility of being laughed at, so considering the matter a family affair and no business of mine, I did not enquire further.

Hearing Peta was doing nothing, and wanting an extra man for a week or two, I sent a message by one of the younger men asking him to come. As he did not turn up I said I imagined he was too lazy. No doubt this went back to him as I meant it to.

Later seeing him sitting amongst his fellows in the street in Otorohanga, I greeted him as usual, and he was correspondingly cordial. I asked him why he was not working, to which he answered pleasantly, "Not working? Me? I am too lacey," in the manner of a man giving a very good and sufficient reason for doing nothing.

He was a versatile fellow though. Presently he developed a flair for variety and burlesque, organising a band, the members of which had paper caps and red paper stripes down the seams of their blue dungaree trousers; with these he fairly convulsed his audience in the wharepuni as the winter nights drew in. Hughes told me it was the best entertainment he had seen anywhere. Thereafter, when anyone died within twenty miles of Otewa, Peta and his vaudeville turn were in demand for the tangi. Everyone agreed that they were the life and soul of the party.

*   *   *

THE CAMP AND THE TOWNSHIP

The Sullivan gang made good progress with the track out and were finished in record time. I now did what I should have done in the first place, borrowed a chain from Crawford and measured it, to find that instead of being " 'pout a mile", it was nearer two. Rowley, when he came over, was highly critical of the work, as well he might be. The Sullivans had made enormous money on it. I wished Rowley had been there when I let them the job, as the track benefited both of us, but the Sullivans had presented themselves early and Rowley had not been present. I debated with myself whether to let him pay his half, but reflected that he had had the benefit of my initial exploration, that MacCracken had opened a good track up the ridge through his leasehold, and that in the ensuing twelve months what with felling, grassing and stocking, he would probably use the track as much as I would.

The Sullivan gang went off in high fettle. I found they had put green timber into the culverts that would not last more than a couple of years, and in fact that they had swindled me properly. In Te Kuiti they found that a recent settler near Pio Pio, named James Wall, was getting a thousand acres felled and letting a number of contracts, one of which they took, and again made big money in a short time.

Laurie Christian, a somewhat disreputable pakeha from Te Kuiti, who had been in financial trouble, was now working for S. W. and was building a substantial whare on the grass patch.

Laurie first erected a frame of timber that he had cut in the bush with an axe and trimmed himself. Over the roof he spread wire netting and on top of that rubberoid. These materials were packed out in handy rolls. He made a wide deep fireplace of tin at the middle of the back wall. The wide front of the building faced the sun, which on the grass patch arrived late in winter. He put up a hinged door, and three glass windows which came out ready made. The sides of the dwelling were made of squared punga stems erected close together, side by side, and the chinks between them caulked up tight with the trimmings.

So much for the outer walls. He now lined them inside with the nice new grass seed bags which he split down the sides and nailed flat. We got a roll of brown paper from the store and pasted this on, making a nice smooth surface to the interior of quite a pleasant colour. Finally he got me to join him with the cross-cut saw and we cut a length of straight rata lying in the bush close by. This he split, selecting three good slabs which he dressed with an adze and planed smooth. Oiled, they looked very well and were erected as two sidepieces or supports to a real wide mantel-piece. He made

103

two easy chairs of timber and sacking with arms; very comfortable to sit in.

Whilst this work was in progress, my father came up to see the clearing and was well satisfied. Laurie was at his best and my father listened to his stories, toned down suitably for his benefit, and thought him an amusing fellow; but of course he had met similar men before. Laurie was very clean and neat about the camp and skilled in everything he did. He had a brother, a respectable fellow, about his own build, in an office in Christchurch, who used to send him his clothes when they were no longer fit for town wear. These Laurie used to take to pieces and turn, stitching the seams up again so carefully and well they looked like new. He was preparing for his return to civilised life once more, which he would be able to begin with funds again, for Rowley, seeing the quality of his work, engaged him, when mine was done, to go and erect a two-roomed dwelling for him on his place at a site close to the track up the mountain, about a mile and a half from the grass patch. This all helped to restore Laurie's confidence to the peak, not that it had ever fallen very far.

My custom at that time, when returning blackened with charcoal from the clearing, was to go across the grass patch to the stream just below, where we drew water for the camp, and plunge into a hole we had made about a foot deep, where I would soap off the day's grime before the evening meal. Laurie, noting this, said it was a poor way to wash; but I thought it was a good one. However he pooh-poohed my ideas and sewed up a canvas saucer bath which he pegged out by the whare. As it meant carrying water to fill it, I continued to use the stream. He demonstrated the use of his bath by sitting in it and doing his own ablutions there. Finding I was still unconverted to its use, he took it down and pegged it on the ground beside my bathing hole and filled it with water.

After that he used to extol the advantages of a canvas bath over a shingle-bottomed stream and ask me each evening I came in, if I had used it, being almost indignant when I said I had not. At last I lied to him, as it seemed to wound his feelings never to try it, and said I had, and that it was a nice bath, most useful. After that he seemed content; but I never got into the thing. There was more room in the creek.

*   *   *

Byrt Jordan came out to value the Crown Land on which was the grass patch. He stayed at the grass patch. We were very anxious to hear his opinion as Crown Lands Ranger, on the merits of our undertaking and the quality of the land. He did not take long to

BUSINESS REPLY POST

POSTAGE WILL BE PAID BY

Authority No.
69 TE ARO, NZ

Promotion Manager
PO Box 6454
Wellington
New Zealand

A.H. & A.W. REED Publishers	General/Educational Books & Records
I would like to receive your attractive free brochures when issued. I am interested in the following subjects. (Please tick ✓).	Name ....
☐ Art ☐ Australia	
☐ Biography ☐ Children	Address ....
☐ Colourful New Zealand	
☐ Crafts and Hobbies	....
☐ Cookery ☐ History	
☐ Horticulture ☐ Literature	....
☐ Maori ☐ Natural History	Please print clearly
☐ New Zealand ☐ Pacific	....
☐ Politics and Economics	I understand I am under no obligation to purchase
☐ Sport	

give it. After riding up the creek and looking round him he turned to us and said, "There is no doubt you fellows are on to the best thing in the King Country."

That seemed to put the hallmark on our work, for he knew the whole district from end to end, and his opinion was quite an unbiassed one, a contradiction of what so many of his friends had been saying. It gave Rowley and me a very happy feeling, though I do not think Rowley had ever had any doubts about the wisdom of our undertaking, being blessed with a sanguine disposition. We were a happy camp that night.

To have my own dwelling was a great comfort to me now. I got all my books and treasures from the south, eleven kerosene boxes full. I had two beds in the bedroom at the east end, and could make another room at the far end by draping a tent fly over a rafter which went right across the whare. To sit in an easy chair in the evenings in front of my own blazing fire reading my own books seemed a milestone on the journey towards prosperous squiredom.

By now I realised I could not expect to marry a girl of my own class for years to come. The life would mean she must give up too much with no compensating advantages. Brittan and Rowley had been very worried soon after my arrival in the King Country that with my ideas I might do something rash. Certainly if I liked a girl I spent as much time as I could in her company. My friends were tactful; when Rowley thought I might make a fool of myself, Britts agreed I might; but there was very little, nothing in fact, anyone could do about it. To be honest, I did not imagine then that anyone I might want, could care for me enough to be ready to share the vagrant existence, in and out of the bush, that I then led.

Now I was becoming more settled, or would have been had I had a wife to make a home for me, or so I thought. I do not now think I would have made a good husband. I had really seen little of the world though I thought that I knew so much. Brittan was in the end the man who brought me to my senses, as we stood one day on the kerbstone outside the hotel. The day had been a wet one. Lewis's coach stopped and down from it climbed three women. They were buffeted by the weather, their hair in wet wisps about their heads; their clothes hung to their figures, shapeless and gaunt through hardship and overwork. The worst part of all was that they looked old before their time. They were wives of backblocks settlers in the Aria district.

Somehow the cruel tragedy of it seemed to strike us both at once. A silence fell upon us, then Brittan said quietly, "That is what happens to the wife of a man who takes her into the bush." I did not answer; but it impressed me more profoundly than any amount of moralising might have done.

Sometimes I took Kereihi Falwasser, Ted's daughter, to the pictures. Kereihi was Maori for Gracie. There was quite a good picture show in Hetet's Hall two nights a week now. The town was coming on.

They were always crowded. My little friend loved them. She had spent most of her life in Kawhia, a growing place; but as yet pictures were not going there. They certainly were a great show. The man who played the piano was a wonderful fellow. The music alone was worth the money. Half the audience were natives. They liked the adventure films best. There was a wonderful fellow called "Foolshead", a marvel of the films, who rode races, fell off horses, dived down cataracts and jumped over cliffs in the most comical manner. That man certainly earned his money if anyone did. There was a very fat man, John Bunny, who delighted everyone with his smile, and made love in the drollest way. We all liked him; but love did not appeal to the natives much. What they liked were the cowboy films where everyone galloped along, firing his revolver, or the Red Indians chasing the pale-faces through the woods. Their sympathies were not with the savages either, but like all nice people, with the pursued. How anxious they were when the hero peered through the undergrowth. "Look out! Look out!" they called from all round the hall, for they could see what he could not, the villainous redskin waiting behind the tree. Fortunately, the latter looked all ways but the right one, enabling the hero to get off to a good start with the heroine.

It was an anxious moment all the same, and we breathed again — for we had been holding our breaths — when they sprinted together across the woodland glade, and along the forest path with arrows flying after and quivering as they struck the tree trunks. "Go on," we yelled, "go on!" as the hunted people paused for a close-up, and to look which way to go. Then when the hero took up the heroine in his arms we were frightfully worried. He could not run like that. "Put her down!" we called. "Let her run. She can do it." It was a great relief when they sprang into a canoe and floated over the rapids to safety and marital happiness.

As the pianist put down the loud pedal, and thundered out "God Save the King", we stood, respectful and bareheaded, before going out into the night.

*   *   *

Now I had to prepare to get sheep out to the clearing. To follow our usual route up the Waipa seemed too risky. The river might be flooded at the very moment we wanted to move the sheep up it. I was used to it by now, and flattered myself that no flood would stop me on horseback, if I wanted to cross; but sheep were a different story. I was afraid to try to take them upstream, though

I believed I could bring them down it in summer.

Once more I turned to the route through Mangaorongo. Mrs David Ormsby had a farm at the edge of the flat there. Behind her house was a valley with a level grass bottom, and stream flowing down it, which ran up into the hills for a mile or two. One could camp sheep there. I believed we could get them there from Otorohanga in one day's drive. The next stage was on across hills, comparatively low, following the track by which I had taken the bushmen in the previous year. I hoped we might manage to get to Macfarlane's grass on the Tauraroa in the hours of daylight. A native track ran along the ridge towards the bush. It went close to my own riding track up the Waimahora, the only serious obstacle being a swamp between.

There were several swamps between the Ormsby valley and the Tauraroa. Horses could cross them; but for sheep they must be opened out and fascined. The tracks through the fern and scrub from the green valley of the Tauraroa and again on to the bush would have to be widened. It meant work — how long I could not judge. I decided to get a man to help me, and do this myself, camping by the track at night as we went. As usual I asked Te Ngoi to let me have a man who could be trusted to live with me without getting lonely and who would stay and see the work through.

The specimen who reported to me did not fill me with confidence, when he told me that he had come to work for me and that his name was Puru Tonga. He was tall and thin for a Maori, slow in his movement, quiet and deliberate of speech. His clothes were disreputable, of course; that meant nothing. He wore a cap and had a long straggling moustache; but what made him look most seedy was that he had weak eyes which peered at one through a pair of blue spectacles. I did not at first like the idea of sharing camp and sleeping beside him; but I prepared to make the best of it.

He proved more useful than I expected. The first night or two at my whare he chopped the wood, and unbidden put the kettle on to boil. He was the first up in the morning, having slept on the floor in front of the fire. Though not a MacCracken or a Hughes, he moved quite smartly along the track in front of me. I found there was something quite likable about him. We began by fascining the first swamp outside the bush and clearing the track over the Tauraroa. When three miles from home we took a pack horse and went round and camped there on the grass.

We soon had a useful track to the Tauraroa. He would go ahead for three chains with the slasher and cut back towards me. Similarly armed, I did the same the other side of the track. In the swampy hollows there was plenty of tall manuka, so fascining was easy. We soon had to move along the track again to sleep, so as not to have to walk too far to and from our work. We left our horses on the

Tauraroa where the grass kept them content, and had a tent pitched there with our heavier things.

The weather was fine, so we slept under a fly fastened down to the scrub behind us, and spread over a cross-piece of manuka about five feet high. It was clear and cold at night, but we always had a good fire at our feet on the open side to the eastward. Our hours of business were dawn to dark. The first sign of daylight took Puru out of his blankets to start the fire. I often lay long enough to see the sky turn from grey to yellow and then to light blue before the sun rose.

Puru Tonga's costume and habits always gave me a cheerful feeling at this hour, as he tended the fire and put the billies on to boil. His outline against the dawning day was a joy to an eye which sought the unique and original in preference to the commonplace. Having slept half-clad, as did I, his first act on casting aside his blankets was to pull on his boots and light the fire. When that was blazing well, he hung the billy over it for tea. He pulled on a coat and lit himself a disreputable cigarette, mostly paper, with the merest whisp of tobacco in it, which he puffed contentedly. It was at this stage, as I lingered before myself turning out, that I enjoyed the sight of him, for he did not don trousers till later. It seemed so in keeping with our wild solitude, a touch of truly picturesque life in the foreground, the hills rolling away to a background of forest.

On these nights I slept in the thick woollen heather mixture drawers that served me for trousers in the daytime. It was easy to comprehend how so many of the early Europeans in the King Country adopted native habits. Environment soon affects character. One of the things I found nauseating was smoking as we waited for the billy to boil, which took about twenty minutes. The reek of Puru's cigarette was indescribable. I said I wondered how he could smoke on an empty stomach.

"This the best time," he told me. "Cigarette he taste very good. You try 'im the pipe. You smoke it, eh? All the same the kai. Not too much hurry for the billy boils eh?"

So in self-defence I lit up my pipe, half-smoked from the night before, found I liked it, and continued the habit while Puru remained with me. Our meals were simple, tinned meat and bread and butter, or ship's biscuit when the bread gave out. Tea and sugar gave us the warmth required. We washed our plates after wiping them with fern if they were greasy, pouring the hot water first into the mugs and then over the plates. That done we put them into a sugar bag rucksack, with the food for midday, and set off for work.

*   *   *

Such good progress had we made beyond the Tauraroa that I felt confident we would have the track ready in ample time, and as we wanted one or two things, and Puru wanted to see his family, we decided to sleep at the Tauraroa on the Friday night and went over there early in the afternoon. To my surprise we found my grey horse grazing there, and determined to catch him. This, needless to say, was not easy. He headed towards the Waipa, more than a mile away. Fortunately he was in no hurry, so we formulated a plan. About half a mile down the river the track ran through a patch of bush along the hillside, with a steep drop to the river below. Puru agreed to ride down the Waimahora and get ahead of the horse without being seen, and crossing the Waipa wait at the far side of the bush to stop Grey Brother when he came that way.

When Puru had been gone twenty minutes I followed on the track, having filled in the interval cutting and knotting a long rope of green flax, the native harakeke, which abounded there. The horse had settled to graze on the wide grassy flat on the right bank of the river. Keeping behind him I gave him the opportunity to be caught like a gentlemen, and tried to walk up to him, but he was not having that, and moved off down the flat. At the same time he showed his contempt for a man afoot by not hurrying, and walked ahead of me, occasionally stopping to take a bite of a shrub by the wayside. No doubt he thought he could precede me in this way until he joined the native horses at Otewa, four or five miles away.

He crossed the river and followed the track beyond. So did I. The water was up to my waist, but I had no socks on, and it squelched out of my boots as I walked on, on the other side. There was no need to run or exert myself as long as he kept to the track, though I was prepared to sprint if he tried a byway. Fortunately he did not, and I saw him enter the bush where we wanted him. As soon as he disappeared from sight I did a fast hundred yards and had the exit blocked at my end. I wondered if Puru had failed me, but felt I need not worry, and I was right, for when about fifty yards into the bush I saw my horse coming trotting towards me, and his look of knowing cleverness had given way to one of quick thinking.

Seeing me, he turned again and tried to head uphill into the bush, but there the undergrowth was too thick for him. I went warily forward, and he, assuming an air of misjudged innocence, allowed himself to be caught almost like a horse that was looking for me with that purpose in view.

Puru now appeared, having done his part by heading the horse.

"Aha," said he, "werry clever the hoiho, he think himself to beat the man. This time too cunning, eh?"

Though he might profess to be a reformed character, we tethered Grey Brother with a double twisted flax rope that night, and he was there in the morning. I had only brought a pack horse to the Taura-roa so had no saddle or bridle. I therefore made a rough bridle of flax and rode bareback, when we started for Otewa next morning.

Puru Tonga went away at a hand gallop. It had been freezing overnight and the animals were fresh. Usually I did not ride as the Maoris did, but this time I let him set the pace. It was all right where the going was straight, but round the bends I would not normally have galloped like that. The ground was slippery with the thaw, not yet having dried. I admired the way Puru's horse kept his feet, and the ease of the rider in the saddle. Where he could go, so could I.

With these reflections in my mind we slowed down to splash across the Waipa at the wide ford, jogged past Te Kooti's old whare, and ploughed along the track through the swamp which was mud up to the belly. Then away went Puru once more, along the flat and round the foot of the hill, his horse sending up the mud in slobs and splashes from the soft clay. As we galloped, I noticed his animal almost change feet as he went round the head of a slight boggy depression, and had scarce time to think as my own horse's feet went from under him, and we came down over the edge of the bank to my right. As my foot struck this bank, the ankle gave two sharp cracks, and I thought the bone had gone.

Fortunately our fall had carried us onto the soft marshy ground so that the horse in rolling over me seemed to crush nothing; but it was an alarming experience. I had some pain in my leg, and as I lay on my face I am afraid I gave some groans.

Puru had dismounted and was back beside me almost at once. As he touched my shoulder, I looked up and saw my horse about ten yards away standing on the track, and coming to my senses said, "Catch the horse before he gets away, quick!"

"I thinka the man was kill," said Puru.

"Never mind; catch the horse," I reiterated, and Puru did so, and tied him to a manuka.

When he came back I was sitting up. I tried to get on my feet, but could not use the right one. I thought the ankle was broken, and derived a melancholy satisfaction from the thought that it was, for although I had had many knocks and falls, I had never broken a bone or had anything much to show for it, and felt my life had been too soft. Now it was painful, but not unbearable, and we decided to go on to the pa for a cup of tea. Puru managed to get me up onto the horse. He offered his own; but the grey was quiet enough.

At the pa, a sympathetic crowd gathered round us with much interest. They sat me on a box in the cookhouse, and made me some tea. As the foot was painful, we took off the boot, but with some difficulty, owing to the swelling. Te Ngoi said, "You cannot go far with a leg like that. We drive you into town," and sent a man to harness up a buggy.

I felt I must see a doctor, and there being none in Otorohanga, I would have to go by train as usual to Te Kuiti. I was annoyed at this interference with my work; but Puru said he would go on with it whilst I was away.

My ankle was not broken, but I had the attention of a doctor in Te Kuiti, and the pleasure of a few days there, and when the ankle was strong enough to carry me, I returned to the bush again. To my gratified surprise, I found that Puru Tonga had cleared the track, right through, and finished the fascining. He had worked as well in my absence as if I had been there. And now the time had come to bring out the sheep, for turnips, rape, mustard and young grass were growing strongly on the burn.

*   *   *

I had first to retrieve my dog, Fly. She was still living at the stable. One of her dog pups had been stolen, and that is why half the Maori curs in the district for years after had sharp ears and white paws. We never knew who stole him. I put in a written report to old Fraser, the constable, but he did nothing. Sly grog cases were more in his line.

Fly had made herself almost indispensable in Otorohanga, where the Ormsby family, besides being large landowners, and running the livery stables, owned a butchers business. First thing in the morning, Fly would trot off round the town and bring up the horses for the livery stables. She was a clever heeler, and could make anything on four legs move. Next she would go off to the slaughter house and as soon as Ormsby's butcher had opened up the yards she fetched up the bullocks for killing. This meant she was fed as never before. About midday she reported to Tony Ormsby to see if there was any further work to do. She was driving cattle for Tony out to the Symes' farm when I met him and claimed her, and was very reluctant to leave them before the job was done.

One dog was not enough for me now that I was going to have stock on the place, so I bought another. This dog, Glen, was not a young one, but a really good sheep dog for which I had to pay £10. Fly was good with sheep too. I had never liked her activities with horses and cattle; but in this rough country she was useful.

Brittan wanted sheep too. We arranged with St Hill, Dalgety's manager, to meet at Whawharua and look at some hoggets, of which I wanted 300, and Stanley the rest. These hoggets proved to be just what we wanted, of the white-faced woolly Romney-Lincoln cross, suitable for bush country, the price 8/6 a head. Brittan and I went aside and had a talk. We agreed the price was not

111

excessive, though our figure was 8s. In order to counteract the idea that we were rich young men, to whom money was no object, we agreed to offer our own figure and stand firm on that awhile. We offered 8s. The vendor stuck out for his own price. We lingered and shook our heads as if there was something wrong, and said we thought it was on the high side. He told us he had already been offered 8/6. The obvious reply to that was that he could take it. I confess I thought the statement an invention, and so hung on a bit longer before giving in with an air of reluctance, though, as I said, they were what we wanted.

These sheep were paid for by Dalgety & Co. We bought them "on the nod" without being asked for a scratch of the pen, or signature of any kind, such was the faith St Hill had in us that we were rich young men and could pay. In my magnificent way I commissioned him to look out for some ewes for me.

*   *   *

By arrangement with St Hill, a drover was sent up from Te Kuiti to take my sheep to Otorohanga and paddock them a mile or two out, on the Mangaorongo road. There were several farms there, the first belonging to an old Mr Clark, who had a large family of strong sons with native connections. He had had the contract for carting the timber from the mill to the railway, and as he said, made a farm out of it, the sons working on the mill and the farm when necessary. It stood on a hill beyond Otorohanga and was conspicuous a long way off for its careful cultivation, growing a variety of crops, especially roots and green fodder.

The next farm beyond belonged to a family called Eveleigh, and the homestead was planted with English trees, well-grown by now. The sheep came through about midday the next day, driven by a drover called Paddy Corcoran, a sturdy fellow who knew every mile of road in the district. I now walked a mile beside him, telling him the route. He had never been beyond Mangaorongo, but said he would find Davy Ormsby's farm from my description. This first night he would try to paddock the sheep on the far side of Eveleigh's farm. I rode out to Otewa and asked Te Ngoi to send me a couple of boys to help get the sheep over the stream at Mangaorongo.

Next morning I was awakened in my upstairs room at Clayton's Hotel in Otorohanga by a knock on the door. Thinking it was the maid with the tea, I murmured a sleepy "Come in". The door opened. A brown head appeared round the edge of it, and a young native with round eyes said, "Tena koe — there you are — I get you now alright. Wait till you come out into the road — I will be there."

He shut the door and I heard him clattering down the stairs. What was this? Who was he? I had never seen him before that I knew of. Why should he want to "get me"? The abruptness of his appearance and departure was startling, though his voice did not sound as menacing as his words. Pondering on this, I got out of bed and dressed.

Looking out of the front door, I saw my native friend (or was it enemy?), walking up and down, like a man on guard, on the other side of the street, from time to time stopping to look up at the windows on the second storey as if in fear that I might escape over the balcony, then resuming his beat. Deciding that whatever the trouble might be, I had better have it out before breakfast, I stepped out into the verandah, when immediately seeing me, he came over, his face expanding into a smile from ear to ear as he said, "Ah ha! Now I am catching you. Alright for us now, eh?"

"And having caught me, what do you want for me?" I replied, for his obvious pleasure was infectious.

"Te Ngoi — out Otewa — you know him eh?" I nodded. "He tell it me you wanting the mans help you with the heepi, crossit the Mangaorongo. Very well I come now; but I have been frightened you go away before now. I catch you all right, I'm werry glad, me."

The position being thus clearly explained, I said I wanted two boys all right, but would not need them till first thing next morning at Mangaorongo. He said he would be there all right. His name was Whati.

"You ask anyone. All know me." He would go back now. "Kia ora." His cheerful friendliness was infectious. I liked him.

* * *

With my raincoat strapped to my saddle, and some ship's biscuits in my pocket, for I never went without this emergency ration, I took the road after lunch. My two dogs, Glen and Fly, made me feel quite the sheepman once more. It was well over a year since I had handled live stock in the South Island, and I liked the prospect. My pony was fresh after the livery stable and the track was soft. I cantered on the level, which was quite a lot, for my route followed the long ridge, and between two and three I came up with Paddy and the sheep descending the easy slope towards the Mangaorongo pa. There was nothing to do. They were travelling well enough, and pointing out the Ormsby homestead, I left Paddy and rode on there to see about paddocking.

Davy Ormsby, whom I had known at the livery stable, introduced me to his wife. She was one of the most strikingly handsome native women I had ever seen, with an air of high-bred

113

dignity. Her tattooed lips did not mar her features. Her expression was amiable and charming, and her voice musical. It was a matter of course that the travellers in those times sought the shelter of the nearest homestead for the night; but she made me feel we were welcome there. Davy said he would show us where to put the sheep, and when, after rejoining Paddy, I returned an hour or so later, he was waiting at the open gate to see them paddocked for the night.

To call it a paddock was, from a sheepman's point of view, a misnomer. Two wires strung to posts and stakes at about five yards' interval enclosed a space of ground of about twenty acres on which grazed usually a few horses and cows; but there were no sheep in the district and fences were not constructed to hold them; I do not think that within eight miles there was a better one. This did not worry us. The sheep were tired and ready to rest. They were not likely to move far that night, and the grass, having only been grazed by cattle, was good; they need not stray in search of feed. If undisturbed we might be sure they would still be there at daybreak next morning.

The Ormsbys' house was built in European style, with about five rooms. Davy entertained Paddy and me in the front room where there was a good fire. We men had our evening meal there. Mrs Ormsby put the food on the table, helped by a native girl, but as is the native way she did not sit down with us. There was the usual number of native dependents in the back part of the establishment, half-relative, half-employee, or rather a combination of both, together with the children of the family. Amongst the latter was an attractive-looking fair haired white girl of about twelve years old, child of Mrs Davy by a former marriage of hers with Bill Standish. I say marriage, for so by native custom it was regarded.

Davy Ormsby also had a family by a former marriage, and one or more children by the present one. All lived as one happy family now together, Mrs Davy mothering the lot. The principal employee was a tall, hard-working Maori called Tokoroa. Paddy Corcoran had known the Ormsbys for the many years that he had worked as a drover in the King Country. He himself came of a farming family long settled on the lower slopes of Pirongia mountain on the Waikato side. He spoke with pride of the "fighting families of the Waikato", many of them being of soldier stock.

He and I slept side by side on the floor in front of the fire that night, sharing the blankets Mrs Davy provided. On the floor, within the glow of red embers, is a very good place to sleep. They can always be replenished if the cold wakes the sleepers. This time it did not. We lay down sleepy enough, and arose as day was breaking. A stroll outside showed the sheep still contentedly on the ground where we had left them, cropping the grass about them. We had a light wash, and sat down to a good breakfast before catching and saddling the horses.

We each left half a crown "as a present for the children when next they go into town". It was unexpected. Then, with the dogs bustling importantly round our horses, we shook hands with our host and rode off to round up the sheep.

The count-out through the gate proved the number correct. We drove the little mob along the track towards the stream. As we did so the native children from the pa came running to see the "heepi", as they called the sheep. Many had never seen any before. As we moved slowly along, Whati rode up to report for duty, accompanied by another boy, Jimmy Rawiri, whom I knew. They had ridden the four miles across the Waipa from Otewa, galloping most of the way in the Maori style, and pulled their horses up to a walk, in a lather of sweat. They had an air of aloofness towards the smaller fry. After all, were they not engaged to help with the sheep? If they did not know Paddy, they soon caught his name from me, and thereafter addressed him by it. They were important personages.

The track came to the ford at the mouth of the grassy valley. It was fairly wide, but not very deep, and had a good shingle bottom. Nevertheless the sheep baulked at it and clustered at the edge. We drove them close, the dogs barking loudly. We threw several into the stream, but they came back and stood in the water on our side and would not venture across. Paddy and I, bidding the dogs "push 'em on" up to us, each collared a sheep, and walking across let them go on the other side. The natives thought this great fun. Whati and Jimmy followed our example; the other boys heaved in more sheep. We kept them moving in the right direction and they began to string across, and then jump in without assistance. We only had to keep the mob up to the edge of the water and the job was done.

The native children stopped at the stream. We caught our horses and rode over. The sheep straggled up the valley, and we followed, but it was slow going as many small trickles of water ran into the main stream, making swampy places that could only be crossed where the track went. So the sheep had to close in at all the wet places, and take the usual crossings, jumping over one by one. I found it best to cut in behind the leaders of the mob and push them forward, Paddy and the boys remaining behind to keep the laggards moving.

The boys had not been expected to come all the way with us when I originally planned the journey. I had meant to let them go once we had got across the first big stream, but they were keen to come, and I now saw we might want them, as we had the Tauraroa and the Waimaohora to cross, and although they had no dogs,

115

they were useful. The mob was a small one, and on a good road one man could easily handle it; but this drive was such an experiment we did not even know if we could make our stages each day. If we found ourselves benighted in the scrub and fern it would mean remaining on the track with the sheep. I would be glad of a man to send forward for food, if nothing else, so I kept them both, to their obvious pleasure.

Already we were behind the timetable we had planned for ourselves. We were well over an hour coming up the grassy valley. The hills now lay before us with their scrub and fern. The sheep would not, of their own volition, enter the narrow track where they could not see to right or left. We crowded up the mob, and I again took a cut ahead. About a dozen or so of the leaders had to be punched along, and they stopped dead if one was not near enough with the dogs to coerce them. Leading my horse, I got them going. Paddy forced more to follow me, but they only moved slowly and reluctantly. I kept going till I came to the first swamp with its fascined crossing. There was a small open space as one approached it. I got up on my horse and pushing him into the fern I let the leaders rest while I rode back to see how the others were coming along.

Paddy, for his part, looked cheerful and confident, and in response to my enquiry said the sheep were going all right. There is nothing better than a cheerful countenance and a willing smile to banish doubt and misgiving, and I moved back to the head of the mob once more, feeling that things were going as well as could be expected after all.

As if to warrant that comforting reflection, I found the leaders had made their way over the fascines and were following the next stage of the track, through the fern and over a low hill. The others joined me at the swamp, the dogs found water and a bit of shade where they lay with their tongues lolling. We lit our pipes before following on.

I reflected that while, as now, I was concentrating on a job, I could exclude all other thoughts from my mind, but that at other times I was far too prone to daydreaming. Even now, as I directed the dogs where to cut in, and encouraged them to give tongue, and rode directly to and fro, my mind went far away to the country squire idea. I felt it was a long way off. I could not foresee that those ferny hills and wide scrubby valleys would one day be covered with rich pasture, or that the unfenced waste through which we were passing would be divided into prosperous farms, served by a solid network of roads and bridges.

Slow as our progress was, time passed unnoticed, as long as we were actively employed. It was not until we reached the next fascined swamp and let the mob close up again, that I realised the sun had long passed its zenith, and was well over to the westward. We had one more stretch to go, with the Tauraroa stream to cross at the end of it, before we reached the grassy flat and men and animals could settle down for the night. The sheep were obviously tiring, and their pace had become a veriest crawl. The dogs, too, were showing signs of weariness. The track seemed to wind interminably. My mind was never free from anxiety as we climbed each little rise in what was otherwise easy country, only to find another before us. If we failed to do the distance it would be by a very narrow margin.

There was a real danger to the sheep in staying out on the track. Amongst the scrub here and there was tutu. I had more than once found a sheep "tuted", as I believed, on my father's place in the south, and had bled it by cutting the roof of its mouth, when it had recovered; but tutu had been unusual there and the sheep in good condition. The real danger from tutu was when stock filled themselves with it when hungry and empty, and there was enough here if they started to eat it, to destroy the mob if they were allowed to remain on it for the night.

It was therefore with a sigh of relief that we came to the last ridge and I looked down on the broad grassy flat across the Tauraroa stream. Calling to Whati to keep the sheep going I leaned back in my saddle and rode slowly down. The sun was setting as I waited on the shingle to assemble enough sheep to start them over the creek. They seemed to come painfully slowly. All the same they kept coming, weary and walking; but they were walking. Whati joined me. I believe we had over one hundred sheep by now. Calling to the dogs to press them, we each hurled a sheep well out into the water, where they stood a moment, then walked over and climbed up the bank the other side.

"Hooray!" I shouted.

"Hooray!" shouted Whati, as he grabbed another hogget and sent it hurtling in after the first two. I did the same. We kept on throwing until finally we were able to let them string across. They seemed to walk daintily as if doing us a special favour.

We both thrust our way back up the hill to see the string kept going without a break and "Push them now, Jimmy," I said, as we came up to him. "Where is Paddy?" I asked, wondering how far the tail of the mob had to come, for it was now getting noticeably dark.

"Paddy, he's back a long ways. Heepi very slow now."

"How far?" said I, for Jimmy was educated. " 'Pout a mile?"

"Oh no! May be a quarter. Half might be. Not sure."

We forced them down until I saw that Whati and Jimmy could keep them moving over. Then I climbed the hill to help Paddy far to the rear. Darkness came as I went up the hill. Small mob though this was, the sheep seemed endless as I worked my way past them, until sensing rather than seeing larger forms ahead of me, I asked, "Is that you Paddy?"

"That's me," said he. "How are we doin'?" He was on horseback, progressing slowly and I discerned was carrying a sheep on the pommel of his saddle.

"Have you got them all?" I enquired.

"Aye. This is the last," said he, "but I've had to go a bit slow to get 'em all on."

"Never mind," I told him, "the leaders are across the Tauraroa. The others are following. We haven't far to go now."

All the same it must have been a full half hour, and seemed like two, before we trailed the sheep we could no longer see down that hill, the running water before us, till the sound of the horses' feet on the shingle told us we had reached the stream. The black shapes of Jimmy and Whati in the darkness said all the sheep were going over fine. Our eyes growing used to it, we could see the gently flowing current and the tail of the mob picking their way over. When the last had gone on its own feet, Paddy rode over and dropped his burden on the far side, where it too climbed the bank and disappeared into the obscurity of the night.

So far we had travelled to our timetable; but I did not feel this a cause for elation. We had only just done it, and tomorrow, with bush to penetrate, and the Waimahora to cross many times, our progress might be even slower, and short of the grass patch there was nowhere to camp with any pasture. But we were weary enough, we now suddenly realised, to let thought of the morrow fade into the background, as we set about getting a meal.

My tent, where Puru and I had pitched it, was standing. There was tinned meat, bread and butter in a biscuit tin, together with tea, sugar and other stores. We had the billy boiling in half an hour, and for the next twenty minutes thereafter, in silence, ate and drank to repletion.

Whilst the boys cleaned up the utensils and put a large billy full of porridge to soak for breakfast, Paddy and I filled our pipes and lit up.

Stretching his legs in their long leather leggings to the fire, he said, "Do you know what I been thinking as we come along today? If the sheep started to get down on the tutu we'd ha' had a mess up."

"They say great minds think alike, Paddy," was my answer. "Have you ever lost much in the way of sheep from it?"

"Not much," said he, "but enough to make me scared. A big mob we was bringing along from Awakino took to it on the Mangataki. They were staggering all over the place. We had a job bleeding 'em, and even then we lost a lot. What's it going to be like tomorrow?"

"Scrub and fern for the first part," I told him. "High fern along the Waimahora, and then bush and creek for the last two miles. A good camping ground for tomorrow night, and next day about a mile of bush before we get them up to the burn."

"Aw, well. If its no worse than today we shan't do so bad," said he; and presently spreading the blankets as far as they would go over the four of us, with our saddles at our heads, our raincoats beneath, and the dogs curled up round the rim of the firelight, we all went off to sleep.

Porridge warmed us up for breakfast. There was a bit over for the dogs, who scoffed it in a twinkling and then sat round on their tails expectant of further morsels, while we completed the foundation for our day with tinned meat and bread. When we had swallowed our last drop of hot tea, we saddled up and got the sheep together. A count showed their number to be correct, and we drove them once more up a long ridge and continued our progress as the day before.

There was little difficulty as we drove them across a fascine over a swamp at the foot of the hill which brought us by midday to the track we used as our thoroughfare to Rangitoto, about three miles from home. Then they began to stick again. The fern on the flat was higher than a horse, stronger than anything we had yet made passage through. When the sheep came to the stream they would not cross. We had to bring the mob into the shingle, and then unite to push them over. The stretch of fern to the next crossing was just as bad. My heart sank somewhat. If they were like this here, what would they be like in the bush where they could not see the sky, and we could not move a yard from the path to force them on?

Two o'clock was approaching as we belted them over the stream again and we still had seven more crossings. I took a cut and drove them at the entrance to the trees. When they came to it the leaders took one look, then they put their heads up and, it seemed to me, almost pranced away from me, without the dogs having to lift their voices. I followed, and the rest of the mob came after almost at a run, nearly crowding my horse and me. From then on we had no more trouble. Even at the fords they needed little persuasion, and in scarcely more than two hours they were streaming out onto the grass patch and grazing round my homestead. What a win!

At the pace they had travelled through the bush we might have done the remainder of the journey up to the clearing before dark; but we decided that fate had been kind enough to us. We had reached our planned objective more easily than we had dared to hope. Men, horses, dogs and sheep had done all that was expected to them. We decided to wait for morning.

A plentiful store of dry wood was to hand. The fire was soon blazing. We swung on billies for tea, rice and potatoes, and we fried

119

in the camp oven our tinned meat and plenty of onions. We meant to make a feast of it. Whilst this was in progress we removed our wet boots and padded about in our bare feet. Finding we had only a small supply of stale bread, I mixed up a sponge and set it to work for baking next day, while Paddy supervised the completion of the cooking for our meal, which we ate at the table like civilised beings.

What a feast we had, and best of all, what an appetite, to enjoy it. Is there anything like good honest toil and hard going to make one appreciate the real blessings of life, good food, warmth, and a dry lie-down at night?

Next day was Sunday. We breakfasted at leisure. There was no hurry now. I pounded up the bread, and put it in the warm camp oven to rise, and leaving Whati to attend to the baking, we once more started the sheep on their last short stage up to the burn. They drew even better up the hill than they had done the previous afternoon. We counted them onto the rich feed, so high they almost seemed to disappear into it. It was only a small beginning in the stocking of Rangitoto; but there they were at last. Jimmy had never seen the turnips growing like this. I told him to pull some of the smaller ones for cooking and we returned to the grass patch for a quiet Sunday of rest.

There now began to be talk of giving a formal ball in Te Kuiti. Rowley Hill had become engaged to a girl named Ruth Stott, and she strongly supported the idea that S. W.'s sister, Erica, and her friend Char Gosset, should come up from the South Island for this occasion. The intention was that they should stay in S. W.'s whare while he shared Rowley's.

Tending the sheep now occupied me for a while. The next lot to come up were some four-tooth ewes which cost me 16s a head in Otorohanga. They soon began to lamb, and very well they looked. They were right out to the top of the mountain the day after I put them out there. Rowley and I often rode into Otorohanga and back together, and on one occasion Rowley was to spend the night in my whare.

We had a good evening meal, steak and onions chiefly, and sat afterwards in the easy chairs, yarning in comfort before the blaze. It was becoming a good place to live in. I had got up from the south the boxes of all my goods and chattels, chiefly books, and these were gradually brought up from Otewa, a couple of cases at a time, whenever the pack train made the journey. Most of them had arrived. They made the place like home. I had ample stores too, and looked forward to the arrival of my sister and her friend, Char, who were coming first to Rangitoto before going out to the ball.

120

We talked late. It must have been nearly 9.30 when we went to bed in my bedroom on the two stretchers. It was very cold, but we had plenty of blankets. Sleep came at once.

At daybreak I stole out to get breakfast. By now I had learned to bank the fire by burying a piece of firewood in the ember which I covered with ash, so that I only had to push the latter aside with a shovel to find a glowing red heart on which to put firewood and start the breakfast cooking. All these tasks I started before going to the creek to wash and dress. I had on my trousers, socks and boots, but still wore my pyjama jacket. In a certain wind we found my fireplace smoked a little. I thought that by having the front below the mantlepiece a little lower, I could stop this. Rowley remarked upon it. It was a tender subject.

The horse in his cover neighed to me, and came up for his feed. I put a few handfuls of chaff in a box and put it out for him about thirty feet from the front of the whare, and he plunged his muzzle into it appreciately. I thought how much easier to feed a horse than man.

The safe was in the verandah. I went out to bring in some meat and potatoes when the porridge pot had boiled and been stirred. Rowley was still deep in the blankets in the bedroom. I said it was about time to move.

He called out, "This fireplace of yours smokes badly. It even comes into the bedroom."

"Go on," I called back. "It's no worse than your own," and went on fumbling in the safe. When I got what I wanted I went to the front door and saw the room full of dense smoke, and the wallpaper opposite me, above the mantlepiece, ablaze.

"Come on," I called. "Get up. The place is on fire," and running to the fireplace removed the billy with the porridge in it so that it would not get any cinders in it and dumped it outside. I was already running in again with a kerosene tin full of water when Rowley appeared through the smoke at the bedroom door, saying, "My God! My God!" I took a pannikin and started throwing water on the flames. He did the same; but the smoke was already stifling and the blaze spreading half-way along the walls, in spite of us. It seemed the little dwelling was doomed. We decided to save all we could. We were breathing hard, and badly needed fresh air to go on.

Fumbling for the door I went into the bedroom. There was air there as yet, for the smoke had not yet become so thick. I rolled up a bed, mattress, blankets and all and handed it through the window to Rowley. I got the other and as I handed it to him, he said, "Look out. Don't get caught in there."

But I was thinking quickly, and saw we could only now save a few

121

things, and those must be the most valuable, and largest. The saddles were in the front verandah and could wait. I fumbled my way into the living room and got hold of a rifle which I threw out. I was feeling for the double-barrelled gun when several cartridges went off near me. Rowley again pressed me to come out. I thought of a box of blasting powder which I could not get near, and felt I must get away before it went off; but I succeeded in retrieving the gun before I went out into the open.

We flung everything well away from the burning house including the saddles and the safe. Those, and the things I have mentioned were all we saved. Such clothes as I had had were gone and all the treasures of my boyhood. We withdrew to a comfortable distance and watched the blaze. The pony never took his nose out of the feed box, even when the powder blew up inside the burning building. I had never imagined that fire would make such a clean sweep as it did. At least we had the billy with the porridge in it, and sat on the ground and ate it, warmed by the flames. That was all we had to eat.

When breakfast was over, we gathered the things together. Of course Rowley's dwelling was open to me. We decided to move the things up there, and got a pack horse from up the track. We arranged that when loaded, Rowley should take it up to his whare, whilst I, in my pyjama jacket, went up the mountain, round my sheep, and joined him later at his whare. The load was topped by the blankets, and a long surcingle round the lot. The poor cat, who at first had taken to the bush, asked to be taken too, miaowing distressfully. We put him in a sugar bag and tied him on top of everything. He objected to this method of conveyance, but there was no other way.

Rowley led the horse up the track, and I climbed the mountain with sad thoughts. Amongst my possessions had been many things I had treasured, pictures from my boyhood days, odds and ends I had collected at school. I would have hated the thought of throwing them away. Now I had nothing to anchor me. I was aware that I was too sentimental about small things. I could now make a fresh start.

*   *   *

The sheep looked well as I climbed the main ridge. Both ewes and hoggets were well woolled and had put on condition since arrival. The lambs, with their long tails, were the picture of health. It is curious how healthy sheep seek the heights. There were far more of them on the mountain top than down the long ridge where the feed was richer. Already on top they had eaten the turnips well down and cleared the rape and mustard. I reflected they could not starve, and I ought to have more of them; but they must find their way back down the slope to feed. The gullies were in dirty condition. They had never burned properly, and there was already sign of green second growth. I had been told cattle would clear this, breaking in where the sheep would not go, but the timber seemed rather heavy for them to break down, I thought.

On the mountain top I examined the wreck of my old camp of last year with special care to see if there was anything there to start afresh with. There was some left-over grass seed under cover; but I had already removed everything useful down to my homestead where it had all perished in the flames. The roof of the galley had been blown away in a heavy gale some time before this incident. I stood on the trig for a short time, and turned to the four points of the compass. In every direction the view was wild, spacious and superb. The clear air made me feel strong and well. I reflected that these days I rarely felt anything else. I had so much to be thankful for.

The morning's experience had been a disappointing one, and the loss greater than it should have been, for I had not even taken the precaution to insure the building. It was unfortunate for me, But "the Lord chasteneth those He loveth" was a saying I had used often enough. It returned now, and again cheered me. Yet I felt a loneliness if I lingered. I must move on. Again the psalm I had often sung as a boy in church, where I so seldom went now, came back to me: "Yea, though I walk through the valley of the shadow of death, I will fear no evil, for thou art with me, thy rod and thy staff comfort me." The words were heartening.

Ridiculous, I thought, for I was in no shadow of death as I stood there; but for all that I liked to use the words up there in the bush where no one could hear and laugh at me. I did not feel so lonely now, as one more quotation came to me: "He shall lead me in a green pasture." As the sun shone out I felt sure He would.

The two dogs, who had been lying a few yards away, respecting my silence, feeling with me, rose happily and followed as I took my way down the track again. I turned down to the right, to the bushmen's camp, still standing. Two tents, in a more sheltered position than my own camp on the mountain top, were in good order, with axes, shovel, spade and slashers. There was also a camp oven I could use. I decided that one tent should go down to Rowley's whare for us to sleep in whilst my sister and Char were visiting me, and that they should use Rowley's whare. This fire would, unfortunately, cut their visit short; but they would be able to see Rangitoto. When they were gone, I would come up and make my headquarters at the bushmen's camp. I walked up into the saddle and went down the hill through the bush.

Rowley was at his hut. He had had an eventful journey with the

123

pack load. The old horse Billy had made heavy going of it. He did not like packing; I never met a horse who did. He pretended the load was too heavy, though it was more bulky than solid. He made a fuss at the steep pinches, and to crown all, went head over heels at a slippery bend, scattering the load and evoking loud protests from the cat. Each of these animals being my property, Rowley abused them in tones of humorous irritation, but he had gathered the load together. The horse was none the worse; neither was the cat, who was performing his toilet in front of the fire and shuddering delicately as he reflected on the day's vicissitudes.

*   *   *

Next day we went up to Te Kuiti by the afternoon train, leaving our horses at the stable, with strict instructions not to lose them, as we should want them for my sister and her friend the following week. As the train drew into Te Kuiti, the girls were on the platform to meet us, having arrived the night before. Erica and Rowley had known each other as children. She said, of his engagement, that she hoped to offer her congratulations when she had met his fiancée. He said he liked that, as he knew she would be honest. When they did meet Erica took to Ruth and they became great friends. Char and Erica brought a breath of southern freshness with them. The cold of South Canterbury, 400 miles south of Auckland, makes a difference. The average southerner is more ruddy, the northerner in the fresh air is tanned.

The two girls were interested in all they saw and heard. The whole surroundings were new to them. Canterbury and Otago, settled by people from the old world forty years before they were born, were ready-made when they grew up. Here all was forming. Their train had arrived at 2 a.m. It brought many natives to a great gathering of the Maniapoto tribe. As they got out on the platform, loud and prolonged wailing of welcome could be heard from the old people in the meeting house at the pa on the hill. Old Maoris, men and women, were crying over each other as they descended from the carriages. The young were shrieking and laughing with eagerness and excitement. Our visitors wondered if a great calamity had fallen upon the people.

They stayed at the Grand Hotel, where also were the Mostyn Jones, who had a Miss Shannon staying with them as a guest for the ball. They had not been bored in wandering round the town. Britts joined us at dinner, and afterwards we all walked up the Awakino road and admired the scenery.

Next day there was much to be done preparing for the ball. The supper was all arranged, but the hall had to be decorated with many tree ferns, much bush foliage and bunting, whilst gangs of us tramped the floor dragging loaded bags over it to polish it. All was in order as we went to dinner. There were many visitors, and people had come in in force from the country. They were grouped in each other's minds by the roads from which they had come. There were the Awakino folk, the Waitomo lot, the Mairoa crowd, and others. A few had wives — if the road was passable and the settlement more than five years old.

The ball came up to people's expectations in every way. It opened with the Lancers and went right through a programme of waltzes, chiefly, with one or two polkas, a schottische, a barn dance, and the d'Alberts — a dance in which I never began to know where I was. The Lancers I had learnt sufficiently to be led round by my partner, and I always found the first Lancers after supper a glorious romp and great fun. We contrived to dance with most of the girls whose brothers we knew, and the strangers to whom we had been introduced. One of the latter rather puzzled me; she seemed so confident. Later I found that she carried a flask of brandy wherever she went, and I often wondered what became of her; whether she took a pull on herself, or became an inebriate. Much as I enjoyed the exhilaration of spirits now and then, I was secretly horrified at a girl drinking them, and it was most unusual.

The orchestra kept us going till about 3 a.m. Sir James Carroll, the native minister, had arrived from his train with his party and joined in the dancing. He had come up for the meeting of the Maniapoto, and proved to be a nice old man with charming natural manners. When at last we had seen our visitors to bed, we bachelors gathered at the club. There was more drinking and rioting and singing in the streets. I drank as much and sang as loudly as anyone, yet with all this I felt I had not enjoyed the whole celebration as much as I had hoped, because the presence of so many nice girls brought home to me again the roughness of the life we normally led, and the impossibility of making in the bush the kind of home to which they were accustomed.

Soon after daybreak we stopped the milkman and had fresh milk and whiskey before going to bed.

*　　　*　　　*

After breakfast, which was not unduly early, we watched the proceedings as Sir James Carroll made his way up to the big carved meeting house at the pa. In front of it on the hill were several thousand natives drawn up in lines to welcome him. A native band went down to his carriage at the railway to play him up the street. When all was ready he came in front of them, accompanied by his staff. He wore good European clothes, with a huia feather in the side of his hat to show his native connection, and carried a walking stick. He knew the procedure expected of him and did not walk too fast.

Meanwhile, John Hetet, as the leading rangatira of the district, had come half way down the street to render proper greeting to this eminent personage. He was not now the well-dressed approachable John Hetet, who normally passed the time of day with us as one of our leading citizens, but a distant, highly dignified Maori chieftain, arrayed in the dress of his forefathers, with a taiaha, or native spear, in his hand. He had a huia feather in his hair, over his shoulders was a kiwi feather mat, round his waist was a piupiu, the native kilt of old time, with a greenstone mere thrust into the belt. For the rest, he was as nature made him, a slim active figure, despite his years. His only concession to his European blood was a pair of boots to protect his bare feet from the stones of the roadway — and they were an offence to the artistic eye and sense of fitness.

He was accompanied by a score of wild-looking fellows whose only dress was the feathers in their hair and the piupius round their waists. Several of these, as the Minister approached, ran towards him, and then back to their leader, with loud and horrifying cries to show what a formidable chieftain, what a big and powerful man was advancing upon them. He for his part took no apparent notice, but strode on steadily, looking neither to right nor left, his gaze being directed more to the feet of John Hetet than to anything else. The welcoming party sprang into the air and gave ground, with many leaps and bounds, to display their agility and fitness for battle, as they joined in the general outcry.

John Hetet stood a moment alone, his spear held in two hands pointing at the feet of the oncoming visitor. Then leaping into the air, with an athleticism astonishing in a man well into his sixties, he suddenly reversed the point of his weapon, and turning about, kept a distance of about fifty paces as he led the way to the pa. The people on the hill now burst into a long wail of welcome as they waved green branches and danced the powhiri, taking the time from several nigh-naked chiefs who leapt and chanted in front of their lines.

There are those who can see in such demonstrations only what is anachronistic, even comic, in the mixture of savagery and civilisation half-absorbed which such gatherings as these display. I always derived interest and pleasure from them. Ted Falwasser, who had grown up where they were common enough, would say to me, "I cannot think what interest or pleasure you derive from a lot of half-naked savages jumping about." He professed to feel no primal urge from his Maori blood.

But I could always do with more of it. It might be primitive. It was natural, superb, thrilling to the blood in its stamping syncopation, and the mixed ferocity and plaint of its cries, even though I could not understand them. There was art in it all. One forgot John Hetet's boots, and sensed the excitement of the moment as the procession arrived at the gate of the pa. The natives, till now vociferous and active, ceased their antics, and the lines on the hill with one long wail broke off. One moment they were there, a stamping, swaying mass, the next they had fallen away in silence and were sitting about on the ground, and the space where they had been seemed strangely empty.

The conference now commenced. Rows of chairs faced the pa. The Minister sat in the central one in the front row, and in the remaining ones sat the visitors, ourselves and our friends, while the local chiefs came forward one by one and made addresses of welcome. The first wore a beautiful old cloak over his European clothing, and carried a mere. He began by calling out, "Haeremai, Timi Kurra, haeremai!" Welcome, Jimmy Carroll, welcome.

Then he strode twenty paces or so, and facing Sir James spoke another sentence. A further perambulation and he uttered another great thought.

This went on interminably for an hour or more, in which doubtless the catalogue of native requirements was well stated, after due compliment to all visitors. The minister sat impassive, his eyes half-closed, his hands on his walking stick. The principal natives sat silent with equal impassivity until their turn should come to talk, all providing a lesson in attentive good manners that might well be imitated in white centres of debate. Well away in the background, the young people enjoyed themselves more vociferously; but if voices rose to a pitch to be heard on the marae, the council ground, they brought on themselves the wrath of a fierce fellow dressed as a policeman, in a battered shako, who shooed them away if they impinged on the conference.

In spite of the comic constable, who took himself very seriously, the women preparing the food for the gathering well behind the scenes, raised their voices in merry chatter, scarcely audible where the speaker stood. To the visitors from afar, no doubt, it was all very novel and interesting. They craned forward for something to happen which never did; but at least they had the pleasure of anticipation. To most of the local Europeans who had become familiar with native oratory, the proceedings were dull enough; but the sun was shining, and having been up all night, one or two people went to sleep where they sat.

Between speeches the band gave items, and various natives provided entertainment. The highlight of the day was a woman and

127

two men, who, to a suitable accompaniment, gave a posture dance. She had the usual ample buttocks of a female of her race, and these she twitched as she wriggled, swayed and writhed to provoke the attentions of her partners, in a manner much appreciated by her audience, who were highly diverted.

Our girls were out to see all they could of this strange life, so utterly foreign and unknown to South Islanders, and in the evening Kereihi took charge of them and escorted them up to see the pa at night. Everywhere the natives were preparing for sleep. The whare was crowded with them to the number of several hundreds; whole families and groups of families, their mats and rugs spread out to cover every inch of space on the floor. What struck the visitors was the noise. Everyone seemed to be talking at once. There was naturally no lack of warmth. Kereihi showed everything, in a manner completely detached from her surroundings. They found her interesting, and she was indeed an interesting little personage, quite unlike anything they had met before.

The two girls enjoyed their visit greatly. They were taken out to Rangitoto, where they slept in Rowley Hill's whare, while he and S. W. slept in the tent outside. They did not stay as long as originally planned, because of the limited accommodation. The overall effect of their visit on S. W. was to leave him a bit depressed and lonely, but he found consolation both in his work and in the growing distractions of Te Kuiti.

There were usually enough people in town for a game of poker in the evenings, and by now I was enjoying it. St Hill, of Dalgety's was a constant player, as was a young lawyer named Howarth. A man called Lethbridge, who was farming fern country at Mangaorongo, was in town frequently at this time, and was also a regular player, and a good one. A nice young clerk in the Bank of Australasia called Bartelman usually joined us too. We played threepenny poker, at which it seemed no one could come to any harm. Sometimes Mostyn Jones and his partner, Mackay, came in to make up a game and finally Rowley Hill. We got a lot of fun out of it, and no one won or lost very much. The salaried men knew what they could afford, and the rest of us, feeling we were on a win in our land transactions, did not notice the small come and go of a pound or two in our bank balances.

In the club there was another gambling set, on a much more expensive scale, who played as much bridge as they did poker, and though we sat in the card room at adjacent tables we seldom joined — at first. Ted Falwasser was a gambler on this bigger scale; but one evening about this time, he and a man called Farmer, finding none of their usual opponents, did, at our invitation, make up a game. There were seven at the table.

The method was for the player next on the left of the dealer to ante one chip for threepence, making it sixpence to buy cards. When it next came to Ted's ante he pushed two counters out and said, "Make it four for cards."

This meant a shilling to buy. We all came in. The betting was brisk and the game seemed more enjoyable. At the next hand, Ted put in his ante and rallied the man on his left saying, "Make it four for cards. Come along."

The player did so, and after that it became the custom for everyone in his turn to make it four for cards. It seemed a much more interesting game, for the winners, and of course the losers felt bound to chase their luck.

That evening I lost a little on the opening hands and paid over cheerfully enough. The deal came round the table, and the man on my right put in two chips saying, "Make it four for cards."

Ted in his lively way said to me, "Come on, you've got to pick up. Make it eight for cards. Put in four chips."

I was at a stage where I considered I had much to learn and was prepared to be instructed by an older player. I put in four chips, which meant two shillings now to buy. I looked at my cards and found a pair of aces. I had no idea of bluffing, held on to the aces, and asked for three cards.

Everyone else came in. Farmer bought no cards, quietly saying, "I'll keep these."

The others bought variously. I bought three.

Ted said, "Come on. Go to the limit; bet eight." He eyed me with an amused smile.

I looked at the cards I had bought, and there was an ace and two threes. Please note that there was already 14s on the table.

"Right ho," said I. "Bet eight." I pushed them forward.

"Make it sixteen," said Farmer.

"And eight more," said Howarth. Rowley and the others all bet in turn. It came round to me again. A full hand looked good; "And up eight more," said I.

Falwasser whistled and threw in his hand. Two others followed suit. Farmer bet again, so did Howarth. Rowley paused, saying, "I'd like to see him."

"Don't be a fool," said Ted. "Chuck 'em in." Rowley put his cards down. The bet was again up to me.

"And eight more," said I. Howarth dropped out. Farmer bet again. So did I.

He lingered a minute, then he said, "I'll see you," and pushed forward the chips.

"I believe I have a full hand," said I.

"So have I," said he. "Kings up, queens."

"Does three aces and threes beat that?" I asked.

"Of course it does," he answered, pushing the stakes on the table towards me. "Why did you not say so before?"

Everyone laughed at my simplicity.

That was the beginning of an astonishing run of luck which lasted for many months. Everyone thought me a fool, which I was. I had no notion of bluffing, and was not in the least clever, and I think that no one, for that reason, could fathom my play. Ted Falwasser, in his free way, would say, "Come on, bet as if you had 'em." No one seemed to realise that I just bet according to the cards in my hand, seeing in my mind's eye the list of values that a friend had written out for me some time before. I rose from the table, winner of over £5 in that night's play. It was a very pleasant sensation.

The luck held, and as the nights rolled by, people would come into the card room to watch me play, laughing to each other at my careless air, and saying, "He can't go wrong." Of course I lost many a hand, and when I did so, pushed the counters over at once. I developed superstition. I could not help believing in luck and hated to win the first hand. If I did, I played with caution thereafter, feeling I would lose as the evening went on, and I found I did so. If after losing two or three hands, I won, I would then bet on everything happily enough, confident my luck was now in for the evening.

*   *   *

When the pictures were on in Te Kuiti, I took Kereihi to see them. I found our friendship was the subject of much speculation and comment, and one evening John Hetet's wife came up and said something in Maori, which upset my companion. After the show she said she ought not to let me walk home with her. I took a firm line, told her not to be silly girl, and took her arm in a masterful way, when she came along obediently, making me feel rather magnificent. Finding I was getting her talked about, I felt I must put things on a more regular basis and saw Ted about it, saying I trusted he saw no harm in my taking her about. He seemed quite affected by this, saying, "My dear boy, there is nothing I should like better for her," which I think shows that I was rather a simple fellow, having no idea of the possible implication of his words.

I now went to the Falwassers' house in the evenings after the picture show. There was time enough to do this and then cut into a game of poker at the club, which always went on till about 2 a.m., when we would go to the station for a coffee and bun, and see if any of our friends were passing through on the train.

One night at the Falwassers I found myself in for a spiritualist seance. Ted was something of what I suppose we should call a medium, and had great communication. He never tried to make money, but some of the results were startling enough. We sat round the table, our fingertips touching in the dark, whilst Ted called up the spirit of the hour. Present were a Maori called Billy Edwards, Ted, Kereihi and I; Ted's wife never came into these affairs. There seldom occurred anything that impressed me very greatly, though it was curious enough to make one go on.

The spirits were of all kinds, it seemed, dismal and cheerful, foolish and clever. One night a Maori started telling us in the native language, "Tame Ponui tahoe pounamu." Translated this meant, "Tommy Ponui stole greenstone." We found there was a Tommy Ponui at Kawhia, and took the trouble to enquire about his whereabouts and doings, and found that he had offered to sell some greenstone. Also that a native family nearby had lost a hei tiki, an ear pendant and one of two other heirlooms, but in the easygoing Kawhia way had done nothing about it. Whether Tommy Ponui heard of the enquiries and became suspicious I do not know, but he made no effort to sell again, and the greenstone was lost track of.

That was a long late session. Coming away about 3 a.m., I discussed the whole thing dispassionately with Billy Edwards, and we agreed that we still wanted further proof. It seemed to us that delusion was possible. I had at first tried to influence matters myself, regarding the whole thing as a game, but I was sure that by now none of us was consciously doing so. I found Billy had done a lot of experimenting in the hope of getting something tangible. At one time Billy had been in the Civil Service in Auckland, but the easy-going Maori side to his character had not bothered to keep up with his work. I was impressed by the enlightened way in which he discussed spiritualism, and somewhat surprised when he said at parting, "Of course the finite mind cannot grasp the infinite."

Not bad for a Maori. I could not have put it as well myself.

The last experience I had of spiritualism was rather disturbing. One evening Brittan was with me when I went to Ted's house, and when spiritualism was mentioned he said he was not an unbeliever and was quite ready to join in a seance, but I knew he just regarded it in a humorous light as I had done. Very soon, however, a spirit announced she was his grandmother and gave the name Templar. She had a message. What was it? "Tell Violet she is not to come," came the reply.

Now I was the only one at the table who could have known what Brittan's dead grandmother's name was, or that he had a cousin,

131

Violet, then living on the West Coast, and I certainly did not influence proceedings in any way. I did not know what to make of what we had heard. Afterwards Stanley told me that it had convinced him to the point of making him very distressed, and if that were so I did not want to go on poking into a business that I could not understand.

*   *   *

At this time Snadden, the manager of the Union Bank, wanted me to go out and see Lethbridge's place with him, and as Lethbridge had asked me to pay him a visit I thought I could not go in better company than that of my quiet, solid, respectable bank manager. We left on the early train at 6.30 a.m., driving up from the station to the Te Awamutu Hotel in the two-horse coach in time for breakfast. Snadden suggested a whiskey and milk to warm us up. We had two, and after porridge, fish, and eggs and bacon with coffee, drove on by coach to Kihi Kihi, a journey which took under three-quarters of an hour.

The coach put us down at Thompson's livery stable, where we ordered a horse and buggy. Whilst the animal was being groomed and harnessed, "What about a drink?" said Snadden to Thompson. Thompson did not mind. We strolled to the Kihi Kihi pub and had one.

"What about another?" said Thompson. Whiskey again.

"Just one more before we start?" It was my turn to order, and we had that too. It must be remembered that nowhere in the King Country could you drink over a bar, and when leaving it, as we now had, everyone had to get used to this new freedom of purchase. Snadden bought a bottle for the journey.

He was more talkative than usual when at length we started, drawn by a big horse at a steady trot. I drove, at Snadden's suggestion.

"He is not going fast," said he.

I told him I thought he was doing well enough.

"Give me the whip," said he, reaching across and securing it, when he proceeded to flick the animal in ticklish parts till he livened up to a canter.

"Steady on," I protested, holding the reins tight; but "Let's see what he can do," said my hitherto steady-going bank manager, continuing scientifically to ply the whip until we were going all out for Orakau at a hand gallop, despite my efforts to stop him. How long this would have continued I know not, for I was saved further worry by being flung over the dashboard into the road, whilst the horse, with the two front wheels attached, relieved of our weight, galloped on out of sight. Snadden had fallen forward with me and seemed to find the situation funny. He roared with laughter as we both lay prone and I joined in. The unexpected always has its humorous side.

Two strange settlers, riding towards town, returned with our horse and two front wheels, none the worse. We found the king pin had come out, and soon fixed the buggy up again and resumed our journey. Snadden said that we had had the distinction of falling on the battlefield of Orakau, which we had been passing over. I believe that on that famous occasion the reserves were held at that point, which was dead ground to the enemy.

Our route soon led us by a native track through the usual unfenced scrub and fern, and presently crossed the Puniu stream. We had left the grass country behind us soon after Orakau. Up till then, since leaving Te Awamutu station, we had been passing through a land of dairy farms, settled at the end of the Maori Wars in Waikato, nearly half a century before. The grass was rich, but too many daisies were noticeable everywhere. Now we were once more in country that was easier, but no more advanced from a farming point of view, than what lay between the Rangitoto bush and Mangaorongo, through which my sheep had travelled.

A cock pheasant got up. Snadden insisted on getting out his gun and going after him. He had no luck, but he continued to walk, on the chance of getting another one, and I followed, driving our conveyance at a walk along the usual waggon track just wide enough for one vehicle. We thought we ought to be getting near Lethbridge's, and a tin whare came in sight about a quarter of a mile away. Snadden, getting impatient at having nothing to shoot at, fired his right barrel. A man appeared at the door of the hut and came towards us. Snadden let off his left barrel. The man disappeared within. Snadden hallooed. The man reappeared and turned out to be Lethbridge, who said that seeing a man coming, firing towards him, he had thought it might be a native he had recently fallen out with and had gone indoors to see that his own firearm was handy.

A visit commencing on such a note, might be expected to be lively; but we really had a quiet and very pleasant weekend. Lethbridge was very comfortable in his way. His walls were papered with pictures from the *Tatler;* a good-looking young Member of Parliament, F. E. Smith, on horseback, "astride across Lancashire"; the Marchioness of Headfort, very lovely; Harry Lauder, the Scottish comedian, and the like. All very interesting, to remind us of a world far removed from our own. Pictures from the *Tatler* and the *Sketch* have a cheering or irritating effect on backblocks settlers, according to temperament. Encouraging to us, to think that

133

there were people who could afford to lead such lives. We liked to fancy we might some day do so; if only for a brief time between more serious affairs.

Lethbridge impressed us by his practical knowledge of how to break in fern land. To me it was a revelation, that one could burn, plough and sow to get so good a take of grass so soon in land which at first sight did not impress one as having any depth of topsoil; but he was doing it. He had some 6,900 acres of native lease, and only needed the capital to bring it all into profit. This, I gathered, the Union Bank was ready to lend, on Snadden's recommendation, which he was prepared to make, having unbounded confidence in the King Country and its future, only seeking men of honesty, energy and enterprise as clients.

PART FOUR

STOCK, SETTLERS AND STORES

Stole away with pack and ponies — left 'em drinking in the town.

PART FOUR

STOCK, SETTLERS AND STORES

DURING THE ENSUING months I often spent a night at Rowley's whare. I was glad to have it to go to. In the evenings he would discuss his plans for the future, and usually I would listen. His fiancée was ready to marry him and come and live in the bush; but she had had a fall from a horse which someone had lent her, and it had affected her health. I could not see her in this setting. The very journey in and out could not be made on wheels; she would have to ride. Climbing the track from my grass patch was enough to daunt any girl. Yet I had not the heart to throw cold water on their ideas. At least I was glad that he was ready to wait till he had sold some land and had some money of his own. In the meanwhile I listened to much poetry from the Sydney *Bulletin;* "The Sentimental Bloke" was constantly quoted. I like poetry; but this was not my idea of the best. It did not appeal to me like Banjo Patterson, Adam Lindsay Gordon, or Rudyard Kipling. Horses and soldiers were more in my line. Though soldiering was not for me — I had put all that behind me — I still read everything about it that came my way.

On the whole then, considering how very dubious I felt — was I not called "The Pessimist"? I do not think I was very unsympathetic, and I listened to a catalogue of my own shortcomings with due humility, though it was not normally my strong point to do so. To the advice that I really ought to have a more serious purpose in life and settle down, I replied that I should probably marry Kereihi someday, as she would be suitable for the bush surroundings. She could ride in and out, and would know how to cook on a wood fire; she could be comfortable sitting on the floor, and really looked very nice when in town. I hadn't suggested it to the lady herself, but was conceited enough to believe that she would not hesitate if I said the word.

With my cat and dogs I now took up my residence on the mountain top, where I was among my sheep, and spent my spare time cutting tracks. The camp, what was left of it, was nothing like so comfortable as the one MacCracken had established and to which I might well have repaired; but I was reluctant to spend the few pounds necessary to do so while I had another tent standing. This one was small, with lower sides, only three feet, and opened right onto the fireplace where I did my cooking. When the weather was fine it was very cold at night; but I had plenty of blankets. When it was warm it was usually overcast, and often rained heavily.

137

In either case the dogs crept under the tent sides at night, and the cat took position on the bed when I went into it. I slept on my side with my legs drawn up, and he liked to lie in the bend of my knees. Sometimes I would wake feeling cramped, but dared not move for fear of disturbing the cat. We were great friends.

A stranger might have said that this was living in great discomfort, but I had plenty to eat, warmth, and a dry place to sleep at night, unless the rain lasted more than a day or so, when the blankets got a bit damp on the outside through the moisture in the tent, but not enough to keep me awake. On the clearing the ewes and lambs looked very well. All the sheep were fat, and I would soon have to cut and tail the new arrivals. Had it not been for the late upset in my style of living, I would already have done so, but I had to erect the yards for which I had got up the wire netting, staples and split posts, and I must have someone to give me a hand. My present quarters were scarcely big enough for a visitor, so I erected a tent at the foot of the mountain, on the tawa flat across the stream for the grass patch.

Then I went out to Te Kuiti. This time I travelled afoot through the bush past MacLuckie's camp as MacCracken used to do. I dressed as he used to, with a sugar bag on my back, but carried a light pair of dungaree trousers strapped to my waist. I felt quite the competent bushman now, as I half trotted down to the Owawenga and climbed the steep grade the other side. Mac received me with his slow smile, not untinged with surprise, about ten o'clock, and swung the billy over the fire to give me a cup of tea. While he set out bread and butter we discussed our affairs. He was getting in some cattle soon; I offered to help him, but he told me Cotter the butcher had promised to do that. I felt that though his opinion of me was improving, he had not sufficient confidence to rely on me yet. In matters of cattle and sheep he knew far less than I did, yet thought me ignorant too. He now offered to help me with my lambs, but I felt I was already too much in his debt to accept. I had used his camp and track as my own. Until I had done a bit for him, I must get someone else. So I said I had business in Te Kuiti and someone was returning with me from there.

Down the Spiral I went, and across the waist-high Waipa, which was up after the recent rain. My clothing dried on me as I followed the track in the open fern and sunshine. It was past four when I topped the hill from which I could look down on Te Kuiti. The little town looked beautiful as the shadows lengthened. Distance toned down the sharp edges of the buildings. The corrugated iron looked a soft blue. The crudities merged into something restful to the eye as the smoke rose straight up against a background of ferny hillside to a sky which already promised to turn lemon colour ere the light went. I paused to feast my eyes. An afternoon train was climbing out of the township to the southward, its presence betrayed by a widening stream of smoke. Closer, our civilisation might be harsh; here the sight of it cheered me. I crept into the fern to put on my trousers in concession to it, then made my entry by back ways, so as not to attract attention.

*   *   *

Old Britts, when he heard that I wanted a hand, offered to come out with me next day. I took Kereihi to the pictures, then hastened back to the club, where I joined a game of poker. I found the card table drew me like a magnet by now. Everything else in town took second place. I liked amusing company, and enjoyed the effect of whiskey, but gambling had got into my blood. The proverbial beginner's luck still stood to me in a sensational manner. I won more often than I lost, and when I had anything good was not afraid to go the limit. When I lost I did so with equal cheerfulness, which seemed the least I could do, and I always paid up promptly, a thing I could well afford to do, as my winnings kept my pockets full of money at this time.

Money was circulating freely in the community, so it was not surprising that so much of it was won and lost at cards. Yet there were times when I had qualms of conscience. There was a particularly nice Englishman called Skelton, who had a run at the Aharoa, playing this night. He lost £17, and I got some of it. He said as he paid, "There go two nice bullocks." I felt it was wrong to take it. Yet he had travelled the world, fought in the Boer War, and been at Spion Kop. He had more experience and was older than I. By now our doings were being trumpeted abroad, doubtless much exaggerated, and a Methodist or Presbyterian minister had spoken in a sermon against what he called "that gambling hell", the club. We thought this a compliment. I suppose it is human and youthful to like to be thought the devil of a fellow.

Britts and I went out to his place next day to get his working clothes and spend the night there. The cat woke us up in the middle of it, playing with a large rat he had caught, as we saw when we lit the candle. It was a proud moment for Britts. We had a walk round his clearing before we climbed the mountain. It certainly seemed a good piece of land on an easy round hill, and the grass had taken well. The cleared area was not large, but the sheep were doing well upon it. He had the hoggets we had bought together and no lambs.

Next day we erected our yards, one large one and a catching pen with a rail to sit the lambs on. It took us some hours, but Britts was a good worker and we each helped the other without having to be

139

shown anything. Posts went in first. I had laid them out, and now dug the holes and rolled out wire netting. The soil was easy digging and I had several holes dug when he began putting in the posts and ramming the earth hard. When this was finished he stapled on the wire whilst I held a hammer against the uprights to hold them steady. We camped at the foot of the mountain, and on the way down I pointed out the lie of the clearing.

The top of the mountain was comparatively easy, under a hundred acres. Our yard was erected on the edge of the bush, beside the track at the south-west corner of the new grass. We decided to muster up the long ridge from the bottom, down which we were now moving. Brittan could do this. Once he had started I was to leave him, cross the gully to his left, climb a spur onto the next ridge, go over into the Waimahora and clear the hundred acres Flint had fallen, and then follow up the wide easy ridge, till I gained touch with Brittan once more. After which, having reached the top I was to go to the left, he to the right, driving the sheep in front of us till the mob were all following the main track to the yards.

Breakfasting in the dark next morning, we crouched by the fire and lit our pipes as we waited for sufficient daylight to see the track. When the tui warned us we might start, we put off our jackets and started our uphill plod, clad in our oldest dungaree trousers and flannels, with sleeves to the elbows only. A shiver came to each of us as we stepped out of the tent into the chill air, but passed quickly as we warmed to the climb. For over a quarter of an hour we plodded upwards in silence. We passed the corner peg, and soon afterwards I left my companion, who slowed down to let me make my way over the long spur to his left.

A roughly cleared track led me down along the hillside into the gully that had never burned and in which the second growth was already showing thick. Crossing this I found myself at the foot of a spur, up which I began to climb. Already I was sweating with my exertions, and breathing hard, but the route was clear enough. I had only to put my head down and put one foot above the other, and twenty minutes brought me to the top. I felt justified in pausing to recover my breath, though second wind had long since come to me.

Looking back, I was rewarded with a worthwhile view. Brittan, proceeding slowly, was abreast of me on the long ridge I had left. His dogs were clearing the gullies to his right and "speaking up" from time to time in response to his whistles and shouts. Above them the sheep could be seen emerging from among the logs, in groups of from two to a dozen, to join one long string that was filing upwards to the mountain top. Daylight had come; the sky was red and the whole scene tinged half crimson. I thought of the old saying, "Red sky in the morning, shepherds's warning," and hoped it would not prove true this time. Then I plunged down the steep slope to the Waimahora.

The sheep, as I noted on the way down, were well spread out. It was not my intention to disturb them more than I could help until I reached the stream at the bottom; but they seemed to have sensed, rather than heard, the activities of Brittan's dogs over the ridge, and here and there a ewe and lamb were moving to join others, and would pause to look at me, giving a stamp and snort before hurrying off. My own two dogs followed meantime silently at heel. Proceeding like this as quickly as possible, I reached the bottom in less than a quarter of an hour.

Along the Waimahora here, as in all the gullies, the fire had scarcely run at all. Dead timber lay thick, with second growth sprouting through it. There were no sheep here, they having camped higher up. A large unburned gully narrowed the clearing down at the foot of the slope. I could see both sides of my beat. As I turned to retrace my steps, a family of wild pigs came trotting down, led by a sow. She was nearly upon me before she saw me and gave a quick "Grumph, grumph," and stampeded them all into the thicket. I laughed as the little tails disappeared, and had some difficulty in restraining the dogs. Usually I could not have done so, I am sure, but their collie instinct seemed to inform them that today we were on work more worthy of a sheepdog.

Always my imagination ran along the lines of war and battle, even though engaged in a peaceful occupation. At last, I felt, I was like a man going into action; I was about to muster my own sheep on my own clearing. I ascended slowly, and when at last I came out on the top of the ridge, my wristwatch told me it was an hour since I had left it, and lost sight of Britts. I soon descried him again on the main spur, waiting for me to come up in line with him. His dogs had cleared the country on the far side and between us well; not a sheep was to be seen below him, and above was a mob of several hundred, moving up in single file. Each of us seeing the other in his place we followed slowly up. As we went I turned and looked back over the way we had come, and over the country I had mustered. A startling sight met my eyes. Halfway down the long slope to the Waimahora I saw through a gap in the logs a sheep proceeding down the way I had come up. As I watched, another followed, and another, until I counted thirteen, an unlucky number. Of course I must get them. I decided the dogs could not head them. They were more likely, in trying to do so in that tangle of logs, to stampede them down the hill out of my sight to the bottom. I must go down, and would be lucky if I got them back to where I then was in an hour.

The task took longer. I tried to get round the sheep by following down the edge of the gully, but clambering over burnt logs and through the tangled second growth took so long I decided there was nothing for it, I must follow the track and hope to head the sheep when I got closer to them. Though I went as cautiously as I could, it was impossible to avoid some noise, and when I got within reach of the sheep I did so rather suddenly. They had been out of sight for some time, and I came upon them over a small rise. Quietly I tried to put Fly round them. She made a gallant attempt, and made off with her usual silent speed, but the sheep were alert, and an old ewe led them with a dash past her. The others followed swiftly. Neither dog nor man could stop them till they reached the bottom of the clearing and ran along its edge. I found a slight depression leading to my left into the bush, under cover of which I made my way laboriously for the next quarter of an hour until I was below the spot where I judged the sheep to be.

My disappearance from view lulled them into a false sense of security, and when, judging that I had reached a position below them, I crept to the edge of the tangled supplejacks and burned logs and looked out, I found the sheep had spread out and were grazing. The sentinel sheep was standing above them, watching the direction in which they had seen me. I made a quick count; there were nineteen of the cunning brutes. I stepped quietly out, followed by the dogs. An old ewe with a lamb, who I guessed to be the leader in all this trouble, was the first to see me. She looked up and stamped her feet as she gave a loud warning snort that brought them all together, gazing at me. I walked slowly towards them until they hurriedly took their track up the hill again.

Naturally I was careful to try and keep them all in view, but it was not always possible, as there were considerable patches of dead ground in front of us, especially when we once again climbed on to the long ridge. As I made my way along its wide top I lost sight of them until they began to climb the last slope of the mountain top in front of me, and then I counted thirteen only. I would like to have seen nineteen, but reflected that the others might have found their way up by a track to the right round a knoll where I could not see them. If they had, Brittan would collect them. I could see him now, waiting for me on the highest point in view, but lost sight of him as I followed the track round the knoll till I emerged at the spot on the top where I had previously rested and looked back. The main mob was grazing over the mountain top before me.

With Brittan standing in his present commanding position, he became the pivot of a wide wheel of which I was on the outer flank. I moved forward to the left, driving everything before me. The sheep were not moving as briskly as they did at daybreak; the dogs had to force them more; but they made progress, and now began to crowd together into what looked quite a large mob. As they did so of course ewes and lambs became separated, and the baaing and bleating raised a din familiar to me, and brought back pleasant memories of past days down south. It took nearly an hour to clear my ground, as I dared not put the dogs too close, but the sheep moved in the desired direction. The leaders were already at the yards. As I got close up, Brittan moved along the ridge to my right and the space narrowed till we were within calling distance.

"How has it gone?" I called. "Got 'em all?"

"Every one I think," he answered. "They ran well."

We had no time for more words as we pressed them in front of us now. Several times little knots of lambs ran together and looked like making a break, but the dogs kept off at just the right distance, and the position of the yard was right for the lie of the country.

The animals drew well; we kept them going till I found the wire netting at my left hand, pulled out the end stake, carried it over to Britts, and pulling it up at the centre, we swept the sheep into the yard, and with hammer and staples made the netting fast to the stakes we had already driven in. This done, we breathed a sigh of satisfaction as we shooed the lambs away from the barrier until they had settled down.

*   *   *

"That was quite a good bit of work," said Britts. "How did you get on? You were a long time over that ridge."

"So I was, but some sheep beat me back, and I had to go after them. What about a bite before we begin?"

"Good idea,"said he, and we went into the old bushmen's camp, which was not ten minutes away. Whilst I got the fire going, Britts went for water, and then sat down and lit his pipe while the billy boiled.

"It's nearly ten o'clock," said he. "Fancy taking all that time to muster 300 acres. Down south we would have had them all in less than an hour."

"So we would," I agreed, "but the country would have been all open, never a log to be seen; men, dogs and horses could go anywhere. Besides which, the country would have been mustered for over fifty years. Sheep would know which way to run; bred on the same place for generations, probably. Dogs would know where to head 'em, and men would have nothing to do but follow on, giving a whistle and a signal now and again."

"Here," Brittan said, "a dog cannot see you half the time if you do want to signal to him. If he doesn't run right from the start, you cannot tell what he may be up to, unless you go to see."

Britts said this with an almost aggrieved note in his voice, which he often assumed when talking of the King Country, as if the land were a living thing, being purposely obstructive. Yet he was a good worker when on a job, as now, and a trusty companion.

"My father used to say," I told him, "that one should never let a dog out of sight if one can help it, as you never know what he is doing the other side of the ridge."

"Well he is about right too. Yet he must have had to do it at Flaxbourne," said he. (My father had been manager of this large station of Clifford and Weld's.)

"I'm not sure whether he did," I answered. "It was not very high country, nor was it rough. It was very open natural grass and tussock. A few men mustering could see every yard of it for miles ahead of them."

"Yes, and do the job riding on horses and in lovely clear weather where it doesn't rain for weeks on end. What a life! Compare it all with this: logs and charcoal, sheep and men black with dirt, and half the time rain and mist hanging over them as it is now." And so saying he cast his eyes gloomily up at the overhanging clouds seen through the tent door.

"Well, the billy boils," said I, as I sprinkled the tea on the bubbling water, "and it isn't raining yet. What about a bit of bread and butter?"

. We ate in silence, and after rinsing the mugs made our way to the yard and filled the pen with ewes and lambs. Britts did the docking, while I held the lambs up on the rail for him. They were big fine ones, and should have been done earlier. Still, heavy though they were, it was cheering to find they handled so well.

"They are fat," said I.

"They are," said he. "There is no doubt sheep do well in this country." He plied the knife as he spoke, cutting off a lamb's tail. I picked up a big ram lamb. Britts used knife and teeth in the usual manner, snipped the punch hole, bit back on the right ear and severed the tail, which he dropped on the heap beside him before he said, "Oh, it wouldn't be such a bad life if there was a little more civilisation, if there were any prospect of a road, and if one could have a bit more comfort." The blood from the next lamb's tail spurted in his eye.

"And cleanliness," he added, as it poured down his face, which was already covered with gore. He wiped it with the back of his hand, leaving a smear.

"Well," I answered, catching another, "cutting and tailing is no cleaner in the south than it is here. You can't blame the poor old North Island for that."

"I don't," said he. "But at least you can have a bath and clean clothes when the job is over."

I sat a fresh lamb on the rail before replying.

"After all, you always have running water somewhere handy in the north; a creek is a good washing place. It may be a bit cold; but the climate is warmer in winter. I notice you never wear a singlet, even in town."

He whetted his knife on the oilstone, whilst I caught the next lamb, and then he said, "Oh, I am not complaining. We are close to nature here all right; but it would be nice to have more of the decencies which we took as a matter of course in Canterbury, and it might not be so bad if there were neighbours, more of our own people settled about us."

The task of picking up the lambs gave me time to think out a reply to each of these criticisms. The nature of his occupation would have compelled him to listen; but he was quiet at all times, and never broke in on an argument till one had finished speaking. I was always rather on the defensive when anyone was finding fault with Rangitoto and the life we were leading, though I saw its drawbacks as well as he did.

"Of course," I now said, "I would like all the things you name; but aren't they going to come?"

He stood knife in hand ready, as I approached the rail with the next lamb, while he replied, "I suppose they are. Sometimes I feel they are a long time about it. I would like some of them here now."

"And if they were," I replied, "do you think you and I could have got hold of this country at anything like a pound an acre?"

"There is that to it, certainly," he said rather grudgingly and as we had to fill up the pen again, that particular discussion ended.

As afternoon came on we watched the sky anxiously, and sure enough it came on to rain steadily. But we agreed to stick to it till the job was done, and at last we reached a stage where short of a blizzard it could get no worse anyway. Grimly we picked up the lambs and in silence attended to them, until some time after four o'clock I dropped the last lamb and he put its tail on the heap. We counted them. We were nearly thirty sheep short, but we thought we had probably not made a clean muster and would do better next time.

"In bush country they always straggle the new burns after a first muster," I said.

"Yes, but they don't let them back on the same country at docking time if they are going to do that, I imagine," said he.

"Come think of it, I suppose they don't." I reflected that I had only the one enclosure, the whole clearing, surrounded by bush, without a boundary fence. Details we had not thought out, or been informed about, were liable to crop up at any time.

The count of tails showed that we had docked 286 lambs.

145

"Very good," said Brittan, "considering we know some to be still out. It means a tally of about a hundred percent. It's a good start."

Going down the hill we did not talk much. The rain increased, the clouds pressed upon us, and early darkness loomed. We had long since been wet to the point of misery, and the one thing that seemed urgent was to get under cover. We kept moving steadily down the slope, but it took us nearly an hour.

The camp seem unusually cheerless. The fire was dead out. I proceeded to light it, the water squelching in my boots.

"How about a bit of civilisation now?" I asked. "A nice warm fire, your clothes dry, spread out on the bed for you, and tea ready as soon as you have changed?"

"Not too bad," said Britts, "and a nice drop of whiskey into the bargain." He looked sardonic as he shrugged his shoulders.

"Peta offered me his second daughter to come and live with us," I said. "His girls are all rather pretty."

"A man's a dam' fool not to take her," was his reply. "At least he would not have to get the fire going when he comes in on a night like this."

"She's only fourteen," I told him. "Capable, but a bit young, I thought."

"Some would say, 'As soon as they're big enough, they're old enough,' but I suppose they do need more age on 'em," he reflected.

As we sat later that evening replete with tinned beef, potatoes, onions and rice, washed down by hot tea, before a blazing fire with a glowing back log, having cleaned the utensils and lit our pipes, "It isn't really such a bad life," said Brittan.

"Kake te puku kahari te ngakau," I replied contentedly, meaning: Full the stomach, contented the mind.

*　　　*　　　*

He returned to his clearing next day. I stayed on to watch my sheep. The lambs mothered up well. I saw no dead ones, which I had feared I might, as they had been allowed to grow rather big for docking. I kept cutting tracks on the burn, but felt I was not a very good hand with axe and slasher when I thought of MacCracken and of the last year. He was getting Rowley's bush down now, and his mate, young Caterer, was a good bushman. He expected another man, Pratt, to come and help him, and I had promised to lend him a horse to bring him out. Next morning I went down the track to catch old black Billy and put a saddle on at the grass patch, and make my way into Otorohanga.

Halfway down the mountain, I picked up the horse's tracks, and lost them again as they entered the bush. I slowed down and listened as I walked. Two chains further on I heard an animal moving. Then Billy staggered out on the track. He was drunk, and had obviously been eating rangiora. He tried to move, and crossed his front legs, then stood and leered at me, with an expression half-humorous, half-defiant. With one ear forward and one back, he reminded me of a man in the same condition with a bowler hat cocked over one eye. I cursed him as I put the bridle on and tried to lead him. It was no use; I could not get him to follow me, let alone ride him. He tottered so much that I feared he might go down in the scrub where I could not extricate him. I lit a fire and tried to smoke him, but he turned his head away from it and I feared he might fall into it. Then an idea came to me. Rowley's whare was not far off. I went to it and got a discarded sack, and filled it with mouldy leaves. Then I tied the sack over the horse's head, slit a hole in the bottom and set light to the leaves, preventing any big blaze by squeezing it out with my hands, till there was a thick, grey smoke pouring out on each side of his ears. Billy was certainly breathing smoke; in fact he breathed nothing else. Never mind; it was kill or cure, and anyway I was standing by ready to remove the bag if it smothered him. I let the process continue, and he blew great gusts out through the sacking at each breath. Curiously enough, it did not seem to discomfort him at all, and presently, after what seemed like half an hour, he began to run at the nose. I let that continue till the bottom of the sack was soaking wet, and he showed signs of objecting to the smoke and became restive and more alert. I took the sack off.

He blew great streams of smoke through his nostrils. His lungs must have been full of it. It had certainly cleared his head, though he was still running at the nose. He could walk straight, so I led him back to the tent, where I changed into riding breeches, saddled him, and rode out. He was still a bit unsteady, but drank at the creek and was getting better every minute. Nevertheless we had to go slow. I did not want a fall, and it was dark by the time I reach Otewa pa.

There I found that Te Ngoi and most of the inhabitants were away at a tangi. An old woman greeted me, but she spoke little English. I decided to push on, but mindful of a previous experience of trying to find my way down the river in the dark, I decided to try and follow the new road. This proved difficult. I could not pick up the end of it in the scrub, and was at a loss. Stopping to look around me, I saw a light through the manuka about a hundred yards to my left, and deciding to give up the attempt to reach Otorohanga, I rode over to it. Coming to some slip rails, I got off and led the horse through. A dog came barking at me. Against the dark skyline I saw the outline of a European cottage.

A door opened, and a man, with a woman holding a candle, stood framed in it.

"Lie down, Toss," called the man. "Is anyone there?"

I made my presence known, said I could not find the track, and asked for shelter. The man bade me let the horse go, and invited me in.

The room in which I found myself was a small unlined kitchen in a weatherboard house of about five rooms. The couple who greeted me were something under thirty years of age. The man was square, of middle height, and in his shirtsleeves. He had a small close-trimmed moustache. He spoke slowly, with a drawling trace of English country dialect unfamiliar to me. I said my name was Westmacott.

He introduced me formally to his wife: "Mr Westmacott, this is my wife, Mrs Hull."

Mrs Hull said she was pleased to meet me, and had heard of me often.

She was a bright little woman, in a clean apron. She was on the thin side, and looked, like all country women in those parts, as if she worked too hard.

They made me welcome. They had had tea, and offered to get me some, but I told them I had had a bite before leaving, which was untrue.

"Never mind," she said, "we'll have a bit of supper before we go to bed."

They put more manuka on the fire and we sat in front of it. I had one of the two chairs, and my host sat on a kerosene box, putting sticks on the blaze from time to time. They had a real stove with a grate, and we all leaned towards it to keep warm. The wife stirred a saucepan from time to time, saying she always boiled her porridge for breakfast overnight. When the kettle boiled she made tea and cut some bread and butter by way of supper, which relieved my hunger. We contentedly sipped our tea as we sat talking. A question or two soon set them on the way of giving their life's history.

He had served seven years in the Hampshire regiment, and had come out to New Zealand "about seven years agone".

" 'Twould be all that now," his wife confirmed his statement. He had worked on her mother's farm in the Waikato, and that was where they had got married three years ago. They had one little boy. They took up this place the year before last. It was about a hundred acres, all scrub and fern when they got it, but there was a nice bit of swamp which would be real good when it was drained, and they ought to have a bit of grass one of these days. They had ploughed a few acres and sown it, but there was not much growth to be seen. They had a cow and a couple of steers; they got a drop of fresh milk, but not all they ought to have. The calf was a nuisance; they kept him tied up, but you never knew when his mother would get over the fence and then he'd get all the milk. They were all right at present; they had him tied in the bails and there were four sheets of corrugated iron nailed over as a roof. She couldn't get through that, but you never knew when she might horn it over.

It was apparent from their description that they were not making a living from the farm, nor even growing their own food. I asked where they got their stores. They told me they bought them from Green and Colebrooke in Otorohanga. I had heard Mr Green on the subject of some of these settlers, and wondered how the Hulls paid for their stores. I did not ask, but presently was told. They had been at work for the Government making the new road for the past two winters, and wondered how they would live when it was finished and open to traffic.

"Wouldn't it be possible to make a living off the farm?" I asked; but my heart sank as I said it, the country around looked so poor and hungry.

"Well, that is an idea," said the host. "That certainly is an idea. If a man done a bit more ploughing he might carry a bit more livestock. The trouble is the grass don't seem to grow too well. I tried some turnips, but the fly seemed to get them. That's no good you know. I put in oats las' year, but only a few of them came up. They weren't worth trying to harvest. We turned cow into 'em. A man wants a bit of a sideline to carry him on for a year or two. The missus now, she says, why not take in some boarders?"

Boarders in such a place seemed a far-fetched idea. Who but a stray traveller like myself would stay here for so much as a night, if he could see a way to get out of it? But my host seemed a man of ideas and enthusiasms, and I did not want to damp them, so I said, "Well, it was certainly very convenient to be able to find accommodation tonight."

"There y'are, Maud. What did I tell you?" He seemed to forget that the idea had been hers.

"Of course, from my point of view it would be very convenient if the township were at Otewa, not Otorohanga," I said. "I mean it is such a business getting stores. I have to hire natives to pack them out. Otorohanga is too far to go and come back with pack horses in one day. Here one could do it."

He sat wide-eyed with approval, and remarked, "That's just what I reckon. A store here would be the very thing."

"But of course," I hastened to add, "there would be difficulties. Otewa is not on the railway. Everything would have to be carted here."

"That's what I say. There's a real good opening for a carrier's business too. A man might get the mail contract from the Post O8ce. There's money in it."

As he was getting a little carried away by his dreams of future prosperity, I made no further suggestions. His wife seemed more practical, and presently I thought her suggestion of bed a sensible one.

She took the candle and showed me to a small box-like room off the kitchen with a stretcher made up with blankets and sheets, and I slept like a top.

This encounter with the Hulls was not destined to be my last.

*   *   *

Shearing was now coming upon me. I moved my camp down from the mountain top so as to have two tents on the grass patch, and made two yards and a catching-pen, over which I rigged a fly. It was hard to get shearers; very few men in the district had handled sheep. I got an old Maori called Kono, from Mangaorongo, who had shorn sheep in Hawke's Bay. Hongi Pork said he had shorn a sheep or two, and wanted the chance to learn to do it properly. Paddy Corcoran came up to complete the yards and help with the mustering, and Rowley to do the odd jobs like picking up and rolling the fleeces.

Paddy and I mustered the front face of the mountain, starting at daybreak and having the sheep yarded and drafted by eight o'clock, when the shearers got to work with the blades. Paddy and I had breakfast, which the others had left prepared, and then he gave a hand in the yards. He more than gave a hand — he practically assumed control there. He was earning a pound a day, drover's wages. When Rowley had done the picking up and rolling, they packed the fleeces into sacks. We could not bale them, as we would have to take the wool out on pack horses.

Such cooking as was to be done we divided between those of us who were not shearing. As I was rather at a loose end for some hours, I went up the track above Rowley's whare to find any stragglers there might be there. In pushing my way down I came out on the edge of the flat-topped manuka ridge, and looked out over the Waimahora and grass patch. The grass patch with the fly spread out, and the sheep in the yards, white on the green ground in the sunlight, made an attractive picture. More important, it looked businesslike.

It was years since Kono had shorn a sheep. He was not a young man, and did only sixty-five. Macfarlane was wisely doing his sheep well and not trying to hurry. He had done thirty-seven. Of course men are supposed to average at least a hundred in a woolshed, most of them nowadays many more, but I had to remember that we were not in a sheep district and that when there were larger flocks, men would improve as real shearers came in. Paddy and I had brought down a mob of over 200 sheep, and at this rate should have enough to carry the men through till next day, but on the following morning more would be needed, so we had to go out at daybreak again next day.

On this occasion we had more difficulty with the sheep, and it was nearly seven in the evening before we had them yarded, by which time the dogs and ourselves were tired enough. The shearing had gone well, however. We listened to the account of the day's work from Rowley as we had our tea in camp. Meat and bread and butter was our solid fare. There is nothing better to work on. We had no potatoes, and the onions were coming to an end. Worst of all, we were almost out of bread. I found I was the only one who could bake it, so I had to get to work and knead my dough as soon as tea was over. The others went to bed. I set the loaves in the camp oven, and while they were rising I tried to read. I found this difficult, as I was so sleepy, but whenever I nearly dozed off I put more wood on the fire, and embers around the camp oven, till at last, the bread having come well up, I put the lid on the oven, piled the glowing embers on top and in three-quarters of an hour it was finished. I turned it out, light and brown on top, and smelling delightfully, and covered it with a clean flour bag. To make sure of the morrow's I began another sponge by filling the pan with flour, and emptying half a bottle of yeast into the hollow space in the middle of it, and putting it, covered by a sack, near the fire to keep warm. It was well after 11 p.m. Everyone else was dead to the world. I pulled off my boots and socks and tumbled into my blankets; blessed sleep after weariness came upon me.

At daybreak Paddy and I were away once again. He was a cheerful, willing fellow at all times here. In town I was told he was quarrelsome in drink, but that was no concern of mine. We had to straggle the whole area this morning, which meant clearing what we had done before, and the mountain top. The sheep moved up all right, but several hundred feet below the summit they entered fog which covered the whole basin, and Paddy and I kicked our heels and smoked our pipes whilst waiting for it to clear. When it did, we were able to dog the sheep round the ridge and to our surprise were in time for the midday lunch.

After that I got Jeff and rode down the Waimahora for a few sheep that I knew to have gone down through the bush across the stream. After three crossings I picked up their tracks, and soon came upon the two ewes with the lambs. I could not pass them in the bush, nor get a dog round them, till they came to the next ford of the Waimahora, and instead of crossing the water ran down a small spit of shingle to the left. I rode over, got in front, and turning

151

them back, recrossed the stream on the pony. Sheep are perverse brutes. Instead of sticking to the wide open cleared track, these dived into a little-used one, much overgrown. As I guessed it would rejoin the main one, I followed contentedly. Jeff knew the track, having grazed the valley in and out of the bush the previous year, and he poked his way through the undergrowth whilst I fended off the supplejacks and lawyers with my right arm.

This brought us to a windfall tree across the track, waist-high as I sat on the horse. I did not notice how firmly it was set, and thought to push it aside as I rode. Jeff got his head under it up to the withers before I realised that it was wedged firmly like a rail by being unable to move my bridle hand under it. Fortunately the tug on the reins, about which I was often apt to be careless, brought the little horse to a dead stop; but my body was right up against the obstacle. I tried to get my feet out of the stirrups and dismount and was horrified to find that I could not do so. My big boots were driven home in them to the instep, and no effort of mine would clear them. I felt that if the horse proved restive and tried to force his way forward so much as a couple of feet, I might be a dead man; and the reins were in a position difficult to handle. I spoke to Jeff quietly, and he stood like a lamb till I succeeded at last in reining him back till he was clear, and I could get my boots free from my stirrups with my hands, and dismount. After that I led him under the log and we went on. I had been frightened.

*   *   *

The men cut out the last of the sheep about five o'clock that evening; the weather had been kind to us. The fleeces did not look well, and to my idea had a dead feel. I had no notion how much wool we had lost through their being broken out along the back, and the dark soiled appearance, from constantly moving among burnt logs and charcoal, seemed to spoil it. I had been told that none of these things matter at the woollen mills; these fleeces scour as clean and white as any others. They looked grubby along the back, where they should have been clean and white, but I consoled myself that the sheep looked fat and well, and the lambs were well grown. I felt nonetheless that after shearing in a southern shed this performance would have been enough to give poor old Britts a fit of the blues, and send him off into odious comparisons. I confess that I myself could not help thinking of the clean white fleeces of Canterbury, that one feels to be alive to the hand, and shining with the bright grease of the yolk. Also I thought of the cleanliness of the board shearing floor, the busy picker-up and roller, the clank of the press as the wool goes down in the bale, and the careful classing.

Here we had to skirt the wool, wetted in crossing the creek, and spread it on the grass to dry. It was all very primitive. Also we were short of our numbers by a higher percentage than I could account for. I liked to think that more had dodged us than we knew, but in my heart I doubted it. Never mind; this was my first shearing; the wool was off the sheep's backs and would soon be sold. Something would come in, as a promise of better things in the future, and it remained for us gradually to improve our methods and conditions, and profit by this year's experience. I was glad to start the mob back up the mountain after keeping them hanging about so long without proper holding paddocks.

When I woke next morning the sun was well up. Hongi Pork was already out by the fire, on which he had put the billy to boil. He had also taken it upon himself to put the oatmeal on, for which I was grateful.

"And where is Kono?" I asked, looking around.

"Gone," said Hongi. "He's hared off at sparrow fart first thing this morning. He's dyin' for a feed of spuds. No Maori can go long without 'em."

Later in the morning we all "hared off" ourselves, after getting the wool under cover in case of rain. I wanted Puru Tonga to help me with the packing. Ever since Te Ngoi had sent him to me to make the track for bringing in the sheep, he had regarded me possessively as his pakeha, which meant that I sometimes guaranteed his account at the Trading Company for a bag of flour when he could corner me in town, and that I had the somewhat doubtful right to his occasional services when he felt like it. As he had bought more than one bag of flour recently, and also one of sugar, it seemed about time that he came on duty again.

He lived at this time with his wife and young family at a whare on the flat some distance across the road from Frank Hull's. He was not at home when I went there. The only sign of the family having been recently in residence was a small pig, who grunted complainingly to me as I rode up to the door and called out. Closer examination showed no sign of blankets and the fire dead out. It looked as if the pig would have to root for his supper or go without. I rode to Frank Hull's, who said the family had departed that morning. When I told Frank what I wanted Puru for, he said he reckoned there was money in packing and carting, and give him "a bit o' time to get a few things together", he would do it himself. As I did not feel I could depend on his "bit o' time" being less than six months, I thanked him and said there was a kind of understanding the Maoris would do it.

"The trouble with Maoris is, you can't depend on 'em," said Frank.

153

*   *   *

Back to the pa I rode to see my rangatira, Te Ngoi. He smiled and said, "Puru is gone to Mangapehi. I think he stays a long time."

"How long?" I asked. "Days or weeks?"

"I can't tell that. His aunt is ill," said Ngoi. "Maybe it will be weeks till he comes home. When do you want to pack the wool?"

"Tomorrow," I told him. "I want to catch the wool sale in Auckland."

"Well, I will help you. You sleep here tonight. We go up tomorrow."

I was astonished at this, as Ngoi was never in need of money, and I took it as a great compliment that he should offer, and accepted straight away.

Next morning we rode up together and spent the remainder of the day packing the loose wool and preparing the loads. We had nothing to weigh with, but put about 50lbs into a sack as near as we could judge. We had four pack saddles complete with sling-straps which we put round eight bags, ready to hook on in the morning.

There was no difficulty about a daybreak start with Ngoi. He had the horses saddled whilst I cooked breakfast, and we loaded up as soon as we had had a meal, slinging a sack on each of the horses, with another longways across his back, strapped firm with a long surcingle, and started off, Ngoi leading a horse, and I driving the others after. We were at Otewa and had off-loaded the wool into the pataka soon after ten o'clock. Ngoi gave instructions to have some potatoes bagged for us to take back on our second trip, and we started on our way up the river, he again leading at a good canter most of the way to the bush, and we lunched in camp about one o'clock. He prepared the loads whilst I boiled the billy, giving him a hand once the fire was going properly, and in an hour from our time of arrival we were off again.

The year Ngoi had spent at St Stephen's College had given him good ideas and encouraged his natural sense of honour. He kept control over the cultivation and food storage, too, and the natives were content to follow his directions, so that now he was regarded as the chief, and those of us who had any dealings with the local natives naturally went to him. I felt grateful that he had made my problems so much simpler for me. Had I not had him to refer to from the beginning, life might have been much harder, almost impossible. He was a pure-bred Maori, but had more delicate features than was usual with them. He reminded me of pictures of natives of India, what is called the pure Aryan type. The old native rangatira families bred men of strong features with high-bridged noses, perhaps the predatory type. They were descendants of men who could prevail in personal combat, where the fittest survive, and were therefore massive in bodily build. It was usual for the Maoris in describing a leader in any walk of life in my time — whether a large landowner or a rich man — to speak of him as a "big" man. The natives, deprived of war as an occupation, and the necessity of laboriously cultivating the land for food, being healthy and strong, quickly grew fat, both men and women. Ngoi never did, and, where as a child he had been inferior to his contemporaries, he was now fitter and move active than most of them. He neither drank nor smoked. He paid his respects at native ceremonies, and at the many tangis which easy money and immoderate living caused, but he did not appear to enjoy the festivities and the heavy eating which took place at them.

Native life, which for these few days I lived with him, was simple and pleasant enough. We ate well and slept warm at night. Our clothing was sufficient. We prepared for bed by removing our boots and coats and turning into the blankets as we were. We washed in the stream. I have heard it said that under such conditions one quickly becomes verminous, that in fact our forefathers must have been lousy before the days of frequent baths, but I have not found it, and I never recall a lousy native. Fleas are another story; some places seem to breed them, as the bush breeds bluebottles. This time we were untroubled by them.

These two days gave me a pleasant rest and a feeling of content. I seldom had a real loaf when at Rangitoto. The habit of going into town so often gave me all the change I wanted. Had it not been so, I might well have followed the line of least resistance, and drifted into the native way of life. Ngoi was a man who might have made his way in civilised society, and was always good company. Unlike Ngahihi he did not spend the long evenings telling me tales of old times and dering-do, but that he liked me I believed when I found he had written with a piece of charcoal on the tent wall, "Tangata atawhai ki nga tangata katoa," which he translated when asked, "The man who is kind to all men."

When the weather cleared we continued our packing until it was finished, and the pataka was crammed with our wool, which was waggoned onto the railway and consigned to Dalgety & Co. in Auckland, where at the following wool sale it averaged a little over 7d a pound; quite good.

That Christmas of 1911 I spent in Te Kuiti. Many of my friends had gone away, but John Rolleston remained. Mrs Mostyn Jones gave a party to which we both went. There were several young people there, including the Spencer girls whose father, a civil engineer, was in charge of the borough. The youngest Spencer was still a schoolgirl, home for her holidays. We played "Up Jenkins" and other children's games, and John said he had not had so much innocent enjoyment for a long time. I felt that too. It was delightful to be excited and amused and interested where there was no gambling, drinking or rabelaisian stories.

*   *   *

The time had come to bring out some sheep for sale. I decided to sell everything and stock up with cattle for the ensuing winter. Dalgety's agent said he could dispose of the lot for me well enough. He had clients wanting sheep if I would bring them out to where a buyer could have a look at them without an expedition into the wilds. I undertook to do this.

To my regret I found that Paddy Corcoran was not available; he was engaged elsewhere. I was recommended to try a fellow named Glenny, who turned out to be a tall man with a lugubrious expression and long features and moustache — most things about him were long — who had horse and dogs and could start with me next morning. I found that he was the son of a carrier at Sumner, whom I remembered as a boy, so that we knew the same ground; but he was not a lively companion.

We experienced no difficulty in mustering the mountain, except that the same few sheep evaded us that had done so before, and I resolved to clear the country of them later on. As the weather was fine, I anticipated no trouble in bringing the sheep down the Waipa. They travelled well, crossing the smaller Waimahora till they reached the first ford of the river. There to my surprise they stuck, and we had to dog them a lot to get them into the stream. I tried to cross them at a point just below the confluence of the Waimahora with the Waipa, as there was an island of shingle there, and I hoped that by getting them over to this we would find it easy to push them over to the mainland on the other side; but they would not face it. Glenny and I had taken them along to this point rather loosely. We now got behind them, and pressing them with the dogs as hard as we could, we pushed them in a solid mass to the water's edge. There they stopped, and the leaders, rather than wet their feet, faced the dogs and ran round to either side.

We two men now went forward, while the dogs held the sheep up to us, and getting hold of a sheep each, threw it into the stream, in the hope that it would reach the island and the others string after. In this we only half succeeded; there was no stringing over. Some did find the right way, others came back upon our side, and others tended to allow the current, which proved stronger than I had realised, to work them downstream, where, instead of crossing, they allowed themselves to come out further down on the bank from which they had started, or worse still to go downsteam until swept into deep water under a steep hillside where the river ran along a sheer rock face. In the endeavour to prevent this happening I was soon standing in the Waipa up to my knees, and being worked downstream too. However, all things come to an end if you keep at it, and we did at last succeed in getting the mob over, though I had to pull out half a dozen of the ones under the rock face and throw them as far as I could before they would try to help themselves over, and I got wet to the waist in so doing.

Getting them off the little island of shingle was not so difficult. Once there, they did string over to the left bank, and having shaken themselves took the track down the river without waiting for the tail of the mob. So we only had to keep the stragglers moving for the mile or so to the next crossing where they had bunched again when we came up to them.

Here the river flowed slowly between high banks, the track approaching the ford down a cut made to allow a waggon to emerge. It was easier, when they were forced into this, to hold the sheep there, but again they baulked at the river, so the only thing was to throw them in as before, and some did begin to file across; but though the current was not as swift here as up above, it was there just the same, and the river being deeper at this point, and wider, the sheep were having to swim in some places. It was here a broad stream, smooth and unruffled. I was in front, throwing the sheep in, Glenny behind, keeping them closed up with the dogs, when I noticed that the animals were, many of them, coming back, downstream from me, under the steep bank, in water so deep that they were all floating. I worked my way down, pulling sheep out and floating them over to the other side, until I was in up to my armpits.

A false step into a hole, and I completed my own immersion by going head-under. Only for a moment, though. I was soon busy again pulling out the sheep, and really very worried to find so many crowded together in the water in this way, in a place so hard to reach. The thick, tall fern, from eight to ten feet long, overhung the water, and increased the difficulty of getting the brutes out on this side. It made it impossible, in fact, and of course if one had been able to, they still had the river to cross, here, and three times more before reaching market. There was nothing for it but to manhandle them as I was doing. The afternoon was getting on, and there seemed by now to be a hundred sheep treading water under the bank, each of which had to be helped out into mid-stream and shoved off with its head in the right direction, in the hope that it would complete its journey.

At this moment Glenny's face, looking longer than usual, peered down at me through the thicket, and in a doleful voice he asked, "Do you think I ought to come in too?"

"I certainly do," I answered, feeling heated despite the cold water, "if the tail of the mob has crossed the river."

"I won't say they have crossed," he moaned, "but they're all in the water; I'll come and help you."

He disappeared from view, and as he was some time reappearing, I took a breather and went back a few paces to find out what had become of him, and saw him standing with his back to me, undressing on the bank beside the track. I noted that he wore long thick woollen drawers, and groaned aloud as I dived for the nearest sheep once more.

Presently he came wading in towards me, looking more and more lugubrious as the water got deeper and deeper.

It seemed like an hour before we had pushed the last sheep over and followed it onto a shingle spit on the other side.

Glenny looked across the water and said miserably, "And the horses are on the other side, too."

"Yes, I'll get them," I answered brutally. "It would be a pity to get your feet wet. Just dodge along the bank and see that all the sheep have left the river. I'll bring your clothes, too."

When I came splashing over the ford on the horses I found that poor Glenny, having satisfied himself that the sheep had all trailed on, had taken cover behind a toetoe bush and was giving his back a kind of loofah wipe with a bunch of fern. I was saved the trouble, having my clothes on, and these would, in time, dry on me. Fortunately I had strapped my jacket to my saddle earlier in the day. It was dry, so I put it on, and finding tobacco and matches in the pocket, filled and lit a pipe while I reflected what was to be done now.

The situation was really serious enough. These river crossings were providing a very difficult problem for us, and the long immersions were bad for the condition of the sheep. Their wool wet and clinging, they did not look half as well now as when they left the clearing that morning. I dreaded the prospect of three more crossings. The next one would take us onto my neighbour, Mr Cruikshank's flat. A man called Barber had a camp close by; he would be out at work on top of the hill. I told Glenny to go there, kindle the fire, await his arrival, and tell him we would sleep there that night, while I went on to see Mr Cruikshank.

The old Cruikshanks were at the door of their camp as I rode up, and invited me in for a cup of tea, of which I was glad. It seemed hard to think of such people beginning life under canvas again, having been used to refinement all their lives. Even there, the bread and butter was cut thinner than was ever seen in my bushmen's camp, and I watched while she warmed a silver teapot with hot water before putting in the tea. They were interested to hear of our progress down, and I told them how concerned I was at the prospect of three more crossings for the sheep. I said I had always heard there was a track along the hilltop through the fern above us, which led to the one between Aharoa and Otewa, and that although it meant climbing the ridge and going further, I would rather do that than cross the river more than once again.

After tea Mr Cruikshank showed me where he had cleared the fern from a track up a spur, and told me that it was like this all the way up, and that it joined the native riding track at the top. I decided it would be possible for sheep and said I would use it next day. He offered to come and give a hand to get the mob over the river next morning, and we parted.

As I rode up the flat to Barber's camp, the sheep were well spread out and eating the grass that grew there, through the fern, and I felt easier in mind about them then I had since we first reached the river. At the camp I found Barber, who had always been grateful for my advice to keep the place, of which, being a great worker, it seemed he was making a success, and he liked his prospects. He said he was glad to put us up, that very few strangers came that way, and he liked a bit of company now and again. He and Glenny appeared to be rather kindred spirits, in that they derived a woeful satisfaction in discussing all the drawbacks of the country and the misfortunes that were the lot of anyone who settled in it. This they did in mournful tones all evening, one listening politely and without interruption to the other's doleful story, before capping it with another more miserable, until I could have burst into tears had not the narration struck me as having its humorous side; and I did not hear of anyone who had been actually hanged, drowned or blown up, although I gathered that most people in this wicked world came next door to it. Barber was a bachelor, who was really making a very good effort of his undertaking, although his outlook was blue. Glenny was a family man who should never have driven stock off a road, where, no doubt, he was very good and reliable. He certainly had not the backblocks temperament, and failed to enjoy sleeping on the floor that night.

*   *   *

Next morning the sheep already looked better. Barber came to the ford to lend us a hand, and I saw Mr Cruikshank approaching on the other side. I called to him to wait while I brought him over a horse, but he either could not or would not hear, but strode into the water which came well above his knees. I was sorry, and said so, but he made light of it. He was the son of a pioneer, and had had his share of roughing it, no doubt. All the same I thought it was too much for a man well over sixty years of age.

This time the sheep crossed the river well, and headed up the hill willingly enough. It was different on the top, though. The sun was high by the time we got there; the small, thirst-making dust arose from the fern. The sheep refused to move, and we had to dog them all the way. A stranger called Macphee passed us as we were progressing thus slowly. I heard afterwards that he testified to the district that I was a good man with sheep, for, he said, "They brought them over an awful bit of country, and had to dog them all the way, yet I never heard him swear once the whole time."

He was a good man with stock himself, I afterwards learned.

So we came out on the flat as the afternoon wore on. Puru Tonga came out to meet us, and riding beside me said, "You camp the sheep on the flat by the whare eh? The missis, she and I look after them. We got the fence one end. Plenty grass, too, werry good."

I was glad to do this, and in any case felt I would disappoint him if I did not. Having a big mob of sheep there gave him mana in the eyes of his fellows at the pa, or so he felt. Besides, he had given them to understand that I was his pakeha. Now he busied himself on my behalf, and having no sheep dogs, shooed off the women and children who came running out of the pa to see the mob pass, just to show what a fine fellow he was.

As I had Glenny with me, we slept at Frank Hull's that night. Hull wanted to know all about the journey down while we were at tea, and Glenny told him something of the miseries of it all. Our host listened to the story with open eyes until the end, then, "There must be money in drovin', I reckon," said he, "if a man knows the country. I've 'arf a mind to get a coupla dogs myself. There ought to be a good thing in it, if a man give his spare time to it."

A ewe died that night. Mrs Puru was skinning it for the larder when I rode over. Otherwise all was well, and the sheep were drying off. We had the open road before us from now on, and a short day's drive. I left Glenny in charge and rode on to get an accommodation field with some grass in it, as there was nothing but fern by the roadside. The trouble was to get a paddock with more than three wires round it. In the end the Ormsbys let me have one, but it was not sheep-proof, and the sheep were all over the town by morning, and had to be mustered out of the back yards of the houses where the owners did not happen to have any dogs.

Carpenter, Dalgety's new agent, brought along a couple of buyers and I sold the sheep at once. Their bath in the Waipa had spoiled their appearance rather, and I had to take 2s a head below what I believed to be their value. This was after some haggling; but

I could not hold them, owing to lack of accommodation. To auction them meant taking them all the way to Ohaupo, the great market town of lower Waikato. We had formed a company to build our own saleyards on Otorohanga, but as yet there were no auctioneers working in the district.

*　　*　　*

The Scotch thistles were now coming up all over my new burn. It was for that reason that I had sold off all the sheep, meaning when I next put more on, to have wethers. We were all glad to see this fine crop of thistles, as it was considered they were proof of good country, in spite of the inconvenience of them.

I commenced buying cattle to stock the place, putting on strong two-year-old steers, which were always cheap enough in the autumn in a bush district, as people had not then reached the stage of winter feed. My clearing was not fenced, but experienced men said I need not worry about that. If they were short of grass they would find their way into the bush and feed on the undergrowth, and I could count on their coming out in the spring, driven by the mosquitoes and other insects, and seeking the sun and the young grass. I commenced with sixty-five steers, mostly shorthorn or cross-bred with other beef-producing breeds such a Hereford and Polled Angus. We would have no Jersey crosses, though that breed was plentiful in the Waikato where dairy farms were expanding year by year. Ayrshires were no use to me either.

To buy the cattle I went to Dalgety's in Te Kuiti, in the hope that they might get me the stock I wanted from down the line; but I found they had not much to offer. I had a theory that it was unwise to buy cattle bred to the north of us to bring onto hill country, and I have found that my judgment on this was sound, for the further south one went for either cattle or sheep, the better they seemed to do, owing to being bred under colder conditions.

The shape of the property at Rangitoto did not remain constant during these first years of development. King Mahuta had agreed to sell to S. W. and his father the land he had originally leased to them, and as soon as they had the title they themselves sold it, and bought other blocks, this time to the north of the range. Everyone else was doing the same kind of thing, and there was constant talk of sales and exchanges and valuations.

In 1912 S. W. had two projects in hand — a new block of bush to be cleared, and tracks and fences to be put in on the land that was cleared already. He had two Englishmen, named Bob and Wilfred, at work on the fencing job, and another pair falling the bush.

161

The piece of clearing I wanted done this year was undertaken by a man named Johnson who, with a mate, undertook to get down a hundred acres. They camped up the valley to the west of my camp and about half way up to Hill's whare; chopping the bush between his clearing and the track to the mountain top. They were honest workers and steady, and the thorough way they cleared the scrub soon convinced me that I need not watch them much. They wanted to return the following year, and I promised that if I got a good burn I would give them double the area to do then.

Back at Rangitoto the track had gone right to the top of the mountain, and I saw that it would be easier to camp there whilst it was mattocked out for horses, than to come back to the foot each day. Bob was the expert, a most intelligent man. He got me aside and pointed out that he was the one who led the work, and asked for an increase in pay. He and Wilfred were getting £2 a week. I felt that he was holding a pistol to my head, in a polite way, and that I was being weak; but I wanted the work to continue.

Our new camp was on the site Flint and his gang had excavated. It was in the bush on a steep south face. We were comfortable enough until the weather changed, when it was always damp. We had the usual sleeping tent with bunks of punga, and a galley attached, with a slab table. The cat, whom we had transported up there, had six kittens under my bunk. I wanted to destroy them, but Bob revealed a tender heart, and persuaded me to let them live. He promised to cherish them, so I gave in. Fly then showed what she could do by having seven puppies under the galley table. I insisted both families must reside outside the living quarters, and shelters were made for them on each side of the galley chimney.

All went well for a couple of days till the weather changed to the north-west and it rained. When we went to bed the creek was getting up twenty feet below us and the water was streaming down the excavated bank on the hill side of the galley. We dug a channel across the floor to carry it away. I went to sleep to the sound of water trickling from the foliage all around us. At about 2 a.m. I awoke to hear Bob and Wilfred stirring and asked what was up.

"It's us," said Wilfred, sitting up in his bunk. "The rain is washing everything away."

"Well, it won't wash us," said I. "We are above the water. It would never reach this."

"Them kittens," said Bob, listening intently, as I heard the cat mewing outside.

"Them puppies," said Wilfred as he lit a candle. "I can hear Fly down the bank by the creek." She came in and deposited a blind wet dripping puppy on the floor between the bunks.

"The rest is out there," said Bob. "I'm goin' to get 'em."

We all turned out, and for a quarter of an hour were scrambling about in the wet darkness, for no candle would stay alight, feeling for little crawlers on the steep bank between the galley and the stream. We were all wet when at last we checked them over under the cover of our tent. There were loud outcries when I had all but one kitten destroyed next day. Bob was almost mutinous about it and made sneering remarks about "them puppies". But I had all but two of them destroyed too, keeping only a little black dog we christened Johnson after the negro boxing champion, and a tan one we called Sanderson. Later, when their eyes opened, they were the favourites of the camp. It was impossible to keep too many dogs and cats. We had no fresh milk for them.

*   *   *

My two men were a curious pair. Bob was always busy, and when in camp did the cooking, whilst Wilfred cut the wood and did the cleaning or washing up. He also did the little butchering there was to do. Bob usually worked in silence. Wilfred was a character, who in quiet tones said many humorous things, which were generally inspired in a roundabout way by the work he was doing at the moment.

One day he and I had to go down to the camp at the bottom of the mountain for some things we needed. We also had some odds and ends at Hill's whare, so we walked back by the old track. We plodded steadily up to Hill's with quite noticeable loads on our backs, and these grew heavier still as we went on. It was a warm day and quite a steep climb, and when, hot and thirsty, we reached the last glade, we stopped to get what cool air there was and have a spell before entering the thicker bush above. As we lay back on the ground in the sunlight, Wilfred said to me,

"Grand country, England, you know, boss."

"Yes," I answered, "I believe it is. I've never been there. I hope to go. But why do you say that now?"

"Oh, it's a grand country. Pub every mile." The poignance of his words made me laugh, and he went on, "You know I went to many strange places when I was carting there, and I'm walking beside my horses one day up a long steep hill that I thought would never end. There is a wide moor at the top, and it's hot and dusty, and I'm thinking how thirsty I'm goin' to be before I reach the town at the other side, when at last we get to the crest, and there just over the brow is a nice little pub, and what do you think it is called?"

I shook my head.

"Boss, that pub is called The Who Would Have Thought It, and a pint of their beer is the best in the world."

163

"Well, it's a long way to a pint of beer here, Wilfred," said I, laughing.

"It is, boss," he continued, in the same solemn tones. "It's what I say, you know; this country is only half civilised yet. No beer, no pubs, nothing to have a joke about, or even make you think. Most of the pubs have grand names, too. They call 'em inns there, but here they call 'em all hotels. Sounds so formal. In England you only find hotels in the larger towns. If you have to go into 'em to deliver packages or anything like that you take your hat off and walk on tiptoe to avoid soiling the carpet. If you have a pint given you, it's a case of drink it quiet and get out. Now give me a nice little bar with a low ceiling and a sanded floor, and a seat outside for the summer days when you can sit and have a pint with your lunch while your horses are having theirs with their nosebags on and you can watch them."

"There are two pubs in New Zealand that call themselves inns," I told him. "One is the Bush Inn and the other is the Plough."

"And where are they, boss?"

"Down in Canterbury, on the way out to Riccarton racecourse. Nice houses they are too. The Plough has a trough outside labelled 'Drink, and let thy cattle drink also'."

"And that's what I call nice and homely," said Wilfred. "Reminds you of the Old Country, and makes you thirsty to think of 'em. I've always heard that the South Island is more English than up here. I'd like to go there. Them names now, they might be in England itself, where all the pubs have fancy ones. Did you ever hear of the Four Alls?"

"No. Is it something like the Three Castles?" I asked.

"Nothing similar. It's a picture of four men, a parson, a lawyer, a soldier and a farmer, and the first says 'I pray for all'; the lawyer says 'I plead for all'; the soldier says 'I fight for all' — but the farmer says 'I pay for all'."

"Well," said I, "that sounds true too. Without the farmer the rest would starve; but if I had my choice, I would like to be the soldier."

"Funny thing, I suppose most of us would. Yet in England they don't think much of 'em."

"Who don't?" I asked rather sharply.

"Oh, most of the people in steady jobs, you know. They reckon a soldier has too easy a time of it, walkin' around in his red coat when they are working, and goin' about with the girls. When a man is takin' things easy in front of the fire in 'is shirt sleeves an' his feet in his socks of an evenin', and 's wife comes in and says, 'Here's Jenny just come in, Dad, she's brought her young man to speak to yer.' 'E's a soldier,' 'What, a soldier?' he shouts, jumpin' up, 'Where's my clogs? Where's my bloody clogs?' He's wild enough to kick 'im out.

Soldiers don't mean business most times, and they don't earn enough to keep a wife, the way a man who gets good wages can."

The picture conjured up made me laugh again, and I felt renewed vigour in consequence as we shouldered our loads and went on.

*　　*　　*

It was now apparent that we needed more sheep, and I had to go up to Ohaupo to get some idea about values. On the way back I collected my horse in the afternoon and rode out to Frank Hull's. As I was weary, I went to bed early, and Frank and his half-witted farmhand, Leslie, were audibly on the move at daybreak. Presently my host came in with a cup of tea, and the loud complaint, "Mr Westmacott, them Maori cattle have been in my grass all night. They've broken down the fence and trampled over everything."

I duly sympathised, and he went on, "A man ought to sue them for damages; but he'd never get any money out of them. What do you reckon I ought to do about it?"

I found it hard to suggest a soothing remedy. Frank Hull's fences were three wires strung to a post here and there. No enterprising animal could be expected to respect them if there was grass to be seen on the other side. Everything about him, except the little house which had been erected on borrowed money under state super-vision, was scrappy. His so-called cowshed fifty yards beyond the house consisted of a bail of light manuka poles, which also served as part of the frame to prop up two walls, little more than wind breaks of brushwood with four old sheets of corrugated iron nailed over the top and strengthened with wire. It kept the rain from running down the cow's sides into the bucket when he was milking, but that was about all.

"There's a heifer there in milk," Frank went on. "I've a good mind to milk her. What'd you do?"

"I would, Frank, I would. Good idea," I said, ready enough to be rid of him. I must have gone to sleep again, for it seemed only an instant before I heard a bang, crash and shouting from the direction of the cowshed, which brought me to the window in time to see half a dozen nondescript cattle and two horses tearing madly past, followed by a terrified heifer with the bails still round her neck, and three sheets of corrugated iron attached, clanging, as she tried by throwing her head about to rid herself of these incumbrances, whilst a pig fled squealing out of the way in one direction, and cackling fowls and quacking ducks on wings and feet took terrified flight for safety.

They were followed by Frank, with an empty bucket.

"There they go, Mr Westmacott," he wailed. "There they go!" — as if I needed my attention drawn to the fact, — "And they've taken my cowshed and bails with 'em, too. I had 'ardly got that mongrel brute with 'er 'ead in the bails when, she doesn't wait for me to do more than sit down beside 'er, she kicks out and the next thing she 'as 'er foot in the bucket — and it's half full of milk from me own cow. It splashes all over me. Then she's not content with that. She pulls back and rips the bails out of the ground. Down comes the roof on top o' me. A man might 'ave been killed the way she went on. Then she don't stop to think, she's off down the track, scarin' everything within miles, and scatterin' my cowshed 'arf way from 'ere to the pa."

It was with considerable effort that I reserved my laughter and tried to look sympathetic.

* * *

I arrived at the lower camp by lunchtime, had some tea and bread and butter, and went into the bush to see what progress Johnson and his mate were making. The work was being well done, and I completed a little tour of inspection before making my way back to the upper camp.

It was pleasant to be able now to ride up the front face of the mountain, and it only took half the time that going round by the long ridge had done. It was undeniably steeper most of the way — one continuous climb in fact, but the track was well made and one could rest the horse, by walking and leading him, from time to time.

On top we were now putting a fence round the clearing. The line was cleared, and we packed the wire up coil by coil, three coils on a pack saddle. The top barb was an unpleasant thing to handle, but by putting it in sacks and slinging them on the hooks we managed it, though the barb stuck through and scratched the saddles badly. Suitable fencing timber was not to be found close to the top. The papamu was plentiful enough and lasts well; we used some of it as strainers, but it was so twisted that we did not like it. I was told that large konini, cut and put in green, was a permanency, and we used a lot of it. For battens we had plenty of mountain totara, which I was told would do very well, but it would not last if we put it in the ground like the totara on the lower levels. We put up three-quarters of a mile of this fencing. It was not a ring fence, but it stopped the stock going back into the bush on the south side of the mountain, our aim being to get them to come forward on the grass down the slope.

It was soon necessary to leave the camp on the top of the mountain and return to the one at the foot of the hill. We were all glad to move from a place where we had had so much rain, no sunshine and were constantly damp. I was resolved, if I ever had to live up there again, to put in a day or two and erect a good camp on the original site near the trig station. Even if it was a little further back it got the sun all day, and yet in summer had the benefit of the cool breezes in the higher altitude. We packed our belongings onto two pack horses, added the cat, bitterly protesting, in an empty sugar bag, and carried our own swags on our backs. Johnson and Sanderson, though only a few weeks old, ran behind us. We had meant to carry them when they got tired, but apart from a whimper now and again, which we took as an enquiry as to where we were going, they kept up all the way, and "Them puppies is little Britons" was Wilfred's comment at the end of the journey.

*   *   *

This time the sheep I bought were wethers, as I was not happy about having ewes on the place. I resolved to sell off what I had next autumn and to keep dry sheep altogether until the place was better broken in and fenced.

I drove this mob out to Otewa and camped the night at some neighbours', the Fergusons. Fergus had never been to my camp, and offered to help me take the sheep on. We set out at daybreak and made such good progress that by ten o'clock we were nearly at the crossing where the Waimahora joins the Waipa. There Wilfred was waiting to help me across, but by now the sky was heavy with clouds, and a light rain began to fall.

The mob was stringing out for nearly a quarter of a mile behind the leaders. We waited for them to straggle onto the flat, and the ten minutes or so which they took to do this seemed very long ones as the rain increased. We lost no time in getting them into a solid mob, and, with the barking dogs, forced them onto the sloping shingle at the edge of the river. There they stuck, obviously having decided that they were not going to cross that day. In an endeavour to make them string over, we threw a number in. They came back again on our side as soon as we let them go. I carried one out to the middle of the stream, which was over my knees, very swift, and showed signs of rising, as it had already been raining in the bush further up. As my sheep immediately turned to join the mob when I left him go, I grabbed him again and did not release him till he was walking up the shingle to the grass on the other side. At least I had one over.

Fergus came in and collared another. Wilfred did the same. From then on we laboriously half-carried, half-floated the brutes over one by one, for by themselves they would not move; though once having shaken themselves on the shingle they went straggling

167

slowly on. This process took time, but we never seemed to notice its passage, though we grew slower and slower as the water rose to our hips and then above our waists, till it was not easy to stand in the current. At last it was up to our chests. We worked in silence, no one complaining, till I was compelled to look at my watch, and it was three o'clock. The rain had become a steady downpour long since, and only half the mob was over. How one hates to be beaten! But there was nothing for it, I had to stop further effort, let the sheep go where they were and take their chance until the weather improved and the river went down again. This decision was to give me much anxiety and many days riding in and out of the scrub to get my sheep together.

It was difficult not to feel depressed as we rode home, soaking wet from head to foot, but no one showed it unduly. It had been arranged for Wilfred to bring a pack horse down and go on to Frank Hull's for some stores, for Frank had recently set himself up as a storekeeper. It was too late now for him to get back in daylight. I told him to stay there and come up next morning. The rest of us were glad to find a roaring fire in camp, dry singlets and trousers, hot tea and and good meal. We had gone foodless since morning, having felt bound to keep on trying until the job became impossible, and to boil a billy would have meant standing about in misery for nearly half an hour till it was ready.

These sheep were shorn wethers; they should have gone well if the weather had not been so against us. But it was only one more experience of what the Waipa could do. I began to wonder if I could not have a swing bridge made, and selected the site. To cross the river in one span meant nearly sixty feet, which I thought a big undertaking, but there was an island of shingle just below the meeting of the waters which would enable us to get over in two, one span of forty and one of twenty; but I had no time to do anything about it just then.

*　　*　　*

Wilfred arrived back next day, but without half the stores I had ordered from Frank Hull.

"Oh, he's a ragtime storekeeper that, boss," said Wilfred. "'E 'asn't 'arf the things a storekeeper ought to 'ave. 'Where's them potatoes the boss ordered, Frank?' I asked him. 'Was it pertaters 'e wanted?' says Frank. 'I got 'im a bag of onions,' I told 'im. 'You know you want to be a bit more careful when you get an order, Frank; the boss's business would be worth a bit to you. If you ain't careful, 'e'll be dealing elsewhere.' "

This rather made me laugh, as there was no possible business rival to Frank Hull closer than Otorohanga; but it made me think, too, and the next time I rode down, I went into Frank's with a list on which were some things I knew he was unlikely to have.

"I want a tin of honey, Frank," I told him.

"Honey! I ain't had no honey in, this spring."

"Right." I drew a line through honey on my list. "Six tins of jam — two strawberry, two raspberry, two melon and lemon."

"Jam," said Frank, "is a thing I sold out of last Friday."

"Right." Again I made the motions of writing. I pursed my lips, and Frank began to look unhappy.

"Now I want a bag of flour."

"Yes, I can do that," said Frank, brightening again.

"And one of sugar," I told him. I could see none in his shelves and he wilted again as he said, "I sold the last of me sugar yesterday."

I then rapidly reeled off a list of stores to make up a pack load, and found he had only about half of them. I closed my note book.

"All right, Frank," I said pleasantly, "you had better cancel the order. I'll have to get these things in town."

"Oh I don't think you need do that, Mr Westmacott," he told me. "When do you want 'em?"

"Wilfred will be down with a pack horse this afternoon," I answered. "He was to have taken them up tomorrow morning; but I've told him to come on to town if you haven't got the stuff. I'm going on now to catch the train to Te Kuiti."

I had not reached the township when with a jingle of chains Frank passed me in his waggon, and with a wave of his whip he shouted, "Them stores o' yours, Mr Westmacott, I'm goin' in to get 'em. I've left a message for Wilfred with the missus so 'e need come no further."

I felt this looked more promising.

*　　　*　　　*

My father was in Te Kuiti, and I was going to spend the weekend there. He came up a good deal these days, as for the moment he had no home, the house at Waimate having been recently sold. He found the King Country Club a pleasant place to rest in while my mother and sister stayed at the Hydro in Timaru, and other such establishments. Miss Mackenzie, who ran Kelvin House, was kind, and made him very comfortable, and the place was cheap to live in. Mrs Finlay and young Mrs Fitzherbert made him welcome in their houses, and he liked seeing me at weekends. He was unselfish, and made few demands on my time, beyond taking me to church with him, where I was glad to go.

169

I sometimes thought people encroached on his good nature, as for instance when some of the younger men got him to sign the complaints book at the Club with them, his age and standing lending more weight to suggestions than they might otherwise carry.

John Rolleston was impressed by the fact that my father, though by then seventy years of age, never grew old or in any way pompous, but was friendly and natural with younger men. John said that he had been too young, and his father too absorbed in public affairs, for him really to know him intimately, and he regretted it.

As I had only about 300 woolly sheep, I decided we would shear them ourselves. I had never been a shearer, but knew how to hold a sheep, open up, and work round the back, after which it only takes practice to become a fast shearer with the blades. I now tried to teach Bob and Wilfred. When I had shorn three sheep, Bob said he was ready to have a go at it. He and Wilfred got to work, Bob commencing slowly and methodically and making steady progress, but Wilfred never really got the hang of it. The job took four days, and at the end of that time Bob was doing twice as many as his mate. We got the wool off, anyway.

PART FIVE

MORE DEVELOPMENT, AND SOME MILITARY INTERRUPTIONS

They will rediscover rivers — not my rivers, heard at night.

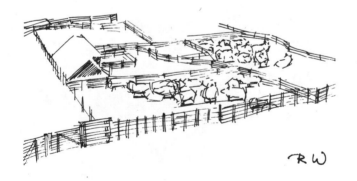

PART FIVE

MORE DEVELOPMENT, AND SOME MILITARY INTERRUPTIONS

That Christmas of 1912 S. W. stayed in camp at Rangitoto, as he wanted to burn bush early in the new year. His life on the property was now punctuated by attendance at annual Military Camps at Trentham, and by regular drill-nights in Te Kuiti. He had been a bugler in the Cadets at Waitaki Boys' High School, and a trooper in the Studholme Mounted Rifles in his South Island days, and had ridden into Waimate and back once a week to attend drills. In 1911 he had accepted a commission in the Waikato Regiment. He regarded these military duties as holidays and enjoyed them immensely, but the result was that he often found the return to Rangitoto depressing, in spite of the fact that he now had a new and more substantial whare.

In January 1913 he felt particularly low when he rode back into the bush, with his new burn to be achieved. He also had the prospect of a visit from the new manager of the Union Bank, Mr Uren, who was to bring a valuer out to look at what was known as the Crown Lands block at Rangitoto, with a view to raising a loan. The necessity for this loan had been on his mind, and his father's, since the latter's purchase of a house in Nile St, Timaru, to replace the family home at Waikakaki.

WHEN NEXT I rode home via Frank Hull's, I found my way blocked by an obstruction called in the north a "Taranaki" gate, and in the south an "Irishman's", consisting of three wires tied to the post and a couple of battens nailed to them to hold it erect and fastened at the opening by a loop of wire at the top and bottom of the opposite post, through which the end batten was slipped. This was Frank Hull's entrance gate. It would suffice to hold in cattle of the house-cow variety, but it would not stop sheep — of which Frank had none — and any self-respecting pig would scorn it. Usually this gate lay open at one side; I had never seen it closed before. Now a young boy sprang out from the short scrub, and said in an accent I had learnt to know as cockney, "'Arf a mo', Mr Westmacott. Let me open the gate for yer."

Guessing he had closed the gate in order to engage me in converse, I said, "What is your name? And where do you come from?"

"Ar! I'm Jack Tighe. I'm living with Mr 'ull. I come from Plaistow."

"And where may that be?" I asked, being vague about it. "In Scotland?"

"Naow! London. Ain't you been there?"

"No, Jack, I've never been in England."

"Go wan!" he said in astonishment. "You talk like it. This is a funny country, ain't it?"

"What's wrong with it?" I asked. His tone accused me.

"Oh, it's a long way off. I came out wiv me muvver, but she's dead now. Me farver's working up the road 'ere. It ain't a bit like what I expected. No one 'as a revolver. It's just like England in some ways, and then it isn't. You'd think a man 'ud 'ave to fight; but he doesn't. All these Maoris, you'd never expect to find them wearing shirts and pants, just like us. I thought they'd be armed with h'assegais, but they don't use 'em. You come from the back country, don't you?"

I nodded.

"Goin' up there now?"

I nodded again.

"They tell me there's wild cattle there. Is that true?"

I said it was true.

"Do they rush you?"

I did not wish to disappoint him, so I said, "Sometimes, if you get in their way."

He said, "Mr 'ull's cows don't rush you. They won't get out of your way. Are there any wild boars up there?"

Again I nodded.

"And have they got tusks?"

I told him the big ones had.

"Mr 'ull's boar ain't got no tusks," he said regretfully. "I wish I was going up to the bush, Mr Westmacott."

I had been taking in this little adventurer who had travelled so much further than I, and crossed the world. I even felt envious. There was a sharpness about him that I was amused at. It was not a bit unpleasant. He was clad in blue dungarees with large boots and carried a big sheath knife prominently in his belt. A grey shirt was open at the neck and he wore the biggest hat I had ever seen, a regular Huckleberry Finn of a hat.

"That's a great scalping knife you have there," I said, looking at his belt.

" 'Tain't for scalping," he replied sourly, "No one gets scalped here." There was a note of regret in his voice.

"Well, Jack, perhaps you will come up to the bush one day."

"And hunt pigs?" he asked eagerly.

"Yes, if you want to," said I. "And now I must jog on." And I bade him goodbye.

He was still there, gazing after me, as I rode round the bend in the road. I do not know why I thought of the Vikings.

*   *   *

Jack Tighe had cheered me up temporarily, but it was not a day to uplift the spirits. The sky was dark and lowering and light mist swept down the valley as I crossed the first ford beyond Te Kooti's old whare.

I reflected that my military commitments did at least give me an added reason for occasional visits to Te Kuiti, even when my father was not there. With Stanley Brittan I still paid my quarter share of half a crown a week for the hire of a bach in town. I could make my visits coincide with Territorial drill, and it was convenient to keep my clothes at the bach. The general use made of it by our friends on their visits to town, as a drinking place when they wanted to be a little exclusive in their parties, had its drawbacks if one wanted to keep clothes, uniform or a sword ready to hand, or if one wanted to go early to bed, but the whiskey and joyous company outweighed these disadvantages, one felt, and it had the good effect of teaching one to put things away where they would not attract attention — under the bed, for preference. I had bought a wonderful trunk second-hand at the auction mart for 5s. It had obviously seen better days, and I found it had belonged to a fat old clerk in Greene and Colebrooke's office in Otorohanga, called Forster. He told me he was glad to be rid of it, and that it had belonged to his father who had been in the Indian Civil Service, and used to take it everywhere with him. In this I packed my valuables, and wondered into what strange places it had gone on camel's or elephant's back. It was indeed a true elephant trunk.

*   *   *

Next time I rode into town I turned in at Frank Hull's for any chance mail. The cockney boy was hoeing the very barren-looking vegetable garden where a few carrots and onions struggled for existence beside some stalks of the cabbage variety. He looked sideways at me without straightening his back when I went in, but when I came out he was resting on his hoe, and I said, "Good morning, Jack."

"Good morning, Mr Westmacott," said he. "Could you give me a job at Rangitoto?"

"What do you want a job for?" I asked. "I'm afraid it is far too lonely for you away back there. You wouldn't like it at all."

"Well, I think if you gave me a chance I'd like it all right," said the boy.

"And what would Mr Hull say if you left him?"

175

"I don't think he'd mind. I'm only here temporary-like," he answered.

Telling him I could promise him nothing I turned to go out of the little side gate into the yard where my horse was tied, when Frank Hull came hurriedly round the corner of the house saying, "Jack, them pigs is out on the road makin' up towards 'ewer's. Run and drive them back, and shut the door of the stye. I don't know 'oo let 'em out. Yer know, Mr Westmacott, with all the people I 'ave round the place I can't trust one to look after things. If I don't do it myself, nothing's ever done. 'Oo fed them pigs this morning?" he asked, turning to the boy and then to me. " 'Ooever did must 'ave left the gate open. No one 'ere uses their 'ead at all."

"You fed 'em yourself," said young Jack.

"Me! Never. I 'ad to go for the mail. No, I didn't. Mail day's termorrer. Well don't stand there talking, Jack. Do as I tell yer. Run along boy, or they'll be in 'ewer's yard in no time."

He turned to me and went on, "Pigs 'ud drive a man balmy, Mr Westmacott. I don't know which is worst, them or cattle. The cows is always where they ain't supposed to be. They were in this garden the other night, walked over the fence. As if that weren't bad enough they ate 'arf the vegetables. They say the brussels sprouts'll grow again. I don't know about the cabbages and cauliflowers. You'd think after all the trouble we 'ave to make 'em grow at all, they'd leave 'em alone; but no! It only wants the pigs in now and they'd root up the carrots and parsnips. H'onions is about all they won't touch, them and leeks. A man ought to grow more of 'em."

"What about artichokes?" I asked.

"Jerusalem h'artichokes grow all right. But the pigs like them too."

I told him Jack had asked me for work, and asked if he was parting from him.

"That's right. He's only 'ere till 'is father finds a home for him. I didn't mind keeping him, but I find he's been bullying Leslie. 'E sleeps in 'is room and Leslie likes lookin' at picture books before 'e puts 'is candle out. It seems Jack don't like it. 'E likes to go to sleep in the dark, and the other night 'e got out and punched Leslie on the nose because 'e would not stop reading when Jack told 'im, and yer know I can't 'ave nothin' 'appen to Les."

He spoke as a man with a valuable piece of property to preserve. I agreed "Nothin' must 'appen to Les."

*   *   *

The clearing looked well as I walked round it next morning, and in the gully west of the hut I suddenly came on a large wild sow with

176

eight plump little piglets contentedly fossicking along the hillside. They did not see me and I quietly got down behind a log, bidding the dogs, in a hoarse whisper, to sit beside me, and putting a hand on Fly's collar as I did so. The sow had stopped and was gazing round suspiciously, whilst the little ones stood frozen, ready to bolt away from the direction of danger. I was well below, and could fade away unseen down the hillside. I did so, and thought how nice it would be to have our own pork on the grass patch whenever we needed it, and so left them there to prosper without disturbance, and made my way up Rangitoto.

As usual at this time of year I found the cattle I met pretty wild. There were not many, as most were in the bush for the winter, but those I did see were in good condition and looking well enough, despite rough coats. The sheep were in grand order. I had no ewes on this year, and these sheep, being wethers, and young, fled before me. Since my experience with ewes and lambs I had decided to carry only dry sheep for the next year or two, as I did not have the same loss as with the ladies and their offspring. At first sight there did not seem as much income to be derived, but a live wether at shearing time is worth more than a dead ewe and an unborn lamb on the hillside.

Wilfred returned two days later to start on a new contract. As Bob was going, he now took up his residence temporarily in the whare. Two days before the day of Bob's departure, I rode out and engaged young Jack Tighe to return with me, which he did next morning, on old Billy, following me on the bay horse. He somehow contrived to look a combination of the parts of Buffalo Bill and the explorer Stanley. It was nearly two o'clock when we got home, hungry for lunch. Telling Jack to off saddle, I kindled the fire and swung the billy on; showed Jack the safe and where to put things, and set a loaf of bread, a pound of butter and a cold roast of beef on the table, with mugs, plates knives, forks and spoons, the boy being bidden to observe what I did, and watching intently, The steam lifting the billy lid showed the water to be boiling. I made the tea, and cutting some large slices of meat gave Jack his share, and we fell to. For ten minutes there was little sound as we ate, and then, looking up, he said, "Grand country, New Zealand, Mr Westmacott."

"Yes, Jack, I suppose it is," I replied. "Why?"

"Always plenty to eat," said the little waif.

"Haven't you always had plenty to eat?" My voice showed astonishment.

"Me? No!" he answered emphatically. "In London me muvver lived in Plaistow. When me farver was at sea, she used to be paid Fridays. By Tuesday it would all be gone, and I used to look for food wherever I could get it."

"What sort of food? How did you get it? There in town, without money?"

"Oh, I'd pick things up. Sometimes I'd find things down by the river, thrown over from ships. I got near a whole loaf of bread, once, only about two pieces cut off it, left by the tide, you know, only a bit wet on the outside, quite good. Sometimes there'd be things in dust cans, or a bit of orange in the gutter. Very nice. But you don't go hungry like that 'ere; there's always plenty."

"Yes, Jack," I said, "and there always will be plenty as long as you are here. Food is never short in New Zealand. However poor you are, you need never go long without it."

I looked at him with renewed interest. I had read of such things; never heard of them at first hand. He was not a big boy, but he was no weed, either, and his face had a good colour and he looked healthy. His eyes met mine honestly, and he smiled when I did, only turning away when I said, "Go on now, have some more," and we fell to again.

After that I set Jack to dig a piece of ground where we were starting a vegetable garden, and went off to where Wilfred was working on the hill above the stream.

Jack proved a ready learner, and we got along very well. I was rather glad to be paying only 10s a week instead of the two guineas which Bob got. Wilfred took up his quarters in the camp where my neighbours Livingstone and Macrae used to come over in the evening two or three times a week, and settled to a steady routine.

Jack was interested in making the garden, and put in a lot of time keeping the soil well worked and clear of weeds. He knew little about seeds, but acquired his knowledge from any of us who would impart it. Frank Barber, when spending a night with us, sowed a packet of tomato seeds by the galley chimney, and they grew well. We had lettuce, cauliflower and cabbage all well started, and were sowing cucumber, marrow and pumpkin, as well as green peas and broad beans. So the coming summer promised an improved diet for all of us. Hitherto potatoes and onions had been our only vegetables, and very good they were for hungry men. I bought a cow from a settler called Hewer at Otewa, who swindled me. She did not look much, but he said I would be surprised at the way she milked. I was. She gave about two pints when she settled down. He left her unmilked night and morning bringing her up to our place, so she did fairly well that evening and we congratulated ourselves. After that she struck her true form and kept it. Jack called her "the goat" and his jokes about her reached Hewer's ears and he talked about taking her back. Instead we dried her off and sold her for beef the next time I took cattle off the place. I bought a springing heifer from Macphee — a shorthorn for which he made no exaggerated claims, and when she calved she gave a steady two gallons of milk each morning, and more than one in the evening. We had milk for all hands, cream with our porridge, and even made a bit of butter each week.

The neighbours passing through the clearing brought us all the gossip, and we were really beginning to feel that we were in the world, and building up a little community of our own. The Barkers, who had bought our first block, took sheep and cattle up onto the rich grass of their new burn. One or other of the brothers dropped in at least once a week, on their way in or out. Tom Macrae and Ken Livingstone had settled on what we called the Taitoki block opposite my grass patch, and were frequent callers too.

* * *

Mr Uren had written that he and a valuer, a Mr Allen of Cambridge, were coming out in two days' time, to value the place. I had decided to burn my bush if I got two more fine days, and so vital a thing is a burn that nothing must be allowed to stand in its way. I would light up the first time the wind came dry from the north. Meantime I cleared along the edge of the standing bush, cutting the branches and throwing them onto the fallen trees. The line of the boundary of the new clearing, which was also the northern boundary of the place, ran up the hill west of the Waimahora, and I had also had a tongue of bush cleared along the flat on top, for about ten chains, having some idea of erecting a fence there before my next clearing.

The weather held; the days were hot; but a change might come at any time, and with it the rain. Even if valuers were expected, I would light up if the wind were right. It might cause them some inconvenience, but I knew no practical man would mind that. On the contrary he would congratulate me on having just the right start for my year's work.

The day Messrs Uren and Allen were due, came up clear and hot, with a slight wind from the north. I sent boy Jack to meet them with horses at Otewa, where they should arrive about ten o'clock, having left Te Kuiti by the early train, breakfasted in Otorohanga, and been driven so far by the livery stable. I gave a note to Jack to be delivered to Mr Uren saying that if the wind improved I would light up along the hill at one o'clock, when he and Mr Allen should have arrived. Even if they had not, they would be very near, and it would be perfectly safe for them to follow Jack on the east side of the Waimahora, as we would light that part last, but it was important to keep going before the flames and smoke became too strong. I impressed this on Jack, and he promised to obey my orders.

The wind improved. Wilfred, Ken and I lunched punctually at twelve, and as I stood outside the whare I wet my finger and held it in the air. The wind was veering to nor'-west — "And that's a wind to bring rain," said Ken.

"I'm lighting up at one," I said, taking up a ready-made torch of cabbage tree, and we filed down the track.

On arrival we found it was three minutes to one. We waited till the hour, and then, crossing the creek, which was low, climbed to our places along the clearing's edge. I took the top end, and when in position yelled, "Let her go!" at the same time applying my torch and moving westwards. Below, along the line I had come, I got an occasional glimpse to show that Wilfred and Ken had lighted up, and then I applied my torch assiduously, forgetting all else as I watched the flames take hold slowly for a few inches, then crackle straight up into the air, until they caught the wind, and then go cutting through the branches with an angry swish and roar like something living. Fascinated, as always, by the terrific powers of destruction I had started on their way, I was suddenly aware of Jack Tighe climbing up to me.

What he could be doing I could not imagine. Had he disregarded my orders to take the valuer and bank manager through, or had they not arrived? Soon we were within shouting distance. He said that Mr Allen and Mr Uren were at the edge of the bush. He had not taken them through because they would not go. They wanted to see me. I did not want to go down. But the fire had by now taken such a hold that I need not stay, so I went, noting with delight the way the fire was travelling in one broad face in front of Wilfred and Ken, and my own fire would soon creep along to join them in one continuous line.

"She's goin' well, boss," said Wilfred, wiping his streaming forehead, and "Ye have Chinese luck," said Ken, as I passed him to go on and have my cup of joy filled by the congratulations of the visitors.

And what was this? I asked myself, as Mr Uren and the elderly man with him waved and shouted frantically as I approached the stream. When I reached them I said, beaming, "Well, it's a wonderful fire."

"And what did you light it for?" demanded Mr Uren, while the other, whom I took to be Mr Allen, said, "You knew we were coming, didn't you? Why could you not have waited?"

By now it was apparent that they were both extremely agitated, and I saw that we must act at once.

"I lit it because it was the most favourable moment and I could not afford to miss it," I said, "but we have not too much time, so if we are to reach the clearing I must ask you to get on the horses and follow me at once. Please do not ask for further explanation till we get through. Are you ready, gentlemen? Follow me."

A variation of the wind brought the smoke billowing down, and I ran ahead along the track. I could hear the hoofbeats of a horse following. When I reached the grass patch I stopped and turned. Jack emerged from the smoke. He told me our two visitors had turned back. There was nothing for it but to return and lose no time about it. Messrs Allen and Uren were waiting at the edge of the clearing. They said they had started but the smoke was too thick for horses, a man could not ride through. I pointed out that Jack had done so.

"His horse's tail is singed," said Mr Allen. "No, I won't ride through."

"All right," I told them, "let the boy drive the horses after me, and you two gentlemen follow on foot; but we must lose no time."

Away I went again. The horses came, and Jack came after; but our visitors were still on the wrong side. I ran back again and expostulated.

No exhortation was any good. Each of those two cowards was past any shame in the matter. I asked if they meant to go home again, and pointed out that their horses were now on the wrong side of the fire, which was by this time crawling into the valley, but owing to its position the wind was not fanning it, as it was higher up. Mr Allen said they would come round through the bush, if I led the way. We started, and as long as he had breath he grumbled all the while.

He said, "There are a lot of supplejacks."

"A sign of good strong soil, isn't it?" I asked. He did not answer. A gust of smoke made him hurry. He stumbled and fell.

"Why don't you clear a track along here?" he asked.

"Because it is a steep hillside and the best route is along the gully," said I. Another heavier gust made him jump to his feet. He plunged forward and was soon tied up in supplejacks, while Mr Uren crowded on top of him.

"We might get smothered here," said he.

"Yes, or burned by the fire if you don't move quicker," said I.

"This is terrible, terrible," said Mr Allen. "It would not be the first case of a man being burnt to death in a bush fire. Why on earth you lighted it . ."

I recalled that above all things I must give the valuer a favourable impression, and said, "Now take my hand, Mr Allen. Try and get on your feet. That's it. Don't hurry. Just take your time. I'll tread down the supplejacks in front of you. Feeling better? That's good. Look out for the lawyer, don't let it catch your head. Right we are."

And so by persuasion and assistance I got those two beauties moving, and presently we reached the track that led down onto the grass patch where the horses were grazing and Jack stood awaiting orders. I sent him ahead to make tea.

"That was a terrible journey," said old Mr Allen. He had been almost hysterical, and Mr Uren little better. They were both too shattered and exhausted to do anything that afternoon, but after a full evening meal the old man was able to sit outside the whare in his shirtsleeves and lay down the law for us. Apparently he did not think much of the King Country. It was not like the Waikato — too rough. Land should be ploughable to farm it properly. All these people felling bush were making a grave mistake. It was a case of throwing money away, in most instances. A lot of the country would never hold grass.

Ken was sitting with us. He had struck his own camp for fear of the fire catching it, and would camp with me. Mr Allen looked up the steep face of Taitoki and said that no one with any brains would waste time clearing land like that. Poor Ken! With true Highland moderation he made no comment.

Sparks were of course flying everywhere. The wind carried them into the treetops. The dry ones crackled into flame, and there were enough of these to illuminate the night and give a faint light all around us. Some broken branches and bark clinging to a standing tree on our side of the creek caught fire and burned angrily. Mr Allen said the tree might fall across the whare and set it on fire. I pointed out that the building was of corrugated iron. The tree was only about thirty feet high and over forty yards away, and was a pukatea, which would not burn in any case. He said it was burning now. I told him it was the remains of other timber clinging to it which was burning. He did not seem happy about it even then, and Uren was the picture of misery. I saw my prospects of an overdraft vanishing. Ken and I slept side by side outside the front door. Our visitors occupied beds within. Ken told me next morning that he had awakened several times in the night to see old Allen come to the door and look up at the pukatea stump on each occasion.

Messrs Allen and Uren slept badly, they told me. By now I felt that they should see the worst and get it over, and was glad to get them going up the mountain. When we had climbed a few chains above the corner peg, Allen asked grimly if I had any better country to show him, and added ominously that he'd seen all he wanted to see. We turned to go down again, and unexpectedly had a good view of my new burn. Allen asked if that were my country. It looked easy and rolling, and for the first time he said something might be made of country like that. But he did not wish to go over it. He could see it. I was glad to get them both off the place.

Afterwards we found he gave the Crown Lands block a good valuation. But the result of the visit in general was to make the U.B.A. tighten up rather than finance us further. If there was a humorous side to this business, I felt the joke was certainly against myself.

In 1913 there was a distraction from farming in the shape of the Auckland Strike. S. W. was among many volunteers who camped on the Domain and stood by to control any violence. This excitement was hardly over when talk of war in Europe set S. W. hoping that after all he might see service. He kept this thought at the back of his mind when he returned from Auckland and re-established himself in his now much more civilised whare.

On my return to Rangitoto I called in at the butcher's in Oto-rohanga and bought ten pounds of good beef-steak and packed it out. It was curious to arrive back and find none to greet me. But Ken Livingstone and his friend Finlayson had milked the cow during my absence. I cut a log of rata about seven feet long, too heavy for one man to lift, and had my evening meal of steak, potatoes, onions and rice. Ken and Finlayson came over to hear the news, and I got them to help me bring in the log. When we had placed it as a back log behind the fire, I knew it would never go out and would last a week. The two Highlanders sat with me till about nine, when I made cocoa, after which they went off — unusually late for us. I had cut my smoking down, and did not light my pipe until I got into the blankets, when after a few whiffs I laid it aside. In this way I had reduced smoking to about two pipes a week. I read a page or two of *From Midshipman to Field Marshal* by Sir Evelyn Wood, and dropped off to sleep with the back log still alight.

It was smouldering next morning when I got up, and a chip or two placed against the centre part, where the ember was, blazed up in a few minutes; I put last night's potatoes on to come to the boil in their jackets, set a billy of porridge on, and boiled another for tea. When these were all ready I put about a pound of beef-steak in the gridiron over the embers, and ran down and cleaned my teeth and plunged my head and shoulders in the stream. I had in this way spent about five minutes by the time that, drying myself as I came, I returned to turn the gridiron. To pull on my shirt and comb and brush my hair took me another five minutes, and I had a breakfast cooked that the King of the Cannibal Islands might envy. After-wards, having put the cut loaf of bread and half a pound of butter in a sugar bag, I wrapped up the remainder of the cooked steak and put that in too, with the billy containing the tea and sugar. I set a sponge for bread, and as an extra luxury filled a small bottle with milk, and was ready to go out for the day's work.

The new burn was looking well; the turnips, rape and mustard would feed a lot of sheep in a few months' time, and everywhere the grass was showing up well. I was erecting a fence across the valley. It had already reached the stage at which it would stop cattle, being wired, but the next thing it would need was battens. These had been split from a rimu log, and I now carried them out on my shoulders to lay along the fence-line. I continued this for half a day, and then while sitting at lunch with dogs beside me, I saw two cattle moving along the ridge on the new burn, and went after them. A tongue of clearing ran along the boundary on the northern side. The animals made for this and I had to work round it to head them. They got into the bush before me and it took me a long time to head them and work them back onto the previous year's grass and up the mountain. By the time I had finished it was half past four and I decided to call it a day and go home to my whare.

When I had kindled the fire and set the water on to boil I was ready to milk the cow, who was, on this night, within fifty yards of the bails. I had set potatoes on to boil. At lunch I had enjoyed my cold grilled steak. I now cut another piece and set it in the gridiron. There is nothing like variety, and as I had time in hand, I sliced the potatoes and onions by way of a change and fried them. Instead of rice I decided to top up with bread and jam, and finding my choice lay between melon and lemon or quince and strawberry I decided to keep the latter until I had company and opened the former. I thought I would have cold stewed fruit with my rice tomorrow evening, so I put some dried apricots on to boil, kneaded my bread, set it to one side of the fire to rise in the camp oven, and settled down to my evening meal. The Highlanders were a little late in coming over and the bread was already baking when they arrived. Such was my day, and one was very like another, except that sometimes it rained when all of me got wet, and sometimes it was fine when only my feet did. These were variations so regular that I rarely noticed them once winter had set in.

*   *   *

Now there was always the dry whare to come home to — a great advance from the days when it was only a tent. If my clothes were wet, they were only trousers and a blue flannel singlet to dry, and the fire was never out. When the back log at the centre would, after several days, burn through, I had only to push the ends together for them to break into flame, almost like a match. Despite my washing so regularly in the stream I was none too clean, inasmuch as the constant drying of clothes hung from a wire in the chimney made them smell of woodsmoke. To wash them I would tie them on a piece of string and let them float in the stream till I returned from work. Of course I kept clean clothes for when I went into town, but otherwise laundry was not my strong suit.

Morton, the big red Irishman down the creek, by the Waipa, had now brought a wife to share his two-roomed shack. She was a bright little soul who had been in good domestic service in the Old Country. As I always made it my business to bring up any of the rare letters for herself or her husband, and did any little commissions they might require in town, she used to ask me in for a cup of tea sometimes, which I was glad to have. Brown-haired and pretty, she was, I am sure, as good and innocent as the majority of her country-women, and it was a pleasure to see the cleanliness and comfort she brought to her small new home. She also kept a very productive vegetable garden, and had a few flowers growing from seeds on each side of the front door. Some wire netting enclosed half a dozen hens and some Indian Runner ducks.

She was ironing by the light of the only window in her little kitchen the next time I went out from Otorohanga. Having asked me in to have a cup of tea, of which I had brought a pound at her request from the store. I ate a piece of bread and butter and remarked on the good looks of a dozen young Holstein heifers grazing in the scrub, that Mick had brought up the previous year as calves.

"Yes," said she,"they are growin' big, aren't they? They'll be calvin' in the spring and we'll be milkin' them, though if Mick gets more work on the new road it might pay us better to sell all but just one for ourselves. He makes good money on a road contract. He thinks of nothing but his work when he's at it. He isn't like me."

"But you work hard, Mrs Morton," I told her. "You are always at it when we ride by. And it shows, too, in the house and garden. Look at the vegetables you have, and that rose outside will be all over the house wall in no time."

"And do you think so?" She looked pleased as she said it. "Faith! It is no good having a home of your own without tryin' to have it nice, and I wouldn't be without vegetables either in a place like this. No, I was never one to be idle, but I like to think while I work, and feel happy in what I think about. Mick, he's a very quiet one, and always used to keep himself to himself when he wasn't working. No, I'm not like that. I did my work in service and I liked it too, but when I'd finished for the day, well, I liked a bit of fun, if I could get out and enjoy myself on evenings off, and always had a boy. Mick never thought of such things. And how do you have your washing done, up there all by yourself?"

I described my methods.

185

"Now that is no good at all, at all. It must be ruination on the clothes," she said, "and it doesn't make them clean. Now ye have very little to be washed, I'm sure, just your own pillowslips and sheets and a shirt or two. Ye wear pyjamas maybe. I am sure ye do. The gentry does."

I admitted that I did, though the sheets and pillowcases had been brought up only recently. Before that I slept on blankets with my clothes folded under my head.

"Ye poor man. 'Tis hard for ye. And ye need not shake your head. Ye weren't accustomed to the likes of it before ye came here, I'll be bound." Her tone had a sympathy that few but an Irish voice could express.

"You forget I was born and bred in New Zealand, Mrs Morton," I said.

"I know that too; but away down the South Island and it's different," she replied. "I have been there in the first year I came out. I had a place in service and it was just like the ould country. The people have the homely ways there, but the like of Mick would have to wait a long time before he could look at a farm; and that's why he came up here and got me to come too, and faith, it's not complainin' I am, for when we've been here a few years we'll have it just the same. Now, about your washing. When you're riding by, will you just put your dirty things in a flour bag and leave them here? I'll wash them for ye, and ye're not to be thanking me either, for 'twill be a pleasure, with all this idle time on me hands; but don't ye go telling Mick, for he might not like to think I'm doing it. So just don't mention it when ye talk to him."

At this time S. W. was writing letters to a girl in Auckland, giving some account of his life at Rangitoto. Gracie Falwasser had somewhat surprised him by marrying somebody else, and although he still held the same views about the impossibility of marrying a girl from his own background till he had more to offer her, it is easy to imagine how much he enjoyed his contacts with such girls on his visits to the city.

These letters show with what good heart he tackled his problems.

January 18th, 1913.

I am in Otorohanga, where I spent yesterday. You have no idea what an awful place Otorohanga is. The population consists of Maoris, pakeha Maoris, pakehas, Syrians, etc., and also mixtures of each kind, and a sort of "Taihoa" feeling comes over everybody who stays there long. The first generation of pakehas got it badly apparently, and their half-caste descendants remain to carry on the tradition.

The influx of new settlers has wakened up the surrounding

countryside somewhat, but the township is slow to move; however it is progressing a little — several loads of gravel have been put into the mud-holes in the main street, and most of the store-keepers object to the pigs sleeping under their verandahs, while one or two are even so inconsiderate as to water their doorsteps to prevent the Maoris sitting on them. But the thing which really stirs the place is the weekly picture show which is given in the Town Hall on Saturday nights. So last night my friend and self decided to remain and see the pictures and ride home in the moonlight.

Billed for eight o'clock, the pictures did not start till after nine, the Otorohangans waiting contentedly while the solitary mechanic wrestled with the engine, but when they got started — what oh!

The star film was *Ivanhoe*, but what I liked was the appropriate music accompanying each film. The half-caste pianist, whose aesthetic temperament calls for a biennial sojourn in Avondale Asylum, really rises to the occasion. When the screen announces that "Sir Brian de Bois Guilbert, flushed with wine, insults the beautiful Rebecca," he strikes up in a mournful key, "Mr Booze, Mr Booze, you're a mischief-making fellow, Mr Booze." And again when Ivanhoe hears that the fair Rowena has been abducted by "Front de Boeuf", he played "I wonder who's kissing her now?" But I really thought his best was "Shall we gather at the river?" when Robin Hood blew his horn to summon his merry men to the greenwood. Altogether I enjoyed myself so much that I sat the whole thing through and stayed in town till morning. Sounds wildly dissipated, doesn't it?

*   *   *

December 16th, 1913

I rode into Otorohanga on Saturday, my sheep having been there on account of the rain for three days. I found however that one man had started with them half an hour before me, while the other one, having looked upon the whiskey bottle, had punched a man and gone to the police station to get himself arrested. The policeman having declined to arrest him, being too tired or unsympathetic or something, I managed to dissuade my man Bill from punching the rest of the population, and brought him out to Otewa, a native settlement to which the sheep had come. Here I found that we were eleven short, so had to ride back to Otorohanga eight and a half miles and find them, bringing them on yesterday.

The river Waipa being in flood, the mob remains indefinitely at Otewa. When bringing the missing eleven on yesterday, one took it into its head to leave, so away he went through three apologies for fences with which pakehas and Maoris alike make a pretence of protecting their crops in this benighted land. Thinking of course that he would stop at the river, I went after him on foot with the dogs, the river being in flood and supposedly impossible to cross; but this dear sheep plunged in and swam across, so singing "O you beautiful doll", back I had to go for my horse and carry him back to the others on my saddle. On arrival I found the others had gone, leaving no sign, so being alone in the countryside I had a soliloquy and preached myself a sermon on the parable of the lost sheep in the wilderness. I found them all eventually and reached the farm-house where I was to stay at about 10 p.m. I came on here this morning in the rain to my own camp and here I am.

You have no idea how miserable one can be for a day or two after returning. Just fancy it is only a week tonight since I was dancing. However I shall get over it just about the time I go south for Christmas, whence I am called at the bidding of a fond mother whom I have not seen for eighteen months. Write to me as follows:

S. Westmacott
    C/o H. Westmacott
        King Country Club
        Te Kuiti.

This will catch me on my way through to the South Island, though it is not my usual address. It seems very lonely here just now.

*   *   *

July 25th, 1914

Now to explain why I have not been able to write before. I have really had a most strenuous time. As it was raining cats and dogs on my arrival, I spent the night at the Hills' and rode out next day, returning to Otorohanga on the Friday as I was expecting sheep from the south.

I sat down to write on the Friday evening in the sitting-room of the hotel while three most violent Ulster sympathisers discussed the Home Rule question, and this is the sort of thing which broke in on my meditations:

"Asquith is a scoundrel."

"That lying hound Lloyd George should be shot."

"Carson is the greatest man alive today," etc., etc.

It was impossible to write under such adverse conditions so I crumpled the paper and threw it in the fire, resolved to write the first time I was alone, and do you know since then I have not had one moment to myself till now.

My troubles began next day at 4.30 in the afternoon when the train arrived with 1300 sheep for myself and a neighbour. There were only three of us, and I was the only man with dogs. The station yards would not hold all the sheep, so the dogs and I guarded the mob while the others unloaded, and a tedious business it was. I had to trust largely to the dogs as it was pitch dark and I was once nearly run over by a train, dogs and all, whilst clearing sheep off the line.

After that we had to take them through the township, and they were all over people's back yards and vacant sections.

They seemed to be thoroughly modern in their tastes, for they made for the lights of a moving picture theatre as if they were rushing for early doors. Unfortunately the show was started and there was full house, so we took them down the main street for which I expect to be summonsed, Otorohanga giving itself airs like a full-blown town, and having bylaws forbidding stock in the main street. It was ten o'clock before we ate that night. We were all over the shop and twice I slipped into mud-holes up to my waist, nearly.

A daylight start next morning, Sunday. The rain pelting down. My socks being wet, I did without any, but ugh! for sheer misery let my bitterest enemy be condemned to put his feet into wet boots on a cold morning at daylight.

However, once on the move we were soon too busy to worry. We got the sheep to Ferguson's that night, and I went on home to muster some more for the sale on the 23rd.

Next day, a beautiful day, another chap and I mustered a lot of sheep on this place at daylight, and drafted them for the sale. We started with them at daybreak next day and I handed them over to a drover when we passed the other mob. We had to cross the two mobs at a certain point on the road and my companion and myself were there full three hours before the others appeared. We lit a fire as we were both on foot without overcoats and contrived to keep warm in spite of the southerly showers which came up at frequent intervals.

When the two mobs had passed I took the homeward track once more with the big mob and two companions, one of whom I am glad to say had dogs. We camped the sheep at the edge of the bush and arrived home a little after dark.

I was up again at five in the morning, cooked the breakfast, and at first streak of dawn away we went for the sheep once more. All day was spent in driving and drafting at my yards, and I had the satisfacton of putting the last sheep across the creek as it was becoming too dark to see. My troubles with that lot were over, except for a few stragglers left behind.

I had caught my horse earlier in the day, so I changed my clothes and had the satisfaction of putting on dry socks and boots to ride into Otorohanga. It was dark as pitch going through the bush, and bitterly cold, and later as I passed lights in several homesteads, in each of which I knew there was a bed for the asking, I was sorely tempted to turn in, but I pushed on, reaching Otorohanga at midnight.

I woke up the boarding house keeper, to find that, being sale night, there was not a bed in the house. What was I to do? I found a vacant bed in a friend's diggings, and a Good Samaritan I knew brewed me a cup of coffee. He is an old member of that famous corps of aristocratic hard cases, The Natal Mounted Police, and he brewed the coffee in milk as he said the Boer farmers do in South Africa. I know it was jolly good and restored me considerably, but I could not sleep for some time as I could not get properly warmed.

I slept long next morning, however, and made a late breakfast off biscuits, the Good Samaritan again coming to the rescue with hot coffee.

I sold my sheep pretty well, and night found me once again on the road to Otewa, where I camped at the Fergusons'. Next morning, leading a spare horse and picking up a few stragglers on the track, I rode home, and as the day was delightfully fine, I puffed clouds of smoke into the still air, or relieved the tedium of the journey with bursts of song, where the track was sufficiently solitary for no one to hear me. They say my voice carries half a mile on a still day, so I have to be careful not to frighten the neighbours' sheep and cattle too much. Like Mark Tapley I contrive to be happy under all conditions.

This country is getting settled and civilised; in former times Hill, Rolleston and myself used to ride up that old river and make the valley ring with song and laughter. Hill is married now, and settled near the township, whilst Rolleston lives on the other side of the range and I seldom see him. Of all the merry souls who rioted over the King Country three or four years back, few seem left today, all are scattered; some dead, some married, and some have departed to fresh fields and pastures new. Yet search Australasia from end to end, I think nowhere would you find such a crowd of carefree souls as we were in those times. A newly opened district like this seems to attract a unique class of men, but as the country becomes settled and civilised the men in it seem to become changed, unconsciously perhaps, or go under. I am wandering, however. A sign of dotage, I suppose.

You have had a fairly accurate description of a strenuous week. I am not often so busy. Bother. That is a mild word for me, but here come two chaps to spend the night and I shan't have another chance to write.

I was awakened yesterday by a Scotch neighbour running in to tell me that "the dogs is playing h---l with the sheep". So out I rushed to find two puppies that I had left untied the night before chasing sheep all over the new burn. I will draw a veil over what occurred when I caught them. Suffice it to say that I went to work on them with my coat off and three supplejacks, two of which I broke in the process.

I hate beating dogs, or anything else for that matter, but when one does it one has to do it thoroughly. They say,

> "A woman, a dog and a walnut tree
> The more you beat 'em the better they be."

I don't believe in it quite, not as regards dogs anyway.

One of the men S. W. brought out to help with the bush-felling, Paddy Crane, gave them all, as it turned out, a good deal more trouble than help. It began when S. W. returned from a trip to Te Kuiti and met Paddy in Otorohanga, as they had arranged.

A somewhat weather-beaten Paddy Crane on the station next morning declared himself ready to come out to Rangitoto. He had fallen among thieves, or in other words boon companions and whiskey. Where he had got these things, or spent his time, I did not bother to enquire. It was a sign of the changing times that he got a lift on a wheeled conveyance to Otewa without assistance from me. There I put his swag on a pack horse and we went on.

He certainly looked the worse for wear, and I got off and made him ride my horse while I walked behind for a while, but he only let me do this once. He was indomitable, and the only reply I got to my enquiry of "How're you feeling, Paddy?" was "Me? I'm fine, boss." We kept steadily on and reached camp about 5.30 to find Wilfred and Jack with an old Maori called Wara, preparing their evening meal. It was a good one — Wara had killed a pig. We feasted on pork and onions, with plenty of potatoes of course. Paddy ate very little, which did not surprise me. Like others I had known, he would take a day or two to recover.

Wilfred was satisfied with his contract, but said he could pay for a man to help him. He was glad when I said he could have Paddy and Wara next day as I wanted to have a good look round again before I settled them down to work. Boy Jack had made quite a good job of the new garden, with Ken Livingstone's advice. I took him with me and climbed the mountain. Everything looked green and fresh, and the stock very well. The days were lengthening out and showed signs of spring. We went to the trig station where some cattle ran before us and went right on across the mountain. I did not feel worried about them now, but was confident they would come out as they had done before. We went on down the mountain track along the ridge above Hill's clearing. I was a little worried here to find that the cattle had gone into the bush westward by an old track across which the bush was now felled. Until the burn should take place, after Christmas, there was no chance of their crossing the fallen timber, and I wanted them out to sell earlier than that. How difficult it is to arrange matters so that everything fits in at the right time. We went along the southern edge of this clearing and home down the valley.

About 5.30 I saw Wara coming along the track from where Wilfred, Paddy and he were clearing scrub. I saw he looked very frightened and on asking what was the matter he replied solemnly, "Paddy have the very bad sick."

Bidden to explain further he said, "He makit the blood come all out the mouth. Ah!" and he spread his hand deprecatingly towards the ground as if showing me what lay there. Wilfred and Paddy now came slowly down, the latter for once looking serious, and very white.

In response to my enquiry Wilfred said, "Paddy has been very sick, boss, just as we were knocking off work. I wouldn't have thought so much about that, but it was all blood. I don't mind telling you it frightened me. I reckon we ought to make 'im be careful for a day or two."

Paddy confirmed the statement about the blood, and said he had never had consumption and "couldn't make head nor tail of it no 'ow".

The only thing I could think of was to tell him not to go out to work the next day, which was Saturday, and only to eat soft things like porridge, bread and condensed milk, or rice pudding. This he promised to do. On Sunday in response to my enquiries he said he felt fine and was getting hungry. I told him he had better be careful about his food for a while longer, but on Monday morning he had another haemorrhage, outside the tent, which I saw for myself. He seemed to bring up about two quarts of blood, and this was largely intermingled with clots. Everyone looked scared, and I felt very alarmed myself. Paddy admitted to eating bread and butter. I told him he must eat as little as he could, and must not go out to work, but must lie down and rest on his bunk. Wilfred told me during the day that Paddy had been eating meat, unknown to me. In camp I exacted a promise that he would do as he was told, and believed he was now sufficiently worried about himself to keep it.

Matters continued like this during the ensuing days, and on the fourth day I was quite hopeful. When I asked Paddy how he felt he said, "I'm fine, boss. Feeling grand; but I'm getting so hungry."

I told him to remain on the same diet a while longer, but weakly asked him what he would like to eat.

"I'd like some chops," he said. "I could eat half a dozen."

It so happened we were having steak and onions for our evening meal; the smell was too much for him. He begged to be allowed to have some, and on his assertion that he was sure it would do him good, I let him have some. He took a mouthful, swallowed it and immediately went outside and had another haemorrhage worse than the last. This time he turned corpse-like and nearly fell down. Old Wara stared in front of him with terrified eyes, muttering native prayers. Wilfred and I helped Paddy into the tent and into his bunk. Ken Livingstone now arrived; he could not help seeing the blood, and joined us with a serious face. I told him we would have to carry Paddy out in the morning.

*　　*　　*

Tom Macrae came riding up about six o'clock. He had been away droving for a few days. While he sat, pannikin in hand, eating bread and butter, we told him all about Paddy and how we must take him out in the morning. I left him, to look at the invalid, who was now in a troubled sleep, occasionally muttering incoherently. He looked like a corpse in colour.

Rejoining the little group sitting on a log outside, I was asked by Macrae, "How do ye mean to carry him out in the morning? Ye have no proper stretcher, and not counting the boy there are just five of us. I don't know if you have ever tried to carry anyone far. I have been one of a party carrying a coffin; there were six of us. We found it no light weight and we had only two or three hundred yards to go on a good road. This is a bush track where two cannot walk abreast in most places. It will be slow going, having to be careful how we carry a live man."

"It won't be easy, I agree," I said, "but as for being alive, I am not sure by the look of him he'll live till morning. But it's impossible to move in the bush at night, and it might finish Paddy."

"I'm going for a doctor now!" said Tom, springing up impulsively. "I'll saddle my horse and be off." It happened that Tom's brother was a doctor, which helped me to make up my mind.

Feeling that it was a right decision, I could only insist that he take the grey horse, which was fresh and grazing on the clearing nearby. I felt that if Paddy died now, I would always reproach myself for not doing something of this kind when he was first ill. I told Tom we would start early next morning if Paddy were still alive, whether he had arrived with the doctor or not. I asked him to call in at Dick Meredith's on the way down, ask him if he would bring his waggon up as far as the track would permit, and tell him I would send boy Jack out on a horse to guide him as near as he could come to us. There was little else to say, and it was with gloomy thoughts that we watched him disappear across the stream into the growing dusk. He would have to ride hard to be through the bush before dark.

For a while we sat by the light of the candle, our bare elbows resting on the table. We smoked our pipes and conversed in low tones. Occasionally a muttered word came for the adjacent tent where Paddy lay, but he was always unconscious when we looked in on him. At last I suggested that we were doing no good sitting up together, that we had a heavy carry next day, and that all but one should go to bed. Each watcher it was agreed should wake up his successor at the end of two hours. It was wise to turn in. Ken Livingstone said he would sleep with us and take his turn at watching. I was the first watcher, and after looking at Paddy by the light of a palm-shaded candle and shaking their heads, the others all rolled into blankets and were soon fast asleep.

It is an eerie business sitting up with an invalid who may be going to die, and for a while I sat by the bunk on which the sick man lay, listening to his troubled breathing and occasional muttering of delirium. Soon I decided it was better to leave him and sit in the galley. I was close enough to hear if he made any sound. It was a silent night, fine but not very cold. I pulled a coat on, and kept the fire up. As time passed slowly I began to imagine sounds, though the chief noise was the flow of the creek less than two chains away. I decided to read for a while, and turned the pages of some papers we had kept for fire-lighting. There was a *New Zealand Herald* for the end of June, and others for July.

The overseas news was that divided skirts had been forbidden by law at Louisville in Kentucky, and quite right too, I thought. Better to put their foot down before things went further. One did not know what women would do if allowed to go on. I had never seen divided skirts. Thank goodness New Zealand had not got as far as that. The Socialists opposed an armaments bill in the Reichstag in Berlin. Did they? It did not seem to make much difference, from what I heard. A man called Rufus Isaacs, M.P., claimed credit for voluntary service, in a speech at Newcastle, England. He was a Liberal, apparently. In London a Sir F. D. Acland admitted that compulsory service must be adopted if necessary, and he was a Liberal too. Well, all Liberals were humbugs anyway. We had them here; but we had compulsory service too. Why could not the Old Country copy us and have done with it? The Kaiser's daughter had been married recently. She sounded sweet and attractive. The Balkan allies were fighting too, it seemed. They were always at it; that was none of our business. There were riots among the miners in Johannesburg. I had heard they earn an average wage of £800 a year — the white miners, that is; it would be riches to me. Serve them right if they lost their jobs. What a lot of unpleasant people there were, away from New Zealand; I was inclined to think our country dull, though.

Turn over, let's look at local news. There never is much. Hullo! A deputation to the Honourable F. M. B. Fisher — good old F. M. B. —Minister of Marine Fisheries, protesting that in Wellington the fish shops were selling oysters to the people at half-a-crown a bottle containing five dozen, while, it was pointed out, they bought them fresh, wholesale, at a 1½d a dozen. Scandalous, this exploitation of the consuming public! The Minister promised to have the matter looked into. He said it might be necessary to fix the price; rather an extreme measure, that; I shook my head. All the same, 6d a dozen was a ridiculous price to pay for bottled oysters. That was what they had charged us in the restaurant in Palmerston for fresh ones with coffee and brown bread and butter thrown in. The rainfall for last six months had been the lowest on record — and at this point Paddy called out. I took the candle and went in to him. He was only muttering in his sleep, I found, so I returned to the galley and made up the fire. The billy began to boil. I looked at my watch and found I had overstayed my allotted time. Wilfred blinked when I woke him, and put his feet out of the blankets and reached for his boots. Otherwise he was dressed in trousers, socks and flannel, as we all were. He was yawning when he came into the galley, and glad to have a cup of cocoa I had just made. We sat sipping the hot beverage. I told him Paddy was quiet, then turned in, to sleep dreamlessly.

*   *   *

Awake before daybreak, I found Ken Livingstone in the galley stirring a billy of porridge. He said Paddy had been talking a lot in his sleep. Wilfred came in and took over the cooking while Ken and I went and looked at Paddy. He woke and smiled at us and said, "What the hell is all this about? I'm goin' to get up." We tried to dissuade him, but he insisted on trying, and it ended in Ken and me helping him. After he had been outside for a few moments he turned slack and faint, and Wilfred came to our assistance to get him back to bed. It was broad daylight now, and Jack came in, rubbing the sleep out of his eyes. I gave him his instructions about going down to meet Dick Meredith, and told him to catch Billy the horse and start after breakfast.

At that meal Wilfred had put the usual massive portions of inch-thick beef-steak on our plates to follow the oatmeal, and we ate in silence.

Presently Wilfred said, "I seen in the paper that a man called Cody was killed trying to fly at Farnborough in the Old Country. What a man wants to h'imitate a bird for I never could understand, not for flying. For drinking, now, I think they got every advantage. An ostrich. What a neck to pour beer into! I ain't sure which has the best of it, him or a pelican. The pelican's got a short neck, it's true, but what a mouth to roll the whiskey round!"

"It's the whiskey that's brought Paddy to where he is today," I said.

"Weel, it's no verra gude whiskey," said Ken "I don't think much of it masel', but gude Scots whiskey never hurt any man. It's poison they sell to Maoris, and Paddy must have got some."

We all agreed with him as we filed out, and there, riding at a trot on a tired grey horse, was Tom Macrae returning. Whilst Wara and Wilfred went into the bush to cut two poles for a stretcher, we gave him his breakfast. He had ridden all night. At Otorohanga after midnight he had got on the telephone and rung the doctor's house, to find that he was away, attending a night call. The housekeeper had promised to give him a message, and Tom had ridden straight back. He had been in the saddle about eleven hours, and covered thirty-six miles. The poor grey horse looked as if he had had enough too. Yet despite the fact that the rider had not rested for twenty-four hours this sturdy Highlander was prepared, after a hasty meal, to take his share of carrying with the rest of us.

Jack had caught and saddled his horse, and now rode off. The confidence and assurance of this cockney urchin were a great testimonial to the lads of London. Yet I wondered, as I saw him go, what a different kind of being he might have become if he had grown up in a town.

Wilfred and Wara each came back from the bush carrying a long pole. We laid these on the ground, parallel, and getting two sacks, cut holes in the two bottom corners of each. Then we threaded the poles through them, putting the end of one sack into the mouth of the other. This made a good stretcher. We lifted it to try how it felt, and even without a load the poles were not light, but we dared not try lighter ones for fear of their not being strong enough. We brought out a blanket and spread it on the stretcher. We were now ready, and went in to carry Paddy out.

"Well, isn't this a beggar?" said he, as we went to lift him.

"Stop! Stop!" cried Tom Macrae, who had just put his pannikin down, "Don't carry him out feet first. Turn him round." He was too much a Highlander to be free of superstition.

With a little difficulty we did this, carried him out, and laid him on the stretcher. We put his clothes under his head and covered him with a blanket.

"Are you warm enough, Paddy?" we asked.

"Aye, I'm warm enough," he said. "But Christ! Fancy a man being like this, with everyone waiting on him. Isn't it a beggar?"

196

We told him not to worry. Fortunately it was a fine morning, with promise of a warm day, but we took another blanket in case it turned cold, and, giving our coats to Wara to carry, Wilfred and I took the head, and Tom and Ken the foot. We lifted the stretcher onto our shoulders, and started to walk away.

A few yards convinced us that we had set ourselves a herculean task. The weight of the stretcher was far greater than I could have imagined. I had heard of a woman who had to be carried in this way out of the Tangitu district over a road, more muddy than ours, but at least a road. Ours was a track. I had heard that the settlers en route had turned out, to give the stretcher-bearers relief, and that at the end of the journey thirty people were trailing the procession, all giving a hand in turn, and that they were none too many. For our own relief, till we should meet Dick Meredith's waggon, we had old Wara and no one else. We rested when we had slowly travelled fifty yards — and that was over a bush clearing. I knew it must be worse in the bush, a nightmare. I asked my companions how they felt and how long they thought it would take to do three or four miles at this rate. Their faces looked grave; their silence gave the answer.

"Wara," I said, "catch old Jeff. Put the pack saddle on him." Bidding the others wait, I went to the tent, got two pack straps, and returning to the stretcher commenced winding one round the end of the right pole above Paddy's head, leaving the ring clear. Tom Macrae watched me long enough to catch the idea, then taking the other strap did the same on the left pole with it. Wara appeared, leading the pony, ready and saddled. On my instructions he backed him towards Paddy, and we lifted the stretcher, one pole on each side of the horse, and hooked the sling straps on. The man's head was almost on the tail, but the pony stood quiet.

"Now, Wara, when I give the word, lead Jeff along the track, Go slow, and hang onto him if he plays up. Wilfred and I will take the back ends of the poles, and follow on, carrying the stretcher. The others can carry the coats and give us a spell when we want it." Suiting the action to the word we got the poles on our shoulders, and set off.

*   *   *

From now on the hero of the journey was old Jeff the pony. He seemed to be entirely aware of the importance of his duty, and that Paddy's life was so largely dependent of his behaviour. Instead of any restiveness, he walked quietly and steadily. He seemed, out of consideration for us carriers, to go slow in the rough places so that we could walk circumspectly, and when he came to the creek he looked round before descending into the water, paused before crossing, and on the other side went gently up the bank, where at the top we stopped and made much of him. Tom and Ken insisted on taking the poles till the next ford, where we entered the bush. It was agreed that we now change carriers at each ford, of which I calculated there would be at least ten before we could hope to meet the waggon. The pony never failed to look back and see that all was well before crossing water or rough places. All the same our progress was slow. We did not average a mile an hour through the bush, as it was only a single horse track in the centre, and we had to watch where we put our feet at the outside edges.

When we reached the outer edge of the bush, we took the end of the stretcher off the pack horse and laid Paddy on the ground in the sunlight while pony and men had a spell. The patient had been more and more awake as we travelled, and repeatedly asked if this were not a beggar. While Jeff contentedly ate the leaves of a mahoe nearby, Ken and I filled our pipes.

"How do you feel, Paddy?"

"All right," was the reply. "I could do with a cigarette." We discussed if it could hurt him, decided not, and Wilfred who was rolling one, gave it to him. We all stood round while a match was held to it and Paddy drew a satisfying cloud. But the results were disastrous, for slowly the life seemed to go out of him. His head went back, and we feared the end was coming.

This had the effect of sending us off along the track again. We seemed to make better progress now as we splashed through the creek and walked on through the fern and scrub, which was soon cleared enough to take a wheeled waggon. After another two miles we saw Jack's head above the fern, and Dick Meredith, driving the waggon. The latter had really done very well in handling the horses thus far, and had brought them over several bad places where wheels had never been before. As it would be necessary to take the stretcher out to get the waggon gently over these places, the bearers continued to come on, but the long carry was over, and it only remained to lavish our praises on the gallant little horse, who had shown such cleverness, and had halved our labour.

The waggon crossed the Waipa once, twice, thrice. Fortunately the river was not high, and not up to the waist anywhere. Dick Meredith drove well. We emerged upon the wide ferny flat, and were making for the deep ford where Barber had camped, when the thunder of galloping hoofs was heard and Dr Macrae, on the big bay horse, Caesar, almost charged into us, so fast was he going. One look at the figure in the waggon and he was off Caesar, whose loose rein I caught hold of, and up into the conveyance beside the stretcher.

"Oh, it's you, Crane," he said loudly, with a strong note of disgust in his voice. "Here have I been galloping all the way from Te Kuiti to tend a man who has not the sense to look after himself."

It seemed that the message he had received had been garbled, and he had the impression he was being called out to his brother, which accounted perhaps for the speed at which he had come, and his reaction on arrival. If his words sounded curt, Paddy was too far gone to hear them, and nothing could have exceeded the care and solicitude with which the doctor attended him.

"And where are you taking him?" he said, after he had heard the history of the case. "Hamilton Hospital? Aye, that's the hope for him. I'll ride back now, and ring them up to have him met, and a bed ready. You can get him in the van on the evening goods train. I'll have to go back now, for there's nothing else I can do." He had a few words with his brother, and soon rode past, and was gone almost as quickly as he had come. After all, Caesar was not a grass-fed horse, but got three good feeds of oats each day.

Four more fords of the river, and an axle-deep jolting and splashing through the mud of the swamp the other side of Te Kooti's old whare, brought us out onto the hard flat track running along the foot of the hills to Otewa pa and the road. It was unnecessary for our foot-carriers, who had come along in case of need, to proceed further, but I felt I must accompany Paddy to hospital. There was something very forlorn-looking about the little group, three white men and the boy, with the old Maori holding the pony, who stood gazing after the waggon till we were out of sight. I sat beside the stretcher, and in another hour or a little more we were in Otorohanga. Three willing bushmen and a railway man helped lift Paddy from the waggon, and placed him on a railway stretcher in the waiting room. The bushmen stood by the stretcher while Dick and I had a meal, and when I returned one of them asked me, "What is the trouble with Paddy, Mr Westmacott?"

"Paddy seems to have been poisoned by this damn stuff they sell as whiskey at 6s the bottle," I told him, which was not quite fair, as I found afterwards he had had sly-grog. "How has he been?" I asked.

"He's muttering away," the man told me. "There's no sense in it, kind of delirious-like."

That continued while we sat and waited for the train. When it came in we carried the stretcher across the rails, lifted it into the van and slung it in comfort. I turned to thank my helpers and found that a Roman Catholic priest was one of them. I had noted him in the township, a good-looking young man, and was glad to hear that he was going on the train, in case the end came for Paddy. The latter presently opened his eyes and asked, "Where am I, boss?"

"You are in the train, on the way to Hamilton Hospital, Paddy," I said.

"And isn't it a beggar, a fair cow?" said he. (I may say "beggar" wasn't quite the word he used.) The priest looked at me.

"Is he one of my people?" he asked.

Standing on each side of the stretcher to steady it from the motion of the train, which had now started, we both leaned forward and looked at the pale green face.

"Are you a Roman Catholic, Paddy?" I asked.

"Noa," said Paddy, loudly and emphatically. The idea seemed to horrify him, and he swooned away and remained unconscious for the rest of the journey.

"Never mind, Father," I said, feeling sorry I had asked the question.

"It doesn't matter," said the priest sympathetically, and stood with us till we reached Te Awamutu.

"I get out here," he said, and taking Paddy's hand, said, "Goodbye, old man. You'll be looked after where you're going. Mind you get well again."

Paddy did say "Goodbye", surprisingly, but I doubt if he knew to whom he was saying it. The priest held out his hand to me, "And you too, my son."

I was glad to take it, saying, "Thank you, Father, we've been glad to have you with us."

From then on I did not seem to notice the passage of time as the train journeyed on into the darkness. I felt drowsy, but remained on my feet beside the stretcher, so did not go to sleep. Paddy's incoherences were not very loud, and quite without sense. I was used to the company of my own thoughts, but was relieved when the occasional light told me that we were approaching Frankton. I think the driver was aware of the load we carried, for he brought the train slowly to a stop by the platform without a jolt.

I got out and was accosted by a man in a long overcoat, carrying a driving whip, who asked, "Is there a patient 'ere for the 'Amilton 'Orsepital?"

I felt I had been personally welcomed. Some porters carried the stretcher and placed it in a two-horsed ambulance. I got up beside the driver, and he drove slowly out of the station.

The journey was not a long one, and when we arrived my jaded senses derived much comfort from the light and warmth and general air of cleanliness and space, all in such contrast to the rough camp where I had been the previous night.

Presently there was an opening of doors and bustling about in the passage, and Dr Douglas came out. He said, "Good evening," and enquired what was the matter, and I told him what had happened

200

to Paddy, and wound up by saying how sorry I was that I had not brought him in at the first haemorrhage. I asked if they could do anything for him. He walked with deliberate steps round the patient, and then, giving Paddy's forelock a tug, said, "All right, Crane. We'll pull you round, but you'll have to stay here a bit."

His tone was confident, and feeling cheered, I said good night and walked to the train, and slept all the way in the second class carriage until we reached Te Kuiti at 2 a.m. Neither express ever stopped at the town of Otorohanga. I went to the bach, where Brittan, the only one in residence, was asleep, and knew no more till daylight.

Paddy recovered; and the next time S. W. went away from Rangitoto it was to attend a course of instruction in Auckland, arranged for the Territorials. Livingstone and Finlayson came in and had a meal with him the night before he left; they too would be off next day, on a contract job. Wild pig was on the menu, thanks to the activities of Fly.

We roasted him in the good old-fashioned style, with potatoes and pumpkin, and some sauce made from preserved apples, and ate heartily as men do with sound teeth and the digestion of those who live their life in the open air. We had little appetite left for the rice pudding cooked with milk — how civilised we were becoming — and the stewed apples and cream, but we topped off on it, and after washing up we sat long talking over the fire. It never occurred to us that we might not have another meal together in this world, as we had our cup of cocoa before turning in for the night. We thought we might live to a ripe old age; some people went to over a hundred. A Mrs Rebecca Clark had just died in England aged 110 years. We would be satisfied with less than that, but the end, whatever it might be was too remote to think of, and of course we did not shake hands when they went down the track next morning. I felt depressed when I watched them go, but that was a common feeling when anyone preceded me out.

The day after that I was going for my course of instruction, and would be away over a week. I climbed the mountain and went round the top, coming down the bush track and going over the lower burn. None of the sheep were where they should not have been, and I was home soon after three o'clock and milked the cow. I had an arrangement to leave her at the Mortons', who would milk her if we were all away at one time. This would be the first occasion. I looked out my things for the morrow and had them all ready, short of rolling my swag, and turned in as soon as I had washed up. I lay long enough reading *From Midshipman to Field Marshal* to be reminded for the unnumbered time that the romantic days were past when men went to war; but if I could not enjoy that experience myself I could recapture some of the excitement by reading about it — and with that thought I soon put out the candle and went to sleep.

Up betimes, I milked the cow, had breakfast, tidied up, saddled my horse and changed out of my dungarees into blue undress uniform, which I thought to carry better that way than rolled up in a swag; I strapped the latter onto my pommel, and mounting my horse I drove the cow before me and rode slowly down the creek. Did anyone ever go to war driving a cow before him? I could not allow imagination to play on that subject, and felt self-conscious and ridiculous as I handed the quiet animal into Mrs Morton's keeping. She, good soul, only admired the uniform and saw no absurdity in it, and so I rode on down the Waipa valley alone.

It was Sunday afternoon, and the date was August 2nd, 1914.

EPILOGUE

I NEED NOT EXPLAIN the reasons why Rangitoto does not feature in S. W.'s Memoirs for a long time after this memorable date. He does describe how, on Te Kuiti station, he arranged for a manager to look after the place, before he left for the First World War, but it reads almost like an afterthought. For now S. W. was to have his wish, and fight for his King and country after all.

He set up a recruiting office in Te Kuiti for the Waikato Regiment, and with this regiment he sailed as part of the Expeditionary Force, being sent first to Egypt. He tells of landing on Gallipoli on the morning of 25th April 1915, and describes his part in the attack, in the course of which he was three times wounded, and was finally evacuated to a troopship lying off the beach. Readers of this book will not be surprised that he concludes his account of 25th April by saying, "So ended the most glorious day of my life."

He was taken to England, where he recovered, and later served again in France, but when he returned to New Zealand after the war he was so disabled that it seemed unlikely he would ever farm again. He and his wife therefore settled in Christchurch and their three children were born there. But in 1926 Rangitoto was clearly in need of closer supervision, and S. W. decided to go and live there and manage it himself. He built a house close to the Waimahora, opposite the grass patch. Access was easier now, and when the family arrived it was in a Model T Ford, although there could scarcely be said to be a road, and the car had to ford the stream seven times.

The family grew up at Rangitoto, and S. W. and his wife remained there until 1958. The farm weathered the Depression eventually, and the Government scheme of giving the unemployed work on the roads did at least bring Rangitoto a better approach-road than the bed of the Waimahora. Gradually more country was broken in, and the Crown Lands block and another adjacent property were acquired. Machinery arrived on the place only slowly, and S. W. himself always did his rounds on a horse. He saw the properties around him being steadily developed, although none of his friends retained their original holdings.

He spent thirty-six years of his life at Rangitoto, and this book describes only four of them. But they were years which marked both the place and the man with a character imposed by their mutual impact. He created a farm, and in return it gave him a great deal; even, towards the end, a few after-breakfast cigars.

INDEX

INDEX

The after breakfast cigar lit

The Squire trott...

An incident of the day.

Please Squire. I've just caught this
here young man a ferretin rabbits
in Scrub Wood.

The bailiff
and the Sq
quite a s